RELIGIONS OF THE EAST

Anne Bancroft

RELIGIONS OF THE EAST

St. Martin's Press : New York

First published in the United States of America in 1974
Printed and bound in Spain
D. L.: S.S. 280/74

Endpapers: Painted tanka in the form of four mandalas, Tibet, 15th century.

Created by Walter Parrish International Limited, London

CONTENTS

TIBETAN BUDDHISM

ZEN BUDDHISM

TAOISM

SUFISM

INTRODUCTION

Many Europeans and Americans have come to realize that there are civilizations outside their own where other values prevail; where the religious *experience*, the awareness of the source of life, is the greatest goal. It is the purpose of this book to describe some religions of the East where that particular awareness is regarded as vitally important, and to show the relevance of their teachings to the predicaments of man today. It is not a history book nor is it intended to be a reference book for academic study. Its aim is to be a guide to those who want to know what eastern religions are about; what they believe in and how they practise their beliefs; and what alterations these practices can make to man's condition. It seeks to show how people in the East have set about looking for a changeless, eternal continuity beneath the capricious and insecure experience of life and death, and what they have discovered. It is concerned with the essence of that discovery in each religion and how it has been brought to the West.

Although it has been my intention to write clearly about the spiritual findings of the East, they have not always been easy to describe because of differences in vocabulary. For instance, the term 'God' is used by the Hindus for the Supreme Beingness of the universe, for THAT from which all arises, rather than as the good Father of Christianity or the just Lord of Judaism. In Buddhism, the term 'God' is even more out of place, as Buddhists do not even believe that man is an independent entity having God as his Essence. Buddhists believe that there is *only* Mind, and that man's idea that he exists as a self-determining individual is a delusion. In Taoism, even more impersonally, God is the Way, the mysterious order and rightness of the world. It is only with the Sufis that God seems nearer to the western idea of him, for they see him as a blend of transcendence and immanence. He is the Sublime Essence and yet also the Beloved. He is the Universal Self to be found when the small self of the individual is abandoned, and yet he is also the companion of that small self on its way.

The two points which all the religions in this book have in common are first, their belief that man is not just a collection of molecules organized into a perishable system of bones, flesh and brain, but that his true nature is THAT—the Formless, the Absolute, the Eternal; and second, their understanding that to find his true nature, man must lose his feeling that he is separate from the rest of the world, complete and final in himself.

The ways of making this Self-discovery comprise the main contents of the book and they range from the motionless trance of the yogi to the ecstatic climax of the dancing dervish. Meditation is a practice common to all, whether with crossed legs or bent knees, and many aspects of meditation are given.

The visual is likewise an important aspect in the East, as it is in all religions; for the worshipper, a visual representation of an idea, of the embodiment of divinity, is often an essential part of the path he follows. The illustrations in this book are designed to help the reader to enter into the spirit of the religions described for they show, in a way that words sometimes cannot do, the nature of the religious path. It is regretted that both illustrations and text have been, perforce, selective. Space was not allowed for descriptions of religious ceremonies, nor for discussion of certain esoteric aspects of religion, such as astrology.

Strictly speaking, the historical sequence of religions is not accurate here. Taoism, an ancient Chinese religion, was practised long before Buddhism came to China and should thus have preceded Zen Buddhism in order of sequence. Its influence on Zen was profound and much of the sheer enjoyment of life which marks the Zen master was the fruit of Taoist sages such as Lao Tzu. Taoism has been placed *after* Zen in this book in order to keep the various schools of Buddhism together.

In Zen Buddhism, where there has been a choice of Chinese or Japanese names, the Japanese have been used.

Readers may be surprised to find the Sufis described in a book about eastern religions, as Islam, from which they sprang, has an entirely different view of the essence of religion from its Eastern neighbours. It should be remembered, however, that Persia, the home of Sufism, was greatly influenced by Hindu and Buddhist thought and that Sufi and Hindu ideas were interwoven even more strongly when Islam invaded India.

References for quotations, a list of books for further reading, a glossary and an index are at the back of the book.

I would like gratefully to acknowledge the help given to me by Burt Taylor, the Secretary of the Buddhist Society; by Christmas Humphreys, its President; by Dr Martin Lings and the staff of the Oriental Manuscripts Department at the British Museum; by Mr Marco Pallis; by the librarian of the Royal Asiatic Society; by Alan Watts; by Douglas Harding; and by my husband. Unfortunately, space does not allow me to mention the names of all the many other people who gave me valuable advice and information.

Anne Bancroft

HINDUISM

*Having realized his own self as the Self,
a man becomes selfless; and in virtue of
selflessness he is to be conceived as
unconditioned. This is the highest
mystery, betokening emancipation; through
selflessness he has no part in pleasure
or pain, but attains absoluteness.*
(Maitrayana Upanishad) *[1]*

WHAT HINDUS BELIEVE

What *is* Hinduism? At its very heart is the belief that this perishable, changing bundle of thoughts and emotions which we call man is really one with the Sublime Essence, the Ground of Being. Westerners call this Ground of Being 'God', or the Godhead; Hindus think of it as Absolute Reality. For the Hindu sees God as transcending all qualities and all human comprehension—certainly all words of description. 'O Thou, before Whom all words recoil,' says the sage, Shankara.

This does not mean that God is remote and unrealizable. On the contrary, he is the unchanging, eternal Ground of all men. He is All. Everything that exists is an aspect of the One Reality; he is the unity in which the world lives and moves. When, through ignorance or blindness, this Unity is lost sight of, then the world appears to be comprised of a vast multitude of separate beings and things including ourselves. But when God is seen as the Whole, transcending all his innumerable parts, although not separate from them, as a man transcends his limbs but yet *is* them all, he is then the true nature of all that exists. To the Hindu, the awareness of God as the undifferentiated Ground of himself gives a feeling of true identity, of having come home to his real self at last. Hence God is often spoken of as the Self, the knowledge of one's own being.

In one of the Hindu scriptures, a father tried to explain this to his young son. He told the boy to put some salt into a cup of water and to come back later. When the boy did so, he asked him to sip it from the surface, sip it from the middle, and sip it from the bottom. Then he said:

'How is it?'

'Salt.'

'Set it aside. Then come unto me.'

He (the boy) did so, saying, 'It is always the same.' (He could not find the salt, as it was completely dissolved.)

Then he said to him: 'Verily, indeed, my dear, you do not perceive Being here. Verily, indeed, it is here.'

'That which is the finest essence—this whole world has that as its self. That is Reality. . . . That art thou, Śvetaketu.' (Chandogya Upanishad) *[2]*

The Self is also known as *Brahman*, the origin of all things. Brahman has many names such as the Supreme Soul, Wisdom Mind, Universal Awareness. Brahman, or the Self, is not usually worshipped by Hindus because they believe it is beyond worship in the ordinary sense. Hindus believe that meditation will bring them to a direct experience of It and they will then be absorbed into It. They believe that at some stage in the mystery of creation, Brahman willed the world into existence by breathing forth the words 'May I be many'. Having created the world by an act of will, he sustains and finally re-absorbs it. In the Chandogya Upanishad, Brahman is spoken of as *tajjalan*—as that from which all things are born, into which they dissolve, and in which they breathe and move.

'He who consists of mind, whose body is life (*prāna*), whose form is light, whose conception is truth, whose self is space, containing all works, containing all desires, containing all odors, containing all tastes, encompassing this whole

Head of Shiva, the god of disintegration and death. Sandstone, India, 10th–11th century.

The dance of Shiva. Bronze, India, 1st century.

world, the unspeaking, the unconcerned—this Self of mine within the heart is smaller than a grain of rice, or a barley-corn, or a mustard-seed, or a grain of millet, or the kernel of a grain of millet; this Self of mine within the heart is greater than the earth, greater than the atmosphere, greater than the sky, greater than these worlds.

'. . . this is the Self of mine within the heart, this is *Brahman*. Into him I shall enter on departing hence.' . . . *[3]*

Within each man, Hindus believe, the Self resides. This eternal Self, Brahman, underlies the conscious personality and the changing, perishable body. All that we usually know about ourselves is subject to time and space, but the *Atman* (the Self *in man*, sometimes called the soul) is man's Essence, the Eternal

Ground from which he sees, hears, touches, feels, and thinks. It is likened to the space within a jar which does not differ from the space without; in the same way the individual soul is identical with the Universal Self. The greatest goal of the spiritually-inclined Hindu is to identify self with the Self; to melt away the barrier which seems to stand between the human mind and That from which it springs.

Unawareness of the Self is the primary cause of man's tormented feeling of separateness; awareness of the Self brings about a transformation in man's understanding and he realizes his own self to be one with the Self, unconditioned, beyond space and time.

'This Self, who understands all, who knows all, and whose glory is manifest in the universe, lives within the lotus of the heart, the bright throne of Brahman.

'By the pure in heart is he known. The Self exists in man, within the lotus of the heart, and is the master of his life and of his body. With mind illumined by the power of meditation, the wise know him, the blissful, the immortal.

'The knot of the heart, which is ignorance, is loosed, all doubts are dissolved, all evil effects of deeds are destroyed, when he who is both personal and impersonal is realized.' (Mundaka Upanishad) [4]

THE FOREST GURUS

Hinduism is a religion without a founder. It started in North India where, some three to four thousand years ago, Caucasian colonizers from Persia and Afghanistan, who called themselves Aryans, settled in the Indus Valley and eventually became known as Hindus. Their language, Sanskrit, is one which has close links with English. They were a gifted, energetic people whose talents found expression in religion—not the primitive, insurance-type religion which seeks to appease the deities by ceremony and sacrifice because of the fear of bad

Agni, the Vedic god of fire. Sandstone, India, 10th century.

crops and infertility and death (although this was probably practised as well)—but the religion which begins with awe at the total mystery of life itself. They longed to know the truth of existence, the meaning and purpose of life, and they meditated and gathered together in the forests to talk about these cosmic questions. Some forest recluses, called *rishis*, received great insights, rather like

Garuda, king of the birds, carrying Vishnu and Lakshmi. Painting, India, 18th century.

the Old Testament prophets, and their teachings were gathered together and passed down by word of mouth. These scriptures are called the Vedas and they contain a great deal which is not always very spiritual—pleas for good fortune, magic incantations, and even love potions. But the greater portion is about direct and overwhelming experience of God, the extraordinary sense of the ineffable which points to eternal truths, and these intuitional teachings are the most profound and the most treasured part of the Vedas. They are called the Upanishads.

The word Upanishad means to 'sit near'. As time passed, many small forest meetings came to be held in secret because to receive holy truths was not considered right for everybody. Many Hindus at that time were concerned with the concept of rebirth—the transmigration of souls—a doctrine which is still an essential part of Hinduism today.

God's power, they thought, is infinite and unknowable; mysteriously, for no apparent reason, souls, called *jivas*, enter this world. They start in the bodies of the simplest forms of life but when the body dies, the soul does not die, for it no more depends on the body than the sun depends on the objects it shines on. As the body of one particular species is spiritually outgrown by the soul, so it moves on through higher and higher organisms until at last it acquires a human form. This process is called transmigration of the soul, or reincarnation, and when the soul has become human, it continues to be reborn in human form until this too is transcended.

The law by which the soul passes from one body to another is called Karma and it means the moral law of cause and effect. 'As you sow, so shall you reap.' One's actions (and not only actions but thoughts and motives too) in this existence determine one's next. The sum total of an individual's life at any one moment is portrayed in his nature—how intrinsically happy, enlightened and serene he is, or how disturbed, insecure and irrational—and this state is the exact culmination of all his past, including his many past lives. It is equally an exact determinant of his future for every thought, word and deed has its precise reaction on himself.

One is thus free to make one's bed, but with the knowledge that lying on it is inescapable. There is no evading the results of actions and consequently Hindus, in so far as they are aware of Karma, accept full responsibility for themselves, realizing that whatever their situation in this life, the cause lies in their behaviour in a previous existence. No blame can be attached to others; the only remedy is to change oneself.

To the early Hindus of the Vedic age, dwelling and talking in the forests, the idea of an unending chain of reappearances on the earth (and in heaven) was unsatisfactory and undesirable, even frightening. But the teaching of the wise men was that to be consciously reunited with Brahman meant release from the cycles of rebirth, for it was believed that true realization of the Self finally breaks the links which keep one bound to this earth and to mortal existence.

But how to achieve this realization? The discovery of the Self became an obsession with the Hindus. They longed for the Truth, not only for its own sake but also as a guide to achieving higher states of being. They turned to the gurus, the spiritual teachers who seemed to manifest a realized and illumined nature; whose purifications allowed the divine to shine through.

THE MEANING OF YOGA

The teachings that the gurus gave are called yogas. There are many yogas. People are not alike; their backgrounds and their individual natures vary and the way that suits one may not suit another. The gurus took great care and trouble to outline the paths which could be followed, not so much dictating any universal way as encouraging each student to find his own direction according to his inclinations. Thus the four main yogas are for four general kinds of people: those who are active; those who are thoughtful and reflective; those who are gifted with a loving heart; and those of an enquiring disposition, who are prepared to study the workings of their minds.

To many westerners, the word yoga means a number of physical exercises

Iyengar in a variation of the scorpion pose, from *Light on Yoga* by B. K. S. Iyengar.

and postures. It may also mean some seemingly odd things like sniffing water up one nostril, gazing at the bridge of the nose or at the navel, and tying the arms and legs into a pretzel shape.

Yoga also means those things to a Hindu, but to him it means much more. The word 'yoga' has the same root as our word 'yoke' and it means to join, or to unite. Hence, in Hinduism, it came to mean a way of spiritual union, a practical discipline to bring the aspirant to oneness with God.

References to yoga practices are found throughout the Upanishads. The techniques do not stem from any one source but go back a very long way: for instance, a seal made some four thousand years ago depicts a horned figure sitting cross-legged in a yoga posture. The philosophy and the techniques grew through the centuries, and at some time between 3000 B.C. and 300 A.D. they were put into simple and cogent language by one Patanjali, in the form of *sutras*. A sutra is a group of bare statements which express only what is essential; there is no elaboration and the revelation is compressed into the minimum number of words. This was because writing was not used till later and the entire work had to be memorized. The teachers would learn an aphorism (a single statement) and then amplify and expound it from their own knowledge.

The name for one who practises yoga is a *yogi* and there are many stories of yogis who can perform amazing feats, such as walking barefoot over live coals and lying on beds of nails, without ever a mark appearing on their bodies. The truth is that we know extraordinarily little about our own minds and the relationship of the mind to the body. Within each of us are higher levels of consciousness than we normally utilize; yoga can bring us to an awareness and mastery of them.

Why do we not usually perceive the hidden powers within us? Because our ability to be fully conscious of our limitless nature has been obscured by false desires, says Hinduism. Instead of pure vision, there are ceaseless mental images projected by a restless imagination; instead of pure being, there is the building up of the ego in competition with others; instead of pure happiness, there is self-indulgence. We do all this because of wrong identification, says Patanjali. We identify ourselves with the passing and the transient instead of with that which is eternal within us. If we can but find the Self within us, our nature will become at peace with itself, integrated and whole.

Vishnu and seven of his incarnations contained in a lotus with movable petals. Bronze, Nepal, 12th century.

KARMA YOGA—THE PATH OF ACTION

'He who works, having given up attachment, resigning his actions to God, is not touched by sin, even as a lotus leaf is untouched by water.' (Bhagavad Gita) [5]

The meaning of Karma Yoga is to surrender one's life to Brahman, or God, the Source of the manifested world. Then one acts in the consciousness that God is the doer, God is the thinker and God is the feeler. When one ceases to be possessive of body and ideas, one realizes that everything, even one's most intimate self, is only 'on loan'. The life that lives me is vastly greater than my small organism and the breath that breathes me is never for one moment my own. Real belief that one possesses nothing in this way means in yoga that one merges with God, and in Karma Yoga, one's purified actions are then directed towards the service of mankind. The individual who has accomplished this is no longer discouraged by failure, for where there is no personal attachment to the results of his deeds, there can be no swinging back and forth between the elation of achievement and the dejection of failure.

Thus the yoga of selfless action leads directly to the consciousness of the Self. In the Bhagavad Gita, one of the most revered Hindu scriptures, Krishna, a legendary incarnation of God, teaches that all things in the world are related and are in a constant state of action and reaction all the time. Nowadays science confirms that there is never a moment of non-action; even the most inert object such as a rock never ceases to react to atmosphere and time; we ourselves, when in our soundest sleep, are still in movement with heart beating, lungs breathing and messages pouring into the brain from the digestive system and the skin. As long as we are alive, we are involved in perpetual action and Krishna's teaching is that we should cease regarding ourselves as the doers of these acts. To renounce ownership of all that one does—to give up the idea of oneself as directing one's life—is to allow life to be itself, to flow unimpeded by the 'I'. For 'I' is always being conditioned, always affected by the results of behaviour, always reacting. 'The world is imprisoned in its own activity, except when actions are performed as worship of God. Therefore you must perform every action sacramentally, and be free from all attachments to results.' (Bhagavad Gita) [6]

Every action taken with the motive of self-interest is another layer to thicken the ego, or small self. But every act performed in the spirit of 'God is the doer and I his instrument' cuts through the struggle for achievement and gives a feeling of lightness and freedom to all that is undertaken.

There is a story of a yogi who was meditating on the banks of a river when he saw a scorpion fall in. He fished it out and it stung him. A little later it fell in again. Once more he rescued it and once more he was stung. Twice more this happened and a man standing by asked the yogi why he kept rescuing it when the only gratitude it showed was to sting him. 'It is the nature of scorpions to bite,' was (his) reply, 'It is the nature of *yogis* to help others when they can.' [7]

According to Hinduism, there are two aspects to work, the subjective and the objective. Subjectively, man must strive to develop his spiritual understanding, his God-consciousness; objectively, he must fulfil his duties in such a way that this inner knowledge is made available to all.

The goddess, Tripurasundari. Miniature painting, India, 19th century.

Many people find their lives engaged in employment which is not congenial to them. There is a Hindu word, *swadharma*, which means one's individual law of development. We are all unique, we all develop in different ways and each one of us has his own personal law of development according to all the factors of upbringing, inherited tendencies, innate aptitudes and for Hindus, the effects of previous lives. Not to take one's swadharma into account when looking for employment leads to trouble, and the usual reason for ignoring it is self-interest —the desire to acquire money or prestige easily. According to Hinduism, it is most important that work should be accepted in accordance with one's swadharma; in this way, one's self will be expressed as perfectly as possible. If this is not understood and the motive of self-centred gain dominates the world, there is much unhappiness.

But if a man finds that in spite of all his ignorance and early mistakes he does his work, however uncongenial, in a spirit of detached service, centring his real identity in God, his feeling of bondage will drop away.

'Egoism in the form of "I am the doer" resembles a great black and poisonous serpent. The antidote to its poison is recognition of the fact "I am not the doer." This knowledge leads to happiness.' (Ashtavakra Gita) [8]

'The body is moved by the Gunas [Nature]; it comes, stays and goes. The Self neither comes nor goes; there is no cause for grief.' (Ashtavakra Gita) [9]

JNANA YOGA—THE PATH OF KNOWLEDGE

'Under whatever name and form one may worship the Absolute Reality, it is only a means for Realizing It without name and form. That alone is true Realization, wherein one knows oneself in relation to that Reality, attains peace and realizes one's identity with It.' (Ramana Maharshi) [10]

The word *jnana* means knowledge, particularly the knowledge of Reality as distinguished from ordinary information. A man who wishes to tread the Path of Knowledge must learn the difference between who he seems to be on the surface and who he really is—the true Self which lies qualityless behind his ego. He must be prepared to see the nature of all that is transient and temporary and, by a process of elimination, arrive at last at what is eternal.

When St Augustine was asked what time was, he replied, 'I know, but when you ask me I don't.' In the same way, we see what we think is Reality but when we try to pin it down, we can't. What, in fact, is one's body? Where does it begin and end? So used are we to the idea of being separate from all other creations in the universe, we have forgotten it is we who have fixed the boundary lines. It is worth doing an experiment here. Try to stop naming everything that is about you. Recognize it namelessly, without memory.

If you succeed in doing this, you may find that your body is not the distinct object you thought it to be. Through your feet, it extends along the floor to everything that lies about you. Through your skin, it extends into the atmosphere. Although we may feel that our skin is the limit of our existence, science tells us that we cannot live without oxygen in the air around us and without the rays of the sun. We are totally dependent on them and as much a part of sun and earth as a plant or a flower is. So where do we really begin and end?

It is our minds which have fixed the limits—by the use of names to define the

A visit of a prince to an ascetic. Painting, India, 19th century.

material of the world. But names are man-made and although they are essential for everyday life they are no more 'real' than an inch or a pint. There is no such thing as an inch on its own, it can only be an inch of something. In exactly the same way, there is no such thing as a Mary on her own or a Tom on his own. We must cease thinking about the universe as definable only in terms of names. The practice of Jnana Yoga is to see through the whole man-devised network of a named world to what lies behind it—the undifferentiated life which *is as it is*.

The words we use are symbols only, but when a man is so bemused that he can no longer see this—when he takes the symbol for the reality—he is living in ignorance, according to Jnana Yoga. We have fallen into this ignorance partly because it is hard to say what a thing really *is*, because, as Alan Watts points out, 'Human beings are very much bewitched by words and ideas. They forget they are mere symbols. They tend to confuse them seriously with the real world which they only represent. The reason for this confusion is that the world of ideas and words seems to be relatively fixed and rational, whereas the real world is not fixed at all. Thus the world of ideas and words seems to be so much safer, so much more comprehensible than the real world. The word and idea 'tree' has

Vishnu with his consorts. Bronze, India, 10th century.

remained fixed currency for many centuries, but real trees have behaved in a very odd way. I can try to describe their behaviour by saying that they have appeared and disappeared, that they have been in a constant state of change, and that they flow in and out of their surroundings.

'But this does not really say what they have done, because "disappear", "change", "flow", and "surroundings" are still noises representing something utterly mysterious.' *[11]*

Similarly, the aim of Jnana Yoga is to 'slash delusion with the sword of discrimination.' We must learn to distinguish between the self, this visible person here who is known by name and attributes and who seems to dictate all our thinking, and the Self from which it has emerged and which lies eternally behind all its changes. Discrimination means the clear understanding of the distinction between the substance and the shadow, between the timeless and the passing. Much of our suffering arises from our failure to make this distinction, so that many spend all their lives chasing shadows.

The final step on the Path is the transferring of one's feeling of identity with one's body, emotions and mind to identify with the eternal aspect of one's Being.

Sarasvati, the goddess of knowledge. White marble, India, 11th century.

For this a yogi may go into a state of constant meditation in order to become fully aware of the Truth. But for those to whom this is not possible, there are other effective ways. One way is to see the happenings of the world as if they were episodes in a film or a play—a play in which oneself is *never* on the stage. Just as the light of a lamp shines through a lens, enlarging the tiny figures of a film to a vast proportion—and continues to shine when there is no film, so we should identify ourselves with the lamp and not the images of the film. To stand back from our life, and watch it as though performed in front of our eyes is one way of discrimination, although this does not mean impassivity.

Sometimes our emotions seem to cage us in like prison walls. We seem so much

Shiva, the lord of sleep, as the god of death. Wood, Nepal, 19th century.

at the mercy of circumstances, and feel that if we could be aware of the true meaning of life, this would not be so. The Path of Knowledge brings us to realize that all our demanding thoughts, even the conditions of life which prompted them, are temporary and passing. They are born and will die. But the *awareness* of them, like the lamp, is of a different nature; it belongs to something undying and eternal. 'Simple, changeless Being is our true nature.'

Thus the yoga of knowledge shifts our identification from the small self to the limitless Self by means of an increasing realization of Being, as distinct from its myriad forms. By this yoga, we come home to our nameless origination, our real nature, instead of being adrift in the world. At last we realize the truth of 'THAT ART THOU', the profoundest statement of all Hinduism.

'It is supreme. It is beyond the expression of speech; but it is known by the eye of pure illumination. It is pure, absolute consciousness, the eternal reality. Such is Brahman, and "That art thou". Meditate upon this truth.' (Shankara) *[12]*

BHAKTI YOGA—THE PATH OF DEVOTION

'The Lord bears the burden of the world. Know that the spurious ego which presumes to bear that burden is like a sculptured figure at the foot of a temple tower which appears to sustain the tower's weight. . . .

'Surrender to him and accept His will whether He appears or vanishes. Await His pleasure. If you want Him to do as you want, it is not surrender but command. You cannot ask Him to obey you and yet think you have surrendered.

Shiva and Parvati. Bronze, India, 16th century.

He knows what is best and when and how to do it. Leave everything entirely to Him. The burden is His and you have no more cares. All your cares are His. That is what is meant by surrender.' (Ramana Maharshi) *[13]*

Reaching the heart of God by adoration and surrender to him is a message easier for many to understand than that of dispelling ignorance by the Jnana light of discrimination, for love has familiar aspects to us and seems to reach us in a deeper way than other forms of wisdom. Many Hindus apprehend God in this more intimate way and have personalized him, giving him the name *Ishvara*.

A famous Hindu poet, Tulsidas, who lived in the sixteenth century, was deeply in love with his wife, Ratnavali. One day, while she was away visiting her father, Tulsidas swam the Jamna River while it was in spate in order to meet her. She rebuked him for this, saying if he had as much devotion for God the earth would become gold. These words were a revelation to him. For love for another person can be the finest of human emotions and when it is turned towards God in a selfless adoration, is the basis of the great Bhakti path. God is to be discovered at the end of this path in an entirely different way from the Jnana path of 'That art thou'. In Jnana the work is to recognize Being behind all manifestation as we recognize the sea behind the individual waves. In Bhakti, God is the object, separate from oneself, whom one worships and surrenders to.

Hindu psychology recognizes that there are different ways of loving, and Bhakti suggests five ways of developing a devotion to God which will mature with every step.

First, the strong and primitive instinct of self-love and self-preservation, from which springs the search for security and happiness, can be deepened and directed outwards to God in prayer, for God is the ultimate preserver and protector of life.

Second, the yoga of love understands man's natural desire to lovingly serve his protector (God). As servant to master, the pious man uses ritual and ceremony to worship his ruler, in a spirit of humbleness and self-sacrifice.

Third, God is regarded as ultimate friend and unfailing, ever-available companion. However lonely man may feel himself to be, he can always know that God is there eternally as loving friend.

Fourth, and nearest to Christian belief, is the dearly beloved God in the form of heavenly Father, or heavenly Mother, according to the emotional needs of the devotee. In our mainly patriarchal society, the concept of God is naturally as a Father, but in India both patriarchal and matriarchal societies have grown up together from earliest times, influencing each other, so that God as Father–Mother can be worshipped with equal devotion to both sides.

Fifth is love of God as a child. One of the strongest forms of love is that of a parent for a child and Hindus turn to God as the beloved, eternal Child, manifesting simplicity, spontaneous happiness and freedom. Christians also worship the Child at Christmas and the myth of the birth of the divine child is known throughout the world and has an inner meaning of a new birth or the blaze of truth bursting forth into man. God worshipped as the Child takes the form in Hindu stories of the infant Krishna, who is an incarnation of divine love as is the infant Jesus.

Finally comes perhaps the greatest of all the ways of love, that of the passionate

A scene from the life of Krishna, the incarnation of Vishnu. Watercolour, India, mid-19th century.

lover. All other feelings are merged into this spiritual transformation of erotic desire. In this, the individual is a bride, whether man or woman, and God is the sublime Bridegroom. When the human surrenders totally to God's will, this is recognized as the divine marriage and mystics in all religions have approached God in this way. St John of the Cross says:

Oh flame of love so living,
How tenderly you force
To my soul's inmost core your fiery probe!
Since now you've no misgiving,
End it, pursue your course
And for our sweet encounter tear the robe! [14]

For Hindus, the sexual aspect of love in worship is to be accepted as naturally as any of the others and God as Creator is worshipped through the symbol of the *lingam* which is shaped like a human phallus. They do not worship the lingam as such but recognize that it is the sacred symbol of all forms made manifest.

In Jnana Yoga, God was the Ground, the immensity of dynamic Emptiness from which springs forth the universe of form. But for those whose disposition is towards love, God must have a more personal aspect or their feelings of adoration and devotion will remain attached to the things of the world. This is where the magnificent array of Hindu gods comes in, and all the rituals of the devotional chants, and the consuming fire into which sweet-smelling herbs are thrown. Westerners often look askance at a religion which, although it professes only one Cause and Self, in its everyday and popular aspect seems to worship a great number of male and female deities. Perhaps it should be remembered that not even in our culture is it frequent for the Godhead, the unmanifest and absolute, to be worshipped. It is more usual for an aspect of God, such as his Truth or his Goodness, to be invoked and when he is prayed to, it is often the image of the Father or of the Son or the Virgin Mary which it is hoped will respond. Many people all over the world have found it easier to reach God through one of his manifested forms, and in Hinduism there are as many gods as there are aspects of the universe. Seen as objects of worship in themselves, these deities could indeed be mistaken for graven images, but this is never their purpose. They are symbols to which man's understanding, weighed down with sense-impressions, can respond, for they point the way to that which they stand for.

For Hindus always acknowledge that THAT is beyond description. Huston Smith tells us that even village priests will frequently open their temple worship with the following beloved invocation:

O Lord, forgive three sins that are due to my human limitations:
Thou art everywhere, but I worship you here;
Thou art without form, but I worship you in these forms;
Thou needest no praise, yet I offer you these prayers and salutations.
Lord, forgive three sins that are due to my human limitations. [15]

The inner meaning of a Hindu god's pose must never be overlooked. The many arms of Kali the Mother, or the three heads of Brahma the creator, can represent a whole profound philosophy and are the gateways for devotees everywhere to approach the Godhead. The Bhakti disciple is advised to seek one of these representations as his ideal, for the whole array would be as hard to

Krishna and the milkmaids. Watercolour, India, 19th century.

Two bronze figures. *left:* A standing figure of Vishnu. India, 10th century. *right:* Hanuman, a monkey-headed demi-god, selfless helper of the god Rama. Ceylon, 14th century.

worship as none at all. Whichever he chooses, he attaches himself to it for life, and the name of this deity is the word which he keeps in his mind all day long as he does his work.

Bhakti Yoga has its own practice for approaching the Divine. As Karma Yoga has non-attachment to the result of actions and Jnana Yoga has discrimination between the real and the unreal, so Bhakti has *japam*, the repetition of the name of God. Whatever one is doing, this name is repeated in one's mind, until gradually there is a deeper and deeper consciousness of the Divine which turns the total person towards It.

Other religions also perform this practice and many westerners have been made aware of it through 'The Way of a Pilgrim', the story told by an anonymous nineteenth-century Russian peasant of his search for a prayer which could be said without ceasing. After much wandering, a holy man at last told him of the Prayer of Jesus—'Lord Jesus Christ, have mercy on me'—and he began to form his life around this prayer, repeating it incessantly until it entered his heart and created a sense of warm gladness which spread through his whole being.

Apsara, an anti-god, on horseback. Carved painted wood, China, 18th century.

This calm, creative joy is the disciplined and channelled aspect of the exuberant and sometimes excessive emotions felt by the devotee, for the raptures of uncontrolled love can lead to an unpractical attitude to life which the wisdom of Hinduism deplores.

'With thought controlled and centred on the Self alone, untouched by objects of desire, he is devoted.' (Bhagavad Gita) *[16]*

RAJA YOGA—THE PATH OF INSIGHT

Let him who would climb
In meditation
To heights of the highest
Union with Brahman
Take for his path
The yoga of action:
Then when he nears
That height of oneness
His acts will fall from him,
His path will be tranquil. (Bhagavad Gita) *[17]*

Raja is called the 'king' of yogas for it is a harder and more specific path than any of the others. It is also called the yoga of meditation, for it teaches the techniques of formal meditation, which include the bodily postures known as

Hatha Yoga. It is essentially the yoga of psychology, for personal experience is its basis. Whereas western religion is largely based on faith, its theology distrusting knowledge based on personal experience, the Hindus have no such inhibitions and from earliest times have considered spiritual truths to be as valid as material ones. Consequently, those people who have determination and desire for direct spiritual experience follow the royal path of Raja.

From childhood onwards, our attention has usually been directed outwards and most of us have only rarely looked at the processes of our mind, so that we have almost lost the ability to do so. To stop the mind from wandering to outside events, to concentrate all its powers, and then to open up the mind itself in order that its whole working nature should be made apparent to it—a self-analysis of the very highest degree—is the hard work of this yoga path. No doctrine or act of faith is necessary. Just belief in what is found out, for truth needs no other prop to rest on.

Raja Yoga states that the external world is a gross form of the subtle, or internal, world of the mind. The external is the effect and the internal is the cause. Thus, by learning to manipulate the internal forces, the yogi will gain remarkable expression of his powers; he will gain control of the manifested world and pass beyond the point where the laws of nature have any influence on him. The West has long thought the opposite—that by control of external forces, the world is ordered and put right. But the yogi says that the meaning of the world is in his own mind and this must be discovered first.

The basis of much of the Raja Yoga philosophy is that perception comes through the senses, which are instruments to carry messages to the mind and from the mind to the soul. The soul receives the message and passes the response back through all the same stages. In this way we communicate with the world. The whole process of communication occurs through physical matter (except for the soul) but the mind is of much finer matter than the external organs of sense, such as the eyes or ears. When the material of the mind becomes grosser it becomes substance, and when it is grosser still it forms the external material of the world. Thus intellect and ordinary earth substance are essentially the same in kind and are only different in degree. The soul is the only thing which is non-material; the mind is its tool and the means by which the soul responds to external life. The mind can attach itself to many senses or to only one—when reading a book, for instance, the mind may be oblivious to what it hears and smells—and it is also able to be attached to none of its sense organs and to turn inwards to itself. It is this inward vision that the yogi wants to catch. He wants to discover the actual composition of the brain and how it behaves in relation to the soul. Above all, he wants to reach the soul.

Another way of understanding this is to say that man is made up of four main attributes, or layers. That which we are most aware of is our body. Next comes our conscious individuality, what we think of as 'I'. Thirdly there is the sub-conscious store of all our experiences and memories since birth. Lastly there is the soul, which is also the Self, the Ground of Being, the immense and the eternal. It is the fourth layer which is the goal of Raja Yoga.

The method for following this great path of self-discovery is made up of eight steps and the first two are ones which should precede all yogas. These are *Yama*, the five restraints and *Niyama*, the five observances.

The self-restraints are:
1. non-injury
2. truthfulness
3. non-theft
4. spiritual conduct
5. non-greed.

These requisites of a moral life often come as a surprise to those new to yoga, but a little thought will show that it is most important to ensure that external conduct is not going to interfere with the results of a new way of life. If one wants to hurt people or to lie or steal, a peaceful and composed mind will not be easy to attain. At least one can give up the *desire*, even if habit should lead one to be tempted again.

The five observances are:
1. purity
2. serenity
3. austerity
4. study
5. attentiveness to God.

Perhaps purity is the key to all spiritual exercises. In a pure heart all that disquiets is resolved and healed; all that distracts is filtered away. Whatever restraints and observances have to be practised, purity of heart grants them a miraculous ease.

Having tilled the ground for his moral self, the student is now ready to go on to a third step, which is Hatha Yoga, a yoga for the body and the one which is practised throughout the world. The *asanas*, or postures, of this yoga are primarily intended for health. A healthy body, untroubled by colds, heachaches and other ills, creates its own harmonious energy and leaves the mind free from its demands.

Iyengar in the lotus posture, from *Light on Yoga* by B. K. S. Iyengar.

To keep the mind clear and tranquil is the real aim of this yoga and the work at this stage is to create a body which responds perfectly to all that is asked of it and demands no attention.

There are said to be eighty-four asanas possible to man and of these, thirty-three give good results, while three can normally be done by everyone. Of these three, one, the lotus posture, has been found best for meditation because the spine is completely erect. It is thought that less energy is needed to keep the body upright with an erect back than if the back is allowed to slump. Westerners who attempt this posture often find it painful to begin with, because of the great strain on the leg tendons, but if they persevere for some months, it becomes comfortable, the whole body relaxed and the mind free to concentrate. A posture of sitting rather than lying means that there is no inclination to sleep, a state which is further held at bay by the eyes, which remain half open and focused on a point between them.

The fourth step in the Raja path is the control of breathing. Although the rest of the body may be completely stilled and at rest, if the lungs cease to act, the body will suffer; uncontrolled breathing can also destroy the settled calm of the mind and thus correct breathing is essential. Moreover, yogis believe in a power called *prana* which shapes the formless matter of the universe into its myriad appearances; it is by the power of prana that we breathe. Prana manifests as motion, energy, gravitation and magnetism. Every lungful of air is a movement of prana and thus to control the breath is also to control this vital force. To allow a cough to shatter the concentration of a yogi's silence or to allow the breath to become too shallow so that it can only be regained with a deep sigh, is to cut across the path of meditation like a train whistle in the night.

Thus the yogi practises breathing exercises, most of which are to help him *hold* his breath, for this will give him mastery of prana. Stopping the breath is called external if it is checked after an exhalation when the lungs are empty; and internal if it is checked when the lungs are at their fullest. The breath is usually held for a given period of time and it is then that the body attains its greatest stillness and the mind becomes disembodied. This practice is considered dangerous for untrained pupils because of the alteration in the oxygen intake; however, a harmless exercise which leads to a quiet mind is to close the right nostril slowly with the right thumb and breathe in deeply through the left nostril. Feel, as you do this, that you are inhaling the vital prana and sending it down the left side of your spinal column. Hold your breath at its peak for a moment. As you release your right nostril, close the left one with the forefinger of the same hand and breathe out all the pent-up air through the right nostril, feeling as you do so that you are throwing out all your body impurities. Then inhale again through the right nostril and continue alternating them for several minutes.

The fifth stage of Raja is control of the mind by withdrawing it from all that distracts it. Most of us have had the experience of a period of preoccupation being rudely shattered by somebody turning on a light or making a noise. When immersed in turning his mind inwards, a yogi must learn to cease reacting to all outward disturbances so that, proverbially, a snake may coil itself around him and he will not notice it. For whatever the fascinations of the outer world, the true enchantment for a yogi lies within and his whole aim at this stage is to check

Varuna, the ancient god of moral order and rightness. Sandstone, India, 8th century.

the mind, which naturally turns outwards, and to free it from the grip of the senses.

But the mind is hard to tame. It has been compared to a restless monkey, incessantly active. It can never think about one thing before it starts thinking about a whole series of other, connected things until it is lost in irrelevancies. One of the exercises to bring it under control is to sit and just let it play on, like the monkey cavorting about. You watch it jump and learn all its tricks. Until you know what it is doing you cannot control it and so, for perhaps a long time, you must let it do what it wants. It will probably start with a whole host of rapid thoughts but as time passes, it will calm down and produce fewer and fewer until at last it will be orderly and peaceful and under control. It is at this stage that the yogi can start the real work, which is concentration—the sixth step.

It is said that if the mind can flow towards the same thing for twelve seconds, this is concentration. Turned on an object like a beam of light in this intense way, the powers of the mind begin to respond like trained muscles and it can hold without effort to whatever is put before it. Its power over any problem thus increases enormously.

An exercise to teach it concentration is to gaze at one thing to the exclusion of everything else for a set time. This confines the *chitta*, or monkey-mind chatter. As one gazes, one may find a change occurring in one's consciousness of the object. From analysing its various qualities, such as colour and texture, it may suddenly become indescribably 'of itself', the wholeness rather than the parts drawing one's attention effortlessly.

Another exercise is to concentrate on a part of the body, to hold it in one's mind. This is supposed to have beneficial effects on that particular part and the heart is often the organ used for this, visualized as a lotus full of light.

Meditation is the seventh Raja step. Meditation is the essential practice of eastern religions, though it is the true heart of spiritual life everywhere, in all religions and is practised in the West by Christian monks and nuns; however, it is not widely recognized by westerners as a necessary practice. According to Hinduism, there is no escaping it. Eventually, whatever the starting point, as one approaches the great inner path of religion, one must come to meditation.

In Raja Yoga, Patanjali describes meditation as the flow of the mind towards an object of concentration *without interruption*. Meditation includes step six, but now the mind is directed away from actual objects to one thought, a spiritual ideal or an apprehension of Reality.

As the yogi meditates, he loses the feeling of himself as separate from the object of his concentration. In the previous stage, the mind was able to be held steadily upon an object but the yogi never lost the consciousness of a distinction between himself and the object. But when concentration becomes meditation, the seer and the seen are no longer two but one. The perceiver has merged into the perceived.

Lakshmi Narayan Hindu Temple, Delhi.

'He whose self is harmonized by yoga sees the Self abiding in all beings and all beings in the Self; everywhere he sees the same.' (Bhagavad Gita) *[18]*

The final stage of this eightfold journey is the culmination of all the work and aspiration. *Samadhi* is the name given to this ultimate state and it means 'together (sam) with the Lord (adhi).' It is the integration of man's time-place-bound mind with the timeless and limitless Ground of existence.

Hindus think of consciousness as manifesting in man in four ways. In wakefulness and in dreams there is consciousness of twoness or duality, of oneself and of everything else. In dreamless sleep, there is no consciousness of duality—it only springs into being when one wakes up. In samadhi, likewise, there is no consciousness of duality but one is wide awake. Dreamless sleep has been likened to a darkened room where it is not possible to see the furniture; but samadhi has been likened to a room full of light and empty of furniture. In this state, man is no longer man only, but realizes himself as one with the Godhead, one with the natureless nature of all that ever was and is.

'For where there is a duality . . . as it were . . . there one sees another; there one smells another; there one hears another; there one speaks to another; there one thinks of another; there one understands another. Where, verily, everything has become just one's own self, then whereby and whom would one smell? then whereby and whom would one see? then whereby and whom would one hear? then whereby and to whom would one speak? then whereby and on whom would one think? then whereby and whom would one understand? Whereby would one understand him by whom one understand thiss All? Lo, whereby would one understand the understander?' (Bhradaranyaka Upanishad) *[19]*

TANTRIC YOGA—THE PATH OF TRANSFORMATION

'In the root divine Wisdom is all-Brahman; in the stem she is all-Illusion; in the flower she is all-World; and in the fruit, all-Liberation.' (Tattva Tantra) *[20]*

This yoga worships the Divine as two principles, male and female, Being and Becoming. Shiva, the masculine, is eternal Being, pure perfection and timeless wisdom. Shakti, the Supreme Mother, is the creative power of Becoming, the origin of created form, and the cause of time. She mediates between the Absolute and the relative, between eternity and the flow of events in time. Thus it is to her that men turn when practising this yoga, for help and guidance in their journey towards perfection.

It is believed that the power of Shakti is present in all living things and gives them movement and life. Shiva is Mind, but Shakti is the vitalizing creative power in matter and she dwells in man in the form of dynamic energy at the base of the spine. This centre of psycho-physical power is called Kundalini (the serpent energy) and is thought of as being coiled while resting, but when aroused it uncoils itself. Most people are ignorant of its existence but it is the aim of those who follow Tantric Yoga to awaken the pent-up Kundalini energy which will then travel up the spine to the brain where it unites with Shiva, the Mind, in an embrace of love which is often portrayed sexually.

When Kundalini is thus released, the individual experiences a great surge of warmth and joyous energy. He feels the Divine Mother guiding and protecting him and turning him towards the spiritual path. The ego no longer seems to be

The three divisions of the day personified as female deities. Painting, India, 19th century.

in charge, but a deeper power has arisen within, which transforms his outlook and makes spiritual practices effortless and spontaneous.

The union of the male and female in man, which Kundalini accomplishes when she reaches the brain, is also the merging of time with the timeless, of action with stillness, of self with Self. It is represented as a supreme marriage between Being and Becoming and this integration gives rise to a flood of joy throughout the body and mind.

Tantric followers believe that it is through fulfilment and not through austerity that man finds Reality. Self-mortification is regarded as an insult to Shakti and it is believed that natural desires should be fulfilled intelligently and attentively. The repression of desires leads to endless trouble and if a man listens to the wisdom of Shakti in his heart, his impulses will gradually become higher and more noble.

Most men want to enjoy the pleasures of the world. Tantra bids them do so, but at the same time to begin to discover in them the presence of God. Tantric Yoga teaches certain practices and mystical rites which, if followed with pure motives, gradually transform the desires of the senses into love of God. In this way, says Tantra, the very chains which bind man to the world are used to free him. Hence, the sexual act as such is never condemned, for it is believed that it will be its own remedy and will bring its practitioners into union with supreme Consciousness.

Hinduism acknowledges three main types of people: *sattva* is the quality of spiritual wisdom and purity and those who are sattvic are the most akin to God; *rajas* can be translated as the quality of becoming, energy and darkness—people

Vishnu and his consort Lakshmi enthroned in heaven. Watercolour, India, 18th century.

Shiva riding on the bull, Nandi, called Joyful. India, 19th century.

of rajasic temperament are the go-getters of the world, involved with their own affairs and ambitions; *tamas*, the quality of brutish stupidity, is usually linked to a life absorbed in animal desires. The practices of Tantra (always conducted under a guru) are prescribed according to temperament.

Some of these practices require a member of the opposite sex. In these rites, the two people are thought of as symbolizing cosmic union, their personalities transcended. It is believed that they will realize the primordial origin of the world as it is shown in male and female, the duality which becomes one. Thus they lose their everyday identities and become Shakti and Shiva. Shakti, the active female principle, is the natural world; Shiva, the passive male, is the mind of the universe, the witnesser of the creation.

Tantra believes that there are six centres in the body which Kundalini (the energy of Shakti) passes, energizing them on the way. The intricate details of these centres have formed the basis of many books. The centres are called *chakras* and they are concerned with the functions of six parts of the body. They are:

Ajna—between the eyebrows
Vishuddha—at the throat
Anahata—at the heart
Manipuraka—at the navel
Swadisthana—at the genitals
Maladhara—at the base of the spine, between the anus and the genitals.

The chakras are sometimes called the lotus centres, each chakra visualized as a lotus whose petals become erect as Kundalini enters them. In each lotus is a letter symbolizing a sacred sound. Not all people are able to visualize unseen things easily, however, nor able to think of the processes of force activating matter. It is easier to refer to the unknown in terms of personal experience and Tantra has ascribed various gods and goddesses as resident in the chakras. These deities are never regarded as real, but as a sort of symbolic language through which the ordinary man can become aware of his centres in a way that is superior to words.

At the throat centre is Sadishiva, with five heads and ten arms. In his hands he holds a thunderbolt, a trident, a battle-axe, a sword, a cobra, a bell, a goad, a noose and a fire-weapon. Round his neck is a garland of snakes and he wears a tiger skin. On his forehead is a down-turned crescent moon.

In the heart centre is Isha, which is another form of Shiva, and he has two arms and three eyes. Just below the heart is a very small centre, an island of gems in the centre of a red lotus, and on the island is an alter where a devotee is in meditation. The description of this island is considered one of the most beautiful poems to devotional meditation in the Sanskrit literature. It is translated here by Ernest Wood:

> Let him find in his heart a broad ocean of nectar,
> Within it a beautiful island of gems,
> Where the sands are bright golden and sprinkled with jewels.
> Fair trees line its shores with a myriad of blooms,
> And within it rare bushes, trees, creepers and rushes,
> On all sides shed fragrance most sweet to the sense.
>
> Who would taste of the sweetness of divine completeness
> Should picture therein a most wonderful tree,
> On whose far-spreading branches grow fruit of all fancies—
> The four mighty teachings that hold up the world.
> There the fruit and the flowers know no death and no sorrows,
> While to them the bees hum and soft cuckoos sing.
>
> Now, under the shadow of that peaceful arbour
> A temple of rubies most radiant is seen.
> And he who shall seek there shall find on a seat rare,
> His dearly Beloved enshrined therein.
> Let him dwell with his mind, as his teacher defines,
> On that Divine Form, with its modes and its signs. [21]

In the navel centre is Rudra, yet another form of Shiva and although red, he appears white because he is covered with ashes. With two hands and three eyes he gives the *mudra*, or gesture, for granting boons. In the genital centre is Vishnu, blue in colour and with a yellow cloak. He has four arms and carries a lotus, a mace, a disc and a conch. Most outstanding is a beautiful garland of jewels which represents the souls of all the lives he sustains as a god of life. In the spinal base is the god Brahma, the creator of the material world, and he has four heads symbolizing the four directions of space, and four arms.

The brow centre has been left to the last because it is different in kind from the others. It is called the thousand-petalled chakra but it is not quite a chakra because it is the goal of Kundalini, the end of her journey where, as Shakti, she is united with Shiva, her husband. Energy and mind are now together in union and are represented by Ardhanarishvara, a being half male and half female. Having resided with Shiva, Kundalini then makes the return journey down

The months of the year illustrated by incidents in the life of Krishna. Painting, India, 19th century.

through the chakras, enriching each chakra with spiritual unity as she goes. Each section of the body is illuminated by her return. From the feet to the knees is considered the region of Earth, which is four-sided and yellow. From the knees to the anus is the region of Water, which is crescent-shaped and white. Fire lies between the anus and the heart and it is triangular and red. From the heart to the middle of the eyebrows is Air, which is hexagonal and a shining black. From the eyebrows to the top of the head is Ether, the all-pervading element, blue and spherical.

It has been said that when Kundalini sleeps, man is awake to this material world (his ordinary desires). But when Kundalini wakes, he sleeps—he loses his attachment to the ordinary world and enters supreme consciousness.

'He who knows the immutable, the pure, the shadowless, the bodiless, the colorless, attains to Brahman, O my friend. Such a one becomes all-knowing, and he dwells in all beings.' (Prasna Upanishad) *[22]*

THE MANTRA

Hindus have always recognized that most people have the greatest difficulty in settling down to anything that isn't for their immediate pleasure. Each of the yogas described involves time, effort, perseverance, and although a man's aspirations may be genuine, they may also be weak and easily deflected.

Very early in the Vedic age, the Hindus discovered that sound can produce vibrations which affect the emotions. Just as a piece of music can alter your mood; just as a sound such as a car horn can jar and arouse you, while another sound such as the mechanical monotony of train wheels can lull you into sleep, so certain sounds came to be recognized in India as promoting deep meditation. These sounds are called *mantras* and they consist of one word or several, or sometimes a series of letters.

They emerged through the realization that it is by name that we come to recognize the universe. A mantra is the name, in the form of a sound, by which the gods who represent all aspects of the universe can be reached. A mantra can only be given by a guru and it is considered a source of power, charged with the spiritual vibrations of the guru. It is the living embodiment of that guru's understanding of the Truth and its vibrations create the right conditions round the worshipper for his chosen deity to respond.

Mantra means 'thought-form' and the sound represents that part of the thought-form which *is* the deity. Thus they are inseparable from the deities they express and are considered the most subtle vehicles of communication possible between worshipper and worshipped. To amplify this, let us imagine that a man is attracted by the ideal of mercy and would like to meditate on this. But the word mercy has no meaning unless it is attached to deeds and so he meditates on the goddess of mercy and all the stories he knows about her. To help him to become open to her so that she can enter his heart and mind, his guru gives him a mantra which is the goddess herself incarnated in sound; repetition of the mantra brings the right response from the goddess so that the man feels mercy penetrating his being.

There are an unknown number of mantras, but the number of sounds of

Lady worshipping at the shrine of Shiva. An illustration from *The Indian Musical Mode, Bhairavi Ragini*, India, 16th century.

which the human is capable is limited by his vocal organs. These basic sounds vary from language to language, but most of them are common to all languages. They are thought of as eternally alive. Each sound has its proper expression in an object in the universe. In other words, everything that we see or think about has its own sound, which is its natural name, and when we repeat its natural (not man-given) name, the object is evoked.

One-syllable mantras are called seed-mantras, or basic thought-forms, and the most famous of these is OM. Properly pronounced, OM is intoned A–U–M. Because it begins with 'ah' which is uttered at the back of the mouth, continues with a short 'oo' in the middle of the mouth, and ends with 'm-m', which is made by the lips at the front of the mouth, it is regarded as the announcer of the Godhead, and the three sounds represent a trinity of gods. A is Brahma, the Cosmic Body of the universe; U is Vishnu, the Cosmic Intellect; and M is Shiva, the Cosmic Consciousness. The meaning of AUM (usually written as OM) is 'I accept.'

'Verily, this syllable is of assent, for whenever one assents to anything he says simply *aum*. What is assent is fulfilment.' . . . (Chandogya Upanishad) *[23]*

All mantras have four levels which must be contemplated as the mantra is being intoned:
    1. the sound
    2. the meaning

3. the idea it represents
4. the spirit.

In the case of OM these are: 1. the ultimate sound, using all parts of the mouth; 2. the acceptance of the Divine Trinity, which is ground for concentration; 3. the ideas implicit in it, which is ground for meditation; 4. the spiritual 'feel' of it.

YANTRAS

These are geometrical figures and they represent the thought-forms of the deities put into visual symbols, as the mantras expressed them in sounds. They are for meditating upon and are constructed of the basic linear elements known to man, such as a straight line, cross, circle, triangle and point, and although drawn on the flat, must always be thought of as three-dimensional.

To the Hindu, there are innumerable yantras in the world; for every natural shape, such as a flower or a leaf can be meditated upon as a yantra, its meaning being the story of creation itself.

Yantras are usually made up of interlaced triangles and other figures and when they are framed by a circle, they are often called *mandalas*. They are an aid to holding the mind steadily concentrated on a form and are much used in Tibetan Tantric Yoga, where, as mandalas, they will be more fully described.

THE CASTE SYSTEM

The social distinctions of caste, strongly denounced by the western world, are thought to have originated with the fair-skinned Aryans who migrated into

left: The mantra, AUM, painted with figures. India, 19th century. *right:* A yantra. Crystal, Nepal, 18th century.

India some three thousand years ago. Their disdain for the dark Dravidian natives was perhaps the breeding ground for the caste system, for the Aryans were an energetic and highly organized people with a strong family tradition. They developed professional guilds which were designed to give cohesion to certain groups and they devised many taboos with regard to sanitation and purification.

The division of the population into four main groups of people (castes) probably took several centuries to crystallize. Hindus believed that the castes were created by Brahma and each caste emerged symbolically from a different part of Brahma's body.

The highest caste, the priests, who were called Brahmins, sprang from his mouth. They were the seers, the contemplatives, their office to study the Vedas and interpret them to the people. They looked after the people's spiritual welfare in the way that priests all over the world are required to do, and they were not allowed to deal with material things. Thus many Brahmins were, and still are, very poor. Artists and musicians were usually Brahmins.

From Brahma's arms came the administrators, the rulers and the warriors. The third caste came from Brahma's thighs and were the farmers, craftsmen and artisans, the producers of the material goods on which everyone depended. These three castes were known as twice-born because at the age of twelve the men were initiated into the secrets of the Vedic teaching, for which purpose they were given a sacred thread. The fourth and lowest caste, who emerged from Brahma's feet, were the unskilled labourers, who spent their lives serving the other three.

The caste system was never thought of as a man-made invention. It was believed to be a natural law, revealed to the Hindus, and originally the castes

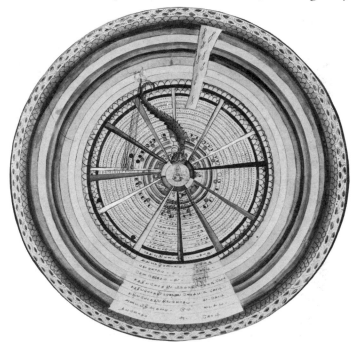

A mandala diagram showing the origin of the waters. Watercolour on paper, Cambodia, 20th century.

were not meant to be hereditary; they stood for rungs on the ladder of spiritual development. Movement upwards from one caste to another was meant to occur with the increase of wisdom and enlightenment for, to the Hindus, all people were at different stages of spiritual development and it was better to express this in the social system.

But the castes became more and more rigid and at last all movement between them was dropped. One remained for life in the caste one was born in. This was not the only distortion that occurred. From the original four castes, two thousand others proliferated. Caste lost its spiritual significance and came to be decided by hundreds of other factors—where one lived, who one's parents were, how one ate and how one washed. Intermarriage was fobidden. A caste scale was introduced to determine the distance at which one caste could approach another, for defilement was considered to have taken place if even the shadow of a person from a lower caste passed over the food of a high-caste Hindu.

But worse than this was to come. The caste scale revealed that there were some people who belonged to no caste at all. They were called the Untouchables and were not allowed to enter the temples, live in the villages, or come within touching distance of any but themselves.

An India gone mad, you might think, and as time went on, various groups denounced the system and refused to recognize it. The groups were the Buddhists, the Jains and the Sikhs. In our time, Mahatma Gandhi was the reformer who fought fiercely against the iniquitous treatment of the Untouchables and since his death, there is by law no such group, for now every Hindu is allowed to go into the temples. Forward-looking Hindus today are working to remove the corruption of exclusiveness in the caste system altogether.

THE FOUR STAGES OF MAN

Hindus believe that everyone has four stages of growth in his life. The first part is youth, when a man must become educated and learn to manage his affairs. His next stage is when he marries and takes on the responsibilities of a householder and head of a family. When his children are grown up—when he has looked at his first grandchild, according to tradition—his duties are over and he begins to detach himself from worldly things, at the same time taking higher responsibilities of a less personal nature. Then, in old age, he retires from the external world altogether, although he may still seem to remain in it.

Closely connected with these stages are his desires. What are the desires of man? According to Hinduism, they are four. Perhaps this sounds oversimplified, until we consider for how long this question has been debated in India.

Man begins with a very natural want—pleasure. Pleasure in the good things of life is considered one of the legitimate desires and the Hindu texts are full of advice as to how to increase enjoyment to its fullest degree. There are infinite possibilities for entertainment in a world that abounds with delights for the senses and wonders for the mind. So long as good judgment and basic morality are observed—go ahead, says the Hindu. Do not suppress the desires for pleasure but fulfil it as magnificently as you can.

Many people do just that and for them, that is exactly what life is about. But for others, there comes a time when seeking pleasure seems too trivial and limiting. They begin to discover that happiness is a state not to be achieved by

Bathing in the Ganges, the sacred river, believed to give immortality.

the satisfying of every wish. In Hinduism, the many wants of man are thought of as animals and feeding one animal satisfies one want. But no sooner is one fed than another starts to howl and it must also be attended to. Sometimes, several cry for attention at once. Because man identifies himself with all these animal voices, he loses his inner wholeness, his true self.

When pleasure ceases to satisfy, man's next great desire is usually for prestige, status, power and wealth. His preoccupation with private, momentary satisfactions turns to the achievement of social success. This, too, is not to be condemned. Worldly success is a very alluring goal for most of us, and it can bring a sense of dignity and purpose which can lead, through self-respect, to true unselfishness. But, on its negative side, it can also bring about an insatiable greed for riches or fame. Then, fierce competition for material gain leads to a nervous anxiety about one's possessions. Then, too, one day each of us will die and that will be the end of it all.

Many men, approaching death, have become conscious of the ephemeral nature of their possessions, whether knowledge, fame, power or wealth. Pleasure and success, the first two steps on the Path of Desire, prove ultimately unsatisfactory. But no one is ever condemned for seeking them. So long as they seem desirable goals, one should pursue them, for they are part of the experience of life. If one never tastes the delights, one will never grow beyond them.

But if a man does find he wants to move on towards another goal, what is the next of his wants? Renunciation, says Hinduism.

When an athlete is in training, or when a student is approaching an exam, all

Holy men at a roadside temple near Delhi.

pleasant distractions are sacrificed for the greater goal. This sort of renunciation is hardly considered as such by those seeking higher prizes. It is different altogether from the so-called renunciation of the person who withdraws from the world because of disillusionment or hurt. Such a person has, out of self-pity, closed the doors on further spiritual development and must remain entombed in his own private world of self until he is prepared to accept life again.

In the same spirit as the athlete, the religious man will prefer to give up the old pleasures in favour of a spiritual objective which is less tangible but infinitely more satisfying. Hinduism stresses that the Path of Desire comes *before* the Path of Renunciation and renunciation is not intended for those who have failed to fulfil their lives. Nor will everybody find the prizes of the Path of Desire inadequate. Many people prefer to live life to the full, confident that this is all they want and that everything is good. They feel no urge towards the inner life of the contemplative and cannot understand how anyone can live life just as richly but find its material rewards unsatisfying. The Hindus explain this difference by the doctrine of rebirth, believing that the enthusiastic hedonist is a 'young soul' tasting the world as a new pleasure, while the other has lived many more times and is now directing his attention elsewhere. For it is the substance that the religious man thirsts for; it is for this that he is willing to leave the shadow for ever behind.

Perhaps he sees how men become their own gods and devote their lives to serving the deity called 'self'. At this turning point, a man is likely to move towards society and humanity at large, believing that his duty is to help man-

kind. He puts the claims of others before his own and by doing so, begins his last journey, for the religion of duty is the first part of the Path of Renunciation and the third recognized desire of human life.

Service to the community represents the wish to give rather than the old desire to gain. The rewards of this attitude are less material but more satisfying. Self-approval, because one has contributed, perhaps at cost to oneself, to the general good; a sense that one is needed in the world; a genuine pleasure in seeing other people benefit. These are strong motives for social service and many people seek no further, but find this their ultimate objective in life.

But even caring for the community has its limitations. This, too, begins to seem inadequate as a goal and although one may still continue the work one has started, the final fulfilment seems to lead beyond the community to another dimension altogether. Then starts the last step on the Path of Desire which has also become the Path of Renunciation.

What does man *really* want? A happiness which is lasting, says Hinduism. At the back of all his actions, even the most base, lies the urge to find a way out of the impasse of his limitations—mortality, ignorance and suffering—and to move towards absolute freedom, immortal existence and untainted, limitless happiness. As a human, he feels small, separate and insignificant. In his ignorant efforts to overcome this, he seeks increasing power over external events and circum- stances. He drives himself ever further and further away from the true Source of all he is looking for, which is within him as God, the Self—the only real fulfilment of life.

What is it that stands in the way of realization of the Self? It is wrong identi- fication, says Hinduism. Within each of us is the Self—that of God which is present in all of us—so that each man lives his life in the presence of God. But instead of identifying himself with the Substance, he identifies with its tem- porary appearance and mistakes the passing for the eternal. He thinks of the body as all there is and fears its death as the end of him.

The goal of Hinduism is the giving up of all the cluttered, muddled sense of separate ego, or small self, which obscures man's true nature, so that the light of the Self will illumine him, just as a crowded, dirty room can be cleaned to show the true proportions within. Then man will know the Reality which is undying and know that his own self is that Reality; then he will know the true happiness of full and abounding life, and the freedom of Being.

THE AGE OF THE WORLD

Like man himself, the world is born and it will die, say Hindus. It passes through great cycles called *kalpas*—a kalpa is one day of Brahma—and within the kalpas are aeons, called *yugas*. Every yuga is divided into four ages, and each age marks a progressive decline in the virtue and happiness of man. Our present age is in kali-yuga, the last and the worst of the four, and Hindus believe that it started in 3102 B.C. and that it will come to an end about 428,000 years from now, when the whole world will be destroyed by fire and flood. But then, as it has happened before, the world will be reborn into a new golden age.

Ganesh, the Elephant god, lord of all that can be counted and comprehended.

MAYA—THE WORLD AS ILLUSION

In their dreams, people may have been climbing a mountain or walking through a forest, perhaps in a situation with unknown companions. Whatever has occurred, they lived it vividly—but then woke up to find that nothing real had taken place at all.

In the same way as a dream, a Hindu who sees God as *Neti–neti* (neither this nor that, i.e. nothing that words can express) regards the whole world as illusion, a projection of his own mind. Hindus call this illusion *maya*. There are three ways of consciousness in which the world appears to us, they say. The first is in dream or in hallucination. The second is the way the world appears to our everyday senses. The third is the world as seen from samadhi, from the state of ultimate consciousness when there is neither 'I' nor 'it', just the oneness of non-duality. This is Reality, and our ordinary world when seen from this state seems like a miraculous appearance only, without any substance.

To explain this further, Alan Watts uses the illustration of a man who has never seen a cat. *[24]* He is looking through a narrow slit in a fence and a cat walks past. First he sees the head, then the furry trunk, and a little later the tail. The cat turns round and walks back and he sees the same regular sequence of

A shrine to Vishnu, the god of duration and eternal life. Carved ivory slightly ornamented with lacquer, India, 18th century.

head, trunk, tail. This sequence appears to be reliable evidence. Once more the cat turns round and once more the man sees the same succession of parts, so he reasons that the event called head is the invariable and necessary cause of the event called tail, which is the head's effect. This confused thinking arises because he failed to see that the head and tail go together and are all one cat. The cat was born all of a piece, but the observer only saw it through a slit and could not see the whole all at once.

In the same way we seem to look at life bit by bit (wherever our attention is drawn) and we use memory to string the bits together. We notice many objects but our conscious attention is fleeting and narrow. Thus we come to think that the world is made up of separate things which we give names to, and we then have the problem of how these things are connected and how they condition each other. But this problem is an unreal one based on our ignorance of the fact that it is just our way of looking at the world which has chopped it up into names and events and causes and effects. We fail to see that the world is all one, like the cat.

This involvement with unreal problems takes all the fun out of life and turns the world into a dreary and complicated place. We seem to be out of step with the dance of life, with all its movement and gaiety, and our trouble lies in identifying ourselves with the parts instead of with the whole. *Lila* is the Hindu name given to this dance of the ever-changing events in all their inexhaustible marvel.

When we take the parts as the only reality, the world appears full of sorrow and confusion. But when we look for the Whole and not for the parts, when we see that a cat in its catness is more than its parts, that the world in its Essence is more than its million appearances, we place ourselves at the centre and not at the periphery of life and are then able to enjoy all the innumerable and amazing parts because we are freed from our bondage to them. To believe that the myriad, ever-changing phenomena of life are in themselves the only reality is to exist as beasts of burden, mindlessly bearing the heavy load of our own existence. But to know that the true nature of all things is the timeless and eternal Ground is to enter the dance and to find ourselves in step with all creation.

THE WESTERN HINDU—RAMANA MAHARSHI

The influence on the West of Vedanta, the highest Hindu teaching, has usually come about through visiting *swamis* (teachers), frequently sages in their own right, who have travelled to the West and found support in countries such as America and England. Ramana Maharshi, perhaps the greatest modern sage that India has produced, did not travel. He remained in his *ashram* (community of disciples) in the town of Tiruvannamalai from the age of seventeen until his death. Westerners travelled in a constant stream to visit him, and received from him unfailing wisdom, penetrating analysis, and deep compassion.

He was born in 1879, in the Tamil land of South India, during the yearly festival of the 'Sight of Shiva' (Shiva is the god who represents the cosmic dance of creation) and he was given the name of Venkataraman. He grew up in a happy Brahmin family and nothing untoward happened until he was sixteen, when he first heard a relative talking of the Holy Hill of Arunachala, thought to be the seat of Shiva, at the foot of which lies Tiruvannamalai. A sudden realization came to him that the holiness men talked of when they spoke of this hill was not a remote abstraction but an awesome actuality. For some months, he contemplated this discovery, becoming more and more aware of the path he must follow. Then he had a strange experience:

'It was about six weeks before I left Madura for good that the great change in my life took place. It was quite sudden. I was sitting alone in a room on the first floor of my uncle's house. I seldom had any sickness, and on that day there was

Shiva's gentle companion, Gauri, the Fair One. Bronze, India, 14th century.

nothing wrong with my health, but a sudden violent fear of death overtook me. There was nothing in my state of health to account for it, and I did not try to account for it or to find out whether there was any reason for the fear. I just felt "I am going to die" and began thinking what to do about it. It did not occur to me to consult a doctor, or my elders or friends; I felt that I had to solve the problem myself, there and then.

'The shock of the fear of death drove my mind inwards and I said to myself mentally, without actually framing the words: "Now death has come; what does it mean? What is it that is dying? The body dies." And I at once dramatised the occurrence of death. I lay with my limbs stretched out stiff as though rigor mortis had set in and imitated a corpse so as to give greater reality to the enquiry. I held my breath and kept my lips tightly closed so that no sound could escape, so that neither the word "I" nor any other word could be uttered. "Well then," I said to myself, "this body is dead. It will be carried stiff to the burning ground and there burnt and reduced to ashes. But with the death of this body am I dead? Is the body I? It is silent and inert but I feel the full force of my personality and even the voice of the "I" within me, apart from it. So I am Spirit transcending the body. The body dies but the Spirit that transcends it cannot be touched by death. That means I am the deathless Spirit." All this was not dull thought; it flashed through me vividly as living truth which I perceived directly, almost without thought-process. "I" was something very real, the only real thing about my present state, and all the conscious activity connected with my body was

A yaksini, a female anti-god who takes possession of children. Terracotta, Bengal, 1st century B.C.

Ramana Maharshi.

centered on that "I". From that moment onwards the "I" or Self focused attention on itself by a powerful fascination. Fear of death had vanished once and for all. Absorption in the Self continued unbroken from that time on.' [25]

At the age of seventeen, he left his home and went to the Holy Hill of Arunachala. He arrived penniless but this mattered nothing to him. He sat, immersed in the experience of Being, for many weeks. A daily cup of food was brought to him and in due course some disciples, sensing the purity of his understanding, begged him to teach. He taught the path of Self-enquiry from then on, for more than fifty years. His name of Venkataraman was shortened to Ramana and he was also called the Maharshi, which comes from *Maha Rishi* or Great Sage, a title given to those who teach a new spiritual truth. But the name frequently used for him by his students was Bhagavan, which means 'Lord', a title given only to those supreme sages who are recognized as being one with God. He died in 1950.

His devotees formed an ashram around him early in his life. Here he lived and taught. He wrote very little. His disciples recorded his answers to the many queries of his students and there are several books of these describing the way to the knowledge of Self in simple and direct words.

Here is one such dialogue between Bhagavan, referred to as 'B' and two Parsi ladies, referred to as 'L'.

L. 'Bhagavan, we have been spiritually inclined from childhood. We have read several books on philosophy and are attracted by Vedanta. So we read the Upanishads, Yoga Vasishta, Bhagavad Gita, etc. We try to meditate, but there is no progress in our meditation. We do not understand how to realize. Can you kindly help us towards realization?'

B. 'How do you meditate?'

L. 'I begin with asking myself "Who am I?" and eliminate the body as not "I", the breath as not "I", the mind as not "I", but then I am unable to proceed further.'

B. 'Well, that is all right so far as the mind goes. Your process is only mental. Actually all the scriptures mention this process only in order to guide the seeker to the Truth. The Truth cannot be directly indicated; that is why this mental process is used. You see, he who eliminates all the "not-I" cannot eliminate the "I". In order to be able to say "I am not this" or "I am That" there must be the "I" to say it. This "I" is only the ego, or the "I"-thought. After the rising up of this "I" thought, all other thoughts arise. The "I"-thought is therefore the root thought. If the root is pulled out, all the rest is at the same time uprooted. Therefore seek the root "I"; question yourself: "Who am I?"; find out the source of the "I". Then all these problems will vanish and the pure Self alone will remain.'

Indra, the personification of law. Sculpture, India, 18th century.

L. 'But how am I to do it?'

B. 'The "I" is always there, whether in deep sleep, in dream, or in the waking state. The one who sleeps is the same as the one who is now speaking. There is always the feeling of "I". If it were not so you would have to deny your existence. But you do not. You say "I am". Find out who is.'

L. 'I still do not understand. You say the "I" is now the false "I". How am I to eliminate this wrong "I"?'

B. 'You need not eliminate any false "I". How can "I" eliminate itself? All that you need do is to find out its origin and stay there. Your effort can extend only so far. Then the Beyond will take care of itself. You are helpless there. No effort can reach it.'

L. 'If "I" am always—here and now—why do I not feel so?'

B. 'Who says that you do not? Does the real "I" or the false "I"? Ask yourself and you will find that it is the false "I". The false "I" is the obstruction which has to be removed in order that the true "I" may cease to be hidden. The feeling that "I have not realized" is the obstruction to realization. In fact, it is already realized. There is nothing more to be realized. If there were, the realization would be something new which did not yet exist, but was to come about in the future; but whatever is born will also die. If realization is not eternal it is not worth having. Therefore, what we seek is not something that must begin to exist but only what is eternal but is veiled from us by obstructions. All that we need do is remove the obstruction. What is eternal is not recognized as such owing to ignorance. Ignorance is the obstruction. Get rid of it and all will be well. This ignorance is identical with the "I"-thought. Seek its source and it will vanish.

'The "I"-thought is like a spirit which, although not palpable, rises up simultaneously with the body, flourishes with it and disappears with it. The body-consciousness is the wrong "I". Give it up. You can do so by seeking the source

Circular pictures of deities.
Colour on paper, India,
19th century.

of "I". The body does not say "I am". It is you who say "I am the body". Find out who this "I" is. Seek its source and it will vanish.'

L. 'Then, will there be bliss?'

B. 'Bliss is co-eval with Being-Consciousness. All the arguments relating to the eternal Being apply to eternal Bliss also. Your nature is Bliss. Ignorance is now hiding the Bliss, but you have only to remove the ignorance for the Bliss to be freed.'

L. 'Should we not find out the ultimate reality of the world as individual and God?'

B. 'These are conceptions of the "I". They arise only after the advent of the "I"-thought. Did you think of them in deep sleep? Yet you existed in sleep, and the same "you" is speaking now. If they were real, would they not exist in your sleep also? They are dependent on the "I"-thought. Again, does the world tell you: "I am the world"? Does the body say "I am the body?" You say: "This is the world", "this is the body", and so on. So these are only your conceptions. Find out who you are, and there will be an end of all doubts.'

L. 'What becomes of the body after realization? Does it continue to exist or not? We see realized people performing actions like other people.'

B. 'This question need not worry you now. You can ask it after realization if you feel like it. As for the realized beings, let them take care of themselves. Why do you worry about them? In fact, after realization, neither the body nor anything else will appear different from the Self.'

L. 'If we are always Being-Consciousness-Bliss, why does God place us in difficulties? Why did he create us?

B. 'Does God come and tell you that He placed you in difficulties? It is you who say so. It is again the false "I". If that disappears, there will be no one to say that God created this or that. That which is does not even say "I am." For does any doubt arise that "I am not?" Only if a doubt arose whether one was not a cow or a buffalo would one have to remind oneself that one is not but is a man; but this never happens. It is the same with one's own existence and realization.

'When the mind unceasingly investigates its own nature, it transpires that there is no such thing as mind. This is the direct path for all.

'The mind is merely thoughts. Of all thoughts, the thought "I" is the root. Therefore the mind is only the thought "I". Whence does this thought "I" arise? Seek for it within; it then vanishes. This is the pursuit of Wisdom. Where the "I" vanished, there appears an "I-I" by itself. This is the Infinite.

'If the ego is, everything else also is. If the ego is not, nothing else is. Indeed the ego is all. Therefore the enquiry as to what this ego is, is the only way of giving up everything.

'The state of non-emergence of "I" is the state of being THAT. Without questing for that state of non-emergence of "I" and attaining It, how can one accomplish one's own extinction, from which the "I" does not revive? Without that attainment, how is it possible to abide in one's true state, where one is That?

'Just as a man would dive in order to get something that had fallen in the water, so one should dive into oneself with a keen one-pointed mind, controlling speech and breath, and find the place whence the "I" originates. The only enquiry leading to Self-realization is seeking the source of the word "I". Meditation on "I am not this; I am that" may be an aid to enquiry but it cannot be the enquiry. If one

The carved marble Jain temple of Mount Abu.

enquires "Who am I?" within the mind, the individual "I" falls down abashed as soon as one reaches the Heart and immediately Reality manifests itself spontaneously as "I-I". Although it reveals itself as "I", it is not the ego but the perfect Being, the Absolute Self.' [26]

SRI RAMAKRISHNA

The intuitive certainty that there is a Godhead, or Ground of Existence, and that it is man's destiny to find It and know It as his own identity, has long been a fervent belief in the West as well as in the East. During the twentieth century, various writers such as Aldous Huxley, Christopher Isherwood, and Gerald Heard spread the teachings of Hinduism in the West, particularly that path to the Supreme Identity called Vedanta.

These three writers, all living in California although British by birth, brought over *swamis* from India, and published books on Vedanta and on yoga. Such works as Aldous Huxley's *Perennial Philosophy* and Christopher Isherwood's *Vedanta for Modern Man* brought interest and revelation to many westerners. A great swami called Vivekananda once wrote that man is like an infinite spring coiled up in a small box, a spring which is trying to unfold itself. Certainly this could be said of western man today, whose religion keeps him coiled up in the small box of humanistic ethics and fails to satisfy his deep need for experience of the sublime, eternal life.

One of the great teachers whose influence, helped by the Californian writers, has been strong in the West, is Sri Ramakrishna. Ramakrishna was born into a Brahmin family in 1836. At the age of six or seven, he had his first experience of spiritual ecstasy when one day in June, walking along a narrow path between paddy-fields and eating the baked rice that he carried in a basket, he looked up at the sky and saw a beautiful dark thunder-cloud. As it spread, rapidly enveloping the whole sky, a flight of snow-white cranes passed in front of it. The beauty of the contrast overwhelmed the boy. He fell to the ground unconscious and was found by some villagers and carried home. He said later that in that state he had experienced an indescribable joy.

When he was sixteen, he went to Calcutta to join his elder brother, who was a priest. The two young men moved to Dakshineswar, a temple devoted to the goddess, Kali. Kali, who symbolizes Reality, and who is thought of as the Mother of the Universe, the Giver of Life and Death, is one of the strangest of the Hindu deities. Because she is the Destroyer as well as the Creator, she is often depicted as a terrifying force of destruction, her sword raised to strike, a garland of severed heads encircling her neck, and her waist girdled by dismembered human arms. Yet, as Christopher Isherwood points out, '. . . Kali embodies a profound spiritual truth. She teaches us to look beneath the appearances of Life. We must not cling to what seems beautiful and pleasant; we must not shrink from what seems ugly and horrible. The same Brahman (Godhead) underlies all experience. When we have learned to regard death and disaster as our Mother, we shall have conquered every fear.' [27]

Ramakrishna found in Kali a great Reality. To her he gave his whole self—his understanding, his devotion and his energy. He meditated on her incessantly, addressing her stone image as a son would talk to his mother. He longed to have

A Brahmin and his wife performing the ceremony of *puja*. Watercolour, India, 1785.

a vision of her living presence, and at last it happened. But this, rather than moderating the pressure of his devotion, merely intensified it, and his austerities began to seem so extreme that they alarmed the temple officials, who feared for his sanity. He even began to doubt his sanity himself and his only recourse was to pray to the Divine Mother for help. To her he would pray, 'I do not know what these things are. I am ignorant of mantras and the scriptures. Teach me, Mother, how to realize Thee. Who else can help me? Art Thou not my only refuge and guide?' *[28]*

He was always reassured and sustained by the feeling of the presence of the Divine Mother, even when most bewildered by his visions and thoughts. Even his critics, the temple manager and his assistants, who had been scandalized by the fact that the young Ramakrishna removed his Brahmin thread (an investiture conferred upon Brahmin boys, giving them certain privileges and imposing upon them strict duties) when meditating, and gave consecrated food to a cat, even they could not help being impressed by his 'purity, guilelessness, truthfulness, integrity, and holiness. They felt an uplifting influence in his presence.' *[29]*

His burning ardour began to attract the attention of religious authorities and after much deliberation, he was proclaimed an *avatar*, an incarnation of the Supreme Reality, regarded in the same light as the Buddha and, indeed, Jesus. Ramakrishna received this staggering announcement with childlike indifference and a certain sly humour. 'Just fancy,' he remarked: 'Well, I'm glad it's not a disease. . . . But, believe me, I know nothing about it.' *[30]*

If Ramakrishna had remained totally dedicated to Kali, his spiritual gifts

Ramakrishna, from a painting by Dvorak.

The goddess Kali in her terrible aspect. Bronze, India, 18th–19th century.

might not have unfolded completely. But in order to find the Supreme Reality, the Self beyond all forms, he had to renounce the Mother, whose image came between him and the formless Ground of God. In 1864, a monk named Totapuri came to Dakshineswar to instruct Ramakrishna. Ramakrishna found it very difficult to break through the illusion of duality created by the beloved Kali. 'At last Totapuri picked up a piece of glass from the ground, stuck it between Ramakrishna's eyebrows and told him to fix his mind on that point. "When Mother appeared," Ramakrishna said later, "I drew the sword of discrimination and cut her in half." For three days, he remained absorbed in samadhi.' [31]

For the rest of his life, Ramakrishna remained at Dakshineswar, his illumined sanity a focal point for many disciples and students. During this time, one disciple, a former headmaster in Calcutta, reverently began to write down all Ramakrishna's statements, which were later published as *The Gospel of Sri Ramakrishna*. Of the many conversations recorded, the following one perhaps best gives a true feeling of the Master:

'*Master*: "There are three classes of devotees. The lowest one says, 'God is up there.' That is, he points to heaven. The mediocre devotee says that God dwells in the heart as the 'Inner Controller.' But the highest devotee says: 'God alone has become everything. All things that we perceive are so many forms of God.' Narendra used to make fun of me and say: 'Yes, God has become them all!

A miniature painting from an illustrated book. India, 19th century.

Then a pot is God, a cup is God!' " (*Laughter*)

"All doubts disappear when one sees God. It is one thing to hear of God, but quite a different thing to see Him. A man cannot have one hundred per cent conviction through mere hearing. But if he beholds God face to face, then he is wholly convinced.

"Formal worship drops away after the vision of God. It was thus that my worship in the temple came to an end. I used to worship the Deity in the Kali temple. It was suddenly revealed to me that everything is Pure Spirit. The utensils of worship, the altar, the door-frame—all Pure Spirit. Men, animals, and other living beings—all Pure Spirit. Then like a madman I began to shower flowers in all directions. Whatever I saw I worshipped.

"One day, while worshipping Shiva (the god representing the force of Death, which resolves all forms into the primordial Ground from which emerges the re-creation of life), I was about to offer a bel-leaf on the head of the image, when it was revealed to me that this Universe itself is Shiva. After that my worship of Shiva through the image came to an end. Another day, I had been plucking flowers, when it was revealed to me that the flowering plants were so many bouquets."

'*Trailokya:* "Ah! How beautiful is God's creation!"

'*Master:* "Oh, no, it is not that. It was revealed to me in a flash. I didn't calculate about it. It was shown to me that each plant was a bouquet adorning the Universal Form of God. That was the end of my plucking flowers. I look on man in just the same way. When I see a man, I see that it is God Himself who walks on earth, as it were rocking to and fro like a pillow floating on the waves. The pillow moves with the waves. It bobs up and down.

"The body has, indeed, only a momentary existence. God alone is real".' . . . *[32]*

Among Ramakrishna's many disciples, two were outstanding—Vivekananda and Brahmananda. Vivekananda was the bearer of Ramakrishna's message to the world, while Brahmananda (regarded by Ramakrishna as his spiritual son) was to remain a great mystic in India. Vivekananda went to America in 1893 and spent some years there, travelling all over the continent to speak on the universality of religious truth. He also visited England and before he died, in 1902, founded the Ramakrishna Order (of which Brahmananda became the head) and also the Ramakrishna Mission in India, an institution which has its own hospitals, schools, agricultural colleges, libraries and publishing house. He founded the Vedanta Society of America, which now has thirteen centres in the United States and one in England. The Society owes much of its continuing strength to a disciple of Vivekananda called Prabhavananda, who has worked with Christopher Isherwood in translating the Hindu scriptures into English for the West.

THE KRISHNA CONSCIOUSNESS MOVEMENT

Some six years ago, young people in America began to be attracted to the teachings of an Indian guru, Swami Prabhupada, and the International Society for Krishna Consciousness was formed. It is now better known as the Hare Krishna Movement. The basis of its teachings is the Bhagavad Gita, one of the Hindu scriptures, in which Krishna, an incarnation of God, gives advice to one Arjuna, when Arjuna is preparing for battle with his cousins.

The Hare Krishna Movement subscribes to the Hindu belief that Krishna was an actual incarnation of God in human form, as Christians believe Jesus to have been. Thus they use the name of Krishna as they would God, and they chant 'Hare Krishna, Hare Krishna' (*Hare* means 'God') in order to reach 'Krishna consciousness', the realization of Krishna in the mind. It is believed that Krishna consciousness brings about a state of spiritual pleasure, and thus the groups of young men and women dance in expectant joy as they go through the streets of American and English cities. They dress in yellow robes and have their hair shaven. They intone 'Hare Krishna' as they dance and believe that the chant, through its power as a mantra, has consciousness-changing vibrations which benefit all who hear it.

The movement is essentially devotional and its followers serve Krishna by thinking of him all the time, so that whatever they are doing—cooking, dancing or studying—the task is devoted to Krishna. They believe that Krishna's disciples have passed his teaching down from guru to guru to the present age, and that his representative today, in direct line of succession from Krishna, is Swami Prabhupada. Swami Prabhupada himself says:

'So what is the object of this Krishna consciousness movement? The purpose of this movement is that we are trying to love Krishna. If I love Krishna or God, then naturally I will be obedient to the laws of God. Is it not? Just like my students. When—say four or five years ago—I came here, I had no students. I was loitering in the street; no one was caring for me. Now I have hundreds and thousands of students; they can do whatever I order. I did not pay them anything, nor did I bring any money from India. But they are executing my orders simply out of love. Is it not a fact? Because they have developed a love for me—the reason may be whatever it may be, but unless they have developed love for me, how could they execute my orders without any personal profit? Therefore this is the first thing required. Religion means to abide by the orders of God. Simple. And this obedience to the laws of God will be automatically performed if everyone revives his dormant love for God.

'We have taken this science. We are teaching everyone how to love God. If one thinks that he has learned how to love God through some particular religion, we have no objection. Whether he is Christian or Hindu or Muslim or whatever he may be, if by executing the religious principles which he is professing he has developed his love of God, then we have nothing to preach to him. The result is there. But because we don't find that love of God is there, we are putting forward a simple formula: here is the way by which—if you utilise or accept it—you'll very quickly love God.' [33]

THE JAINS—THE PATH OF SELF-DENIAL

Between 500 and 600 B.C. two historic figures arose in India, leaving the main Hindu teachings behind them. One, the Buddha, was to become a spiritual teacher known throughout the world, his words carried to all the countries of the

The manuscript of a Jain legend. India, 15th century.

Jain statue of Gometeswara, Mysore, India.

East, including China. The other, Mahavira, was to remain relatively unknown to the outside world, his sect, the Jains, remaining in India as a branch of Hinduism, where they number about two million today.

Mahavira was born the son of a tribal chief. The family had never followed Hindu practices but instead were already Jains, believing in the teachings of one Parshva, who had lived two hundred and fifty years previously and was said to have been the twenty-third Tirthankara (spiritual guide). Very little is known of Parshva but it is likely that he was an austere monk who practised asceticism of an extreme nature because the parents of Mahavira, who called themselves Parshva's disciples, decided to starve themselves to death when Mahavira was thirty years old. Their gesture was considered to be a deeply religious one, resulting in a truly holy death. But to Mahavira, it was a great loss and for twelve years afterwards he renounced the world and wandered through his native state of Bengal as a silent beggar-monk.

He longed for release from the suffering of endless rebirths, the world seemed to him a dreary and frightening place and he himself an evil presence within it. To rid himself of the burden of wicked karma he practised vigorous austerities during these years. He suffered extremes of heat and cold and he gave up wearing clothes in order to be altogether free of possessions.

At the end of this time of self-mortification, he declared that he had gained samadhi, or enlightenment, and gave himself the title of Jaina—the conqueror. He began to preach and soon many were attracted to him and became his disciples. He died at the age of seventy-two of voluntary starvation, as his parents had done.

What Mahavira preached was self-denial to the utmost degree. He did not believe in Brahman, the Absolute, as did the Hindus. Rather, he took the more materialistic view that the universe is divided into two un-created (and thus everlasting) but independent categories—jiva, the soul, and ajiva, all that which is not soul. Ajiva consists of space, time, matter and the principles of movement and stillness, and it is lower than the soul. The soul must always, from its higher plane, be trying to subdue the non-soul, or body, in which it is encased. The soul is naturally pure and bright but is constantly hidden behind a sort of black cloud-stuff called by the Jains *karma*. Whereas to the Hindus, Karma is simply the natural law of cause and effect carried from life to life, to the Jains, karma is a subtle substance which obscures the everlasting light of the soul. A fresh amount of this substance is liable to adhere to the soul with every word, thought and deed and this conditions the life of the person and also his rebirth. Selfish actions cause large amounts of heavy karma to accrue, but good deeds cause little karma and have no bad effects. Thus it is essential that the Jain must live as worthy a life as possible in order to become free from all matter, for when the soul has freed itself from the body, it will rise through natural lightness to the highest point of the universe, where it will stay for ever in bliss.

Not only the monk but the layman, too, must practise good conduct and because of this the Jains are a sect with high ethical principles. There are five rules, called the Commandments of the Soul, to be observed by all Jains:

    1. Not to destroy any kind of life.
    2. Not to lie.
    3. Not to use anything which is not given.

4. To observe chastity.

5. To limit needs and not to covet anything.

Of these rules, the first is the one by which the Jains are best known. It has led to the practice of *ahimsa* (pronounced ahingsa) which means non-violence. It is an extreme form of what Albert Schweitzer came to call, reverence for life. We cannot live in the world without unintentionally destroying thousands of minute creatures daily but the Jains, although acknowledging this, believe that they must do as little injury as possible. This means that every Jain must be a vegetarian, for to injure the higher forms of life is worse than harming the lower ones. Even inert matter has qualities which must not be maltreated and thus Jains cannot be farmers, for to plough land is to cause injury not only to small animals, insects and worms, but also to the earth. Most manual crafts, involving the manipulation of material, fall into similar harmful ways of livelihood and so the Jains have adopted the safest method of earning a living, that of trade. They have become, through the centuries, a wealthy and respected business community, among whom there are many teachers and bankers.

The Jain monk, who is a recognized part of this community, lives a life rigidly bound by ahimsa. Traditionally, he must never move about in the dark in case he injures some living creature and he must always in the daytime carry a little feather brush with which to gently move away any insect which crosses his path. His mouth is covered by a mask so that he will not hurt the air itself, and he must not bathe, for this injures the vermin on his body.

Although Jains have the images of the Hindu gods in their temples, they believe that the gods can only bestow passing blessings on their worshippers; true reverence goes to the twenty-four Tirthankaras, the evolved souls, of whom Mahavira was the last. The Tirthankaras cannot bestow blessings, for they have nothing to do with the earth at all, having completely removed themselves from matter, but they are the real inspiration of the Jain religion.

Thus the Jains, although not believing in any Supreme God, live a life which is gentle, altruistic and self-disciplined. Like the Quakers, in times of war they do not fight, although they will do all they can for the sick and wounded. They have established many hospitals, particularly for sick animals, and aid is given to any in need. Each Jain is required to carry out at least one act of charity every day (they use the word 'sharing' rather than charity). However rich they become, they are expected to lead simple and austere lives, following the advice in their scriptures: 'A pious man eats little, drinks little and sleeps little.'

One of their most vivid parables is that of a man who carried, with a pair of iron tongs, a dish full of burning coals. He took these to a group of three hundred and sixty-three founders of philosophical schools, all of whom differed in their practice and understanding. They formed a circle, and the man with burning coals asked each philosopher to take them from him with his bare hands. But every one of them held back, saying that if he took the coals, his hands would be burnt. 'Ah,' said the man, 'this is a true principle, one which can be applied everywhere: all creatures are averse to pain. He who causes pain to any creature will himself suffer many pains.'

BUDDHISM

Know, Vasettha, that from time to time a
Tathagata is born into the world, a fully awakened
one, abounding in wisdom and goodness, happy, with
knowledge of the worlds, unsurpassed as a guide to
mortals willing to be led, a teacher of gods and
men, a Blessed One, a Buddha. He, by himself,
thoroughly understands this universe, seeing it
face to face. . . . The Truth does he proclaim both
in the letter and in the spirit, lovely in its
origin, lovely in its progress, lovely in its
consummation: the higher life does he make known,
in all its purity and in all its perfectness. (Tevigga Sutta) *[1]*

Sakyamuni Buddha, the sage of the Sakyas. Bronze gilt, China, 5th century.

THE GREAT AWAKENING

Buddhism, emerging from Hinduism, has come to be one of the greatest religions of the world. It began as a branch of Hinduism in the sixth century B.C. and many of its ideas are shared with Hindus. But it is not just another form of Hinduism, its own understanding is unique. It is a historical religion with a founder who was born the son of a king of a small North Indian state.

At the conception of the Buddha it is said that the whole universe was in commotion and all the ten thousand worlds were lit with a radiance never seen before. The fires were put out in all the hells and everywhere there were strange miracles of healing. On the night of his conception, it is said that his mother, Queen Maya, dreamt that a silver-white elephant entered her side and occupied her womb. When she told this dream to her husband, he was immediately concerned to find out its meaning. He sent for Brahmins (Hindu priests) who, after deliberating together, told the king not to be anxious, for a male child had planted itself into the queen's womb. This son, they said, would become a great ruler and a unifier of men if he remained within the kingdom; if, however, he forsook the world he would become a Buddha, an Enlightened One, and would roll back the clouds of ignorance and folly which covered the world. The word *Buddha* itself comes from the Sanskrit word *budh*, meaning 'to wake', and 'Buddha' is the title given to one who knows, in the sense of having become one with the highest object of knowledge, Supreme Truth.

When the birth was nearly due, the queen walked into a beautiful grove of trees and flowers, called Lumbini Grove, and came to a great tree in the middle.

The birth of the Buddha. Part of a bas-relief from Gandhara, India, late 2nd or early 3rd century.

As she approached it, one of the branches moved towards her, and the moment she put her hand on it, the birth pangs started. While she held on to the branch, the Buddha was born, emerging pure and spotless. The story continues that as he flashed from Queen Maya's womb, four angels received him on a golden net and he was bathed by two heavenly sprays of water. He at once gazed in the six directions—north, south, east and west, up and down—and then took seven strides forward, proclaiming himself at one with creation.

The stories surrounding the Buddha's birth are full of magic, legend and beauty and, as in other birth stories, reflect man's reverence for his real liberators. They should not be taken as literally true. It is true, however, that Prince Siddhartha Gautama, who was to become the Buddha, the historic founder of Buddhism, was born about 563 B.C. His father's small kingdom lay at the foot of the majestic Himalayas and from birth onwards, Siddhartha was surrounded with every pleasure in order to attach him to the world; for the king had taken seriously the prophecy that he might become a Buddha, and much preferred that his son should be a great ruler. At the age of nineteen, Siddhartha married his beautiful cousin, who bore him a son, Rahula.

He then had everything he could desire but, nevertheless, a discontent came over him. One day he went driving through the countryside and for the first time saw a sight which his father had tried to shield him from. He saw old age in the form of a bent and decrepit old man, who wandered trembling and leaning on a staff. Siddhartha asked his charioteer the meaning of such a sight. 'It comes to all men,' answered the charioteer. On further drives, they encountered three other sights which had been denied before through the vigilance of the king—a man full of disease, a corpse and, lastly, a yellow-robed monk with a begging bowl. On each occasion, Siddhartha learnt from his charioteer what had taken place and his mind began to realize two truths. One was that ultimate fulfilment could never be attained on the physical plane because of the inevitable mortality of the body; the other was that there were men, monks, who sought for a way of life which was not bound by decay and death, by withdrawing from the world.

From then on, Siddhartha could no longer take any pleasure in palace life. He felt repelled and mocked by the perpetual round of fleshly living, the sumptuous feasts and hunting trips, the endless riot and profusion of processions and festivals. One night, he fell asleep while watching a troupe of dancing girls and when he awoke, they were spread all round him, resting in various seductive postures. Suddenly he knew that it was time to make 'the great retirement' and he sent his charioteer to saddle his horse. Silently, he visited his sleeping wife and son, and then he and his charioteer rode off together to the edge of the forest. It was daybreak when they stopped, and in the shade of the cool, sweet-smelling trees they changed clothes, Siddhartha sending all his princely apparel and his horse home with the charioteer. He shaved his head and entered the forest depths to find the answer to the problem of suffering and death.

For six years, he followed the life of an ascetic. First he sought out two Hindu sages, famous for their self-mastery and philosophical insight. He studied hard with them, particularly the practices of Raja Yoga, but there came a time when he decided there was nothing more they could teach him.

Then he joined a group of wandering monks, whose life was purposely one of intense hardship. He outdid them in all the austerities they practised, learning to subdue every demand of his flesh, to conquer fear and to control his mind. Sometimes he ate only one grain of rice a day, or a bean, and he came to look like a skeleton. It is said that his limbs resembled withered reeds and his hips stood out like a camel's hoof. His ribs were like the rafters of a ruined house and when he touched his stomach, he felt his spine. But still he did not find enlightenment.

At last he decided that he would never discover what he was looking for in austerities and, emaciated to the point of death, he accepted a bowl of curds from a milkmaid. His five companion monks, disgusted at this weakness, left him; and he, having eaten and bathed, regained his strength.

He wandered on to Gaya in north-east India and there, one evening, he sat beneath a tree which has since become known as the Bo Tree (*bo* being short for *bodhi*, which means knowledge). He was thirty-five years old and it was a May night of full moon.

According to legend, Mara, the evil one, now came to him and tempted him with a longing to go back to his wife and child and to give up the quest that had taken such a terrible toll of him. All his attempts to find enlightenment had led to defeat and discouragement. He had come to the end of all he was capable of and he had failed. To return to an ordinary, normal life in comfort and honour must then have been a strong temptation, especially since some records tell us that he suffered from loneliness and found the solitude of the silent forest groves hard to bear.

But his will to find enlightenment remained steadfast. His longing for ultimate truth was greater than any other desire and his very powerlessness to move any nearer that goal on his own—his knowledge that he had reached the end of his own efforts—brought about the final stage necessary for enlightenment: the abandoning of self. Recognition of his own total inadequacy and of the futility of all the attainments of his disciplined mind caused the final emptying of self,

The Buddha touching the earth. Terracotta, Nepal, 16th–17th century.

which is also its transcendence.

In that moment, he became the Buddha. He continued to sit and Mara, unable to deflect him with temptations, tried to kill him with hurricanes, thunderbolts and torrential rain. But all turned to flower petals as they came near the Buddha. At last, Mara challenged his very integrity by asking him by what right he was sitting there. The Buddha touched the earth with his fingertip and, with a great roar of thunder, it replied 'I bear you witness'. Mara fled, vanquished.

The Buddha's meditation now became a clear, luminous knowledge. The barrier of self fell away as his mind penetrated the meaning of life. Because, finally, he had become nothing, so, now he was at one with everything, but an everything that was stainless, restored to its true being. This was the Great Awakening, when the man Siddhartha was transcended and the Buddha emerged.

For seven weeks he sat, deep in bliss. But Mara had one final temptation. This time he pointed out that no words could ever really describe what the Buddha had experienced. How could such a blaze of illumination be translated into speech which the ordinary world would understand. Why not stay the rest of his life in a state of bliss and never go back to the world? And indeed, this troubled the Buddha. Would it be best to keep the whole experience to himself? What could he possibly say to others that would help them also towards this experience? But at last he decided that all his self-sacrifice would have been in vain if he were to adandon the troubled world. 'There will be some who understand me' he said, and ended Mara's temptations for ever.

Members of the army of Mara. Terracotta, Burma, 16th century.

THE TEACHING ABOUT SUFFERING

The Buddha died at the age of eighty. Between his enlightenment and his death, nearly half a century, he wandered the paths of India, teaching all people. He recognized no caste or social differences and taught kings and robbers, outcasts and Brahmins, without distinction.

He taught that the teachings themselves must not be taken as dogma, to be imbibed and believed, but must be tested by each man for himself. He refused to be regarded as divine. His disciples would happily have worshipped him but he would have none of it. They must be content with calling him *Tathagata*— the Thus-Come. His emphasis on intense self-effort was consistent to the end and on his death-bed he said to one of his disciples, Ananda:

'Therefore o Ananda, be ye lamps unto yourselves. Rely on yourselves, and do not rely on external help.

'Hold fast to the truth as a lamp. Seek salvation alone in the truth. Look not for assistance to anyone besides yourselves.' . . . [20]

'Those who, either now or after I am dead, shall be a lamp unto themselves, relying upon themselves only and not relying upon any external help, but

The place of the Buddha's enlightenment, Buddhagaya.

holding fast to the truth as their lamp, and seeking their salvation in the truth alone, not looking for assistance to anyone besides themselves, it is they, Ananda, among my *bhikshus* (disciples) who shall reach the very topmost height! But they must be anxious to learn.' . . . [3]

This approach was designed to penetrate the miasma of discouraged fatalism which had settled on the majority of Hindus, who saw no hope of release from the eternal round of death and rebirth. Nothing vexed the Buddha more than the way in which the Brahmins had turned themselves into a privileged caste by keeping the right teachings back from the people and holding them as secret, powerful possessions. The ordinary Hindus had been deprived of the highest knowledge and had been given instead a superstitious rigmarole of rituals and divinations, which had to be bought in cash from the Brahmins. Their religion had sunk to endless disputes and speculations about questions such as whether there were other worlds, what the soul consisted of, and what the substance of thought was.

As Martin Luther opposed the hypocrisy of the priests who sold indulgences, so the Buddha broke the hold of the Brahmins by preaching a religion which was devoid of authority and which relied on the individual to tread the path by his own power. It was a religion in which there were no secrets and no speculation. The Buddha refused to be drawn into discussions, even on the existence of a First Cause. He neither affirmed nor denied a Source of manifestation but made it clear that his teaching was not concerned with this question. This was not

The Deer Park near Benares where the Buddha preached his first sermon.

always pleasing to his followers. One, Malunkyaputta, once pointed out to him that there were many problems left unexplained by him. Was the world eternal or not eternal? Did the Buddha exist after death or not? Or did he, at the same time, both not exist and not not-exist? If the Buddha knew the answers to these questions, he should say so and if he did not, he should admit that he did not. The Buddha answered by saying that the holy life did not depend on answers to questions such as those:

'Malunkyaputta, if anyone says, "I will not lead the holy life under the Blessed One until he explains these questions," he may die with these questions unanswered by the Tathagata. Suppose, Malunkyaputta, a man is wounded by a poisoned arrow, and his friends bring him to a surgeon. Suppose the man should then say: "I will not let this arrow be taken out until I know who shot me; which caste he is; what his name and family may be; whether he is tall or short; the colour of his complexion; and which town he comes from. I will not let this arrow be taken out until I know with what kind of bow I was shot; what sort of arrow; what colour feather was used on the arrow." Malunkyaputta. that man would die without knowing any of these things. Even so, if anyone says, "I will not follow the holy life under the Blessed One until he answers these questions, such as whether the universe is eternal or not,"—he would die with these questions unanswered by the Tathagata.' [4]

THE FOUR NOBLE TRUTHS

The essence of the Buddha's teaching, his analysis of man's condition, its cause and its cure, is contained in what he called the Four Noble Truths.

The first of these truths is Suffering (*dukkha*). By 'suffering,' the Buddha meant the miseries of existence common to all life—the pain of birth, the pain of old age, the pain of sickness, the pain of death. Frustration is painful and so is aversion. Separation, grief and despair are painful. Even if one is free from these sorrows oneself, one sees others suffering and cannot remain indifferent.

All beings suffer and the Buddha analyzed what it is in them that actually feels the pain. He defined human life as being composed of five strands, called *skandhas*. These are body, sensations, feelings, ideas, and consciousness.

All these five are involved in suffering. Animals suffer physically but humans, with memory and insight, have the additional suffering of the feeling of bondage to their imperfect selves—a sense of unsatisfactoriness and unfulfilment which few escape.

The Buddha, seeking to lay bare to all men the nature of their condition, separated suffering into three categories. The first is physical suffering, including sickness and death. The second is mental pain, the despairs of life and the impossibility of fulfilling all our desires. The third is the existential sort of suffering that comes through clinging to what is known—home, friends, one's own personality—and not daring to face the unknown. Some people never experience the third. Others may experience all three together.

At first sight, the fact of suffering seems so self-evident that to base an entire religion on it would seem to make that religion limited and uninspired. But the

A standing Buddha. Limestone, China, 6th century.

Buddha's teaching was both obvious and profound. The real truths *are* the most simple and do not depend on books or teaching, he stated. All men, whatever their condition, can understand that they suffer. In outlining the truth of suffering, the Buddha was being not pessimistic, but objective and realistic. He wanted people to see for themselves the human condition, to see facts about life which are universal and have nothing to do with speculation.

The second Noble Truth is *tanha*, the ignorant thirst for existence which is the cause of suffering. Craving for pleasure, craving for existence, and craving for death.

Constantly the Buddha came back to one point—that there is nothing wrong with life or death but only with our attitude to them. We try to possess life and so we cling to it. We desire states of mind, such as happiness, and cling to them. Most of all, we cling to our own personality, to the feeling of 'I', but it is just this—the feeling of being a person—which creates the consciousness of separateness and makes us want all the things which will satisfy that separate existence.

As a child grows up, it needs to take in food of all sorts, material and mental, in order to grow. It also must learn to distinguish the known from the unknown. So many new things inundate its senses that it must classify those which are similar to each other or it will live in chaos. In this way, an organizing activity is built up in the brain, based on the recognition of relationships. It is this centralizing force, composed of memory and the ability to discriminate, which is the basic of the 'I'-feeling, the ego-consciousness which belongs to humanity. A child without this directing, organizing drive would not develop mentally into an adult.

Where people seem to have lost their way, however, is that when adulthood is reached (no set age) and the need for this centralization dies away, the ego or 'I'-consciousness does not die with it but, in cancerous fashion, grows large, no longer a by-product of a natural human activity, but a monstrous growth in its own right, feeding on its desire for separate existence as a permanent entity in contrast to the rest of the world.

When the ego is not outgrown, reality is distorted, because everything is valued in accordance with the need to keep the 'I' fed. Insofar as it is fed (and it is never satisfied for long) the objects which feed it are clung to and those which hurt it are avoided or fought. These two forces, clinging and avoidance, are the ones which bind man to existence, for karma, the law of cause and effect, ensures that every action has its result.

Thus, out of *avidya*, or self-delusion, we cling to a construct, the ego, which we ourselves have kept alive and fostered; and in our clinging we lose our natural harmony with life, and our understanding of its meaning and purpose.

The third Noble Truth is the cessation of suffering, liberation from the insatiable ego, and extinction of craving. It is supreme happiness, which is called *Nirvana*. It is seeing the Truth.

According to the Buddha, the truth of the world is that every *thing* is conditioned and relative, including the five skandhas which make up each person. Really there is no person as we feel it here at all, nobody whatever, no separate, lasting entity. Instead there is the Void, eternally present, which contains 'I' and everything else. If we attend carefully to our thoughts and feelings, trying to find the 'I' which directs them, we may discover this fact for ourselves. The

King Vidudabha visiting the Buddha. Sculpture, Barhut, 2nd century B.C.

English philosopher, Hume, once discovered it:

'For my part when I enter most intimately into what I call "myself", I always stumble on some particular perception or other, of heat or cold, light or shade, love or hatred, pain or pleasure. I never can catch *myself* at any time without a perception, and never can observe anything but the perception. . . . We are nothing but a bundle or collection of different perceptions, which succeed each other with an inconceivable rapidity and are in a perpetual flux and movement.' [5]

In this way, it seems as though all our feelings are attached to objects and that everything we experience is brought into being by the outside world. To make this clear there is a good experiment: shut your eyes and then, without any preliminaries, feel amused. Or feel sad. Or feel angry. Or feel amazed. Or feel old.

You may have found that it is impossible to have these feelings in a vacuum and that you were just numb, without any feeling. This is because they are dependent on objects and activities in the outside world. Even age can only be felt in relation to the body's activities.

To realize that here, one's centre, is not filled with 'I' but is everlastingly clear and empty of the world, is to realize the Truth. The Buddha gave the name *Anatta* to this Emptiness of self, and its realization leads to happiness and serenity and the end of suffering, for Emptiness is without boundary and is not at the mercy of the demanding ego. When Emptiness is found to be one's true centre, the ego is seen as the construct of one's own mind, and it dies away. With its death go the cravings and aversions which kept it alive and one is free in oneself, unselfconscious, living spontaneously from the heart of life.

Many Hindus were afraid of Anatta, this teaching, believing it to mean annihilation, the end of consciousness, the losing of the known; and they did not have sufficient faith to believe that Emptiness could sustain them. The Buddha disliked fear and confusion, and although he would not speak about anything which could not be discovered by the senses, he did commit himself to a reassurance of their doubts. 'O *Bikkhus* (monks), there *is* an unborn, uncreated. unmade, and unformed. Were there not, there would be no release from the world of the born, created, made and formed.'

THE EIGHTFOLD NOBLE PATH

The last of the Four Noble Truths is the way by which the end of suffering can be accomplished, the way to Nirvana.

There are eight steps by which one can approach Nirvana and at first glance they seem to be ordinary, ethical common sense and not at all difficult or mystical. To actually live them, however, requires a dedication which is likely to take one to the end of suffering anyway.

left: Seated Sakyamuni Buddha. Dry lacquer, painted, Burma, 17th–18th century. *right:* An ancient stupa—a mound containing the relics of a holy person.

They are:
1. Right Understanding.
2. Right Thought.
3. Right Speech.
4. Right Action.
5. Right Livelihood.
6. Right Effort.
7. Right Mindfulness.
8. Right Concentration.

The Buddhist scriptures contain hundreds of discourses said to have been given by the Buddha during his long teaching life, but nearly all of them are centred on one or other of these eight steps, his explanations adapted to the capacity of his audience to understand him. This is because the steps themselves encompass the whole of human nature. They can be taken at any level and each one of them (they are not meant to be taken consecutively) can be the starting point of a truth-seeking life. The Buddha wanted to reach all men, not just the scholarly, and therefore his message was that there are certain actions, clearly outlined, which can be started *now* by *anybody*, from the lowest outcast to the greatest king.

In Buddhism, there are three main principles: Moral Conduct, Mind Training, and Wisdom. Three of the eight steps are included in Moral Conduct and Moral Conduct itself is based on love and compassion. We must become aware of our own tendencies towards wrong speech (unkind gossip, lying, and the harshness and unawareness of other people's feelings which brings about hatred and unhappiness); towards wrong action (destruction, cruelty and dishonesty); and wrong livelihood (taking advantage of others or harming others by one's occupation). If we become aware of these tendencies in ourselves, we cease to project them onto the outside world and we learn to tolerate and love all people in the compassionate and selfless way which leads to a harmonious society. Without Moral Conduct, the Buddhists say, spiritual understanding will not develop.

Right Effort, Right Mindfulness and Right Concentration come into the principle of Mind Training.

Right Effort is the energy and will to get on with the job, not to be deflected more than one can help, and to be constant in one's determination to tread the path.

Right Mindfulness is a particularly Buddhist practice. Its goal is to bring about complete awareness of what one is doing so that one remains alert and in proper control of one's actions. It is capturing one's attention and bringing it to bear on what is happening now, without any memories or anticipations to cloud the scene. When one is able to do this, one finds a new and wonderful sense of being —whatever one is looking at appears extraordinarily clear and marvellous, itself in itself, unaffected by category and judgment. But this is an incidental reward, the whole aim being to bring about complete awareness of all the processes which go to make up the inner mind as well as the outer world.

Right Concentration is practised during meditation. It is a form of mind training in which thought is persuaded to die down altogether and a tranquil 'one-pointedness' is encouraged, which is usually accompanied by feelings of joy and

A monk in Ceylon with his begging bowl.

well-being. Then these feelings themselves are allowed to die away so that all that remains is a clear transcendent awareness.

The two steps of the path which are included in Wisdom are Right Understanding and Right Thought. They are the most difficult, for Right Understanding means the understanding of the Four Noble Truths and therefore the understanding of Ultimate Reality itself. When we think we understand a thing, we usually mean that we understand it according to the facts about it. This is called 'knowing accordingly' and it is the way in which we cope with ordinary life. But real understanding is the pure awareness of a thing in itself without need for label and this is called penetration (*pativedha*).

Right Thought prepares the mind for Right Understanding. Right Thought is the acceptance of self-sacrifice, the knowledge that the life of the ego is coming to an end to be replaced by a selfless and illumined love for others. For, said the Buddha, real insight into one's fundamental nature brings about four sublime states benevolence, compassion, joyous sympathy and equanimity.

'Be not afraid of good works, brethren. It is another name for happiness, for what is desired, beloved, dear and delightful—this word "good works".' [6]

Amida Buddha, the Buddha of Infinite Light. Limestone painted and gilded over a coating of gesso, China, 7th–8th century.

THE SPREAD OF BUDDHISM—THERAVADA

The Buddha was concerned that all men should learn to look within their own natures for the answers to the cosmic mysteries which perplexed them, and the essence of his teaching is contained in the following famous saying:

'. . . in this very body, six feet in length, with its sense-impressions and its thoughts and ideas, I do declare to you are the world, and the origin of the world, and the ceasing of the world, and likewise the Way that leadeth to the ceasing thereof.' [7]

As he moved through India, his fame spread and he attracted more and more followers, numbering many thousands, many of whom wanted to live as monks, dedicating their lives to the practice of his Way. An order of monks was founded, called the Sangha. Their purpose was that of imparting the Buddha's teaching and their vows were those of poverty and chastity. They owned nothing except the yellow robes which they wound around their bodies and the food put into their begging bowls. There is a story that the Buddha was once found meditating during a frost, sitting in his thin robe on some leaves spread over a rutted cow path.

'Rough is the ground trodden by the hoofs of the cattle; thin is the couch of leaves; light the monk's yellow robe; sharp the cutting winter wind,' he admitted. 'Yet I live happily, with sublime uniformity.' [8]

The Sangha is today very much the same as when it began, 2,500 years ago, and the relationship between monks and laymen remains close. The Buddha's teaching was for everyone, but the monks are able to study the teachings and interpret them to the lay people. In return they are provided with food, robes and shelter. A monk need not remain as one for life. No dishonour is attached to him if he leaves the monastery and returns to ordinary life. The Christian concept of obedience to the head of the monastery did not come into existence in India. When a monk has spent some time in a monastery, learning the Path, and learning the rules which govern a monk's life, he is free to go where he will, practising alone or under other teachers.

After his death, those monks who valued the Buddha's intellectual powers, his great gift for rational thought and analysis, his ability to dissect a problem to its bare bones, making clear the significance and meaning of every aspect—in other words, his head—these monks interpreted his words to mean that anyone who seriously wanted enlightenment must become a monk. Buddhism, in their eyes, was largely a religion for monks, dependent on rules; an austere religion in which each man must work for himself at quelling his body and imagination, his liberation dependent entirely on his own efforts. Their ideal was the *Arhat*, the Enlightened One, the personification of wisdom who, liberated, returns no more to the world. They called their kind of Buddhism Theravada, the Way of the Elders, and it became the religion of the south, spreading to Burma, Thailand and Ceylon.

Theravadins took all that the Buddha had said in a literal way. Scholarly disputations arose over the exact meaning of words and disciples underwent a concentrated but narrow training, with the doctrine of karma, the impersonal but just law by which one reaps as one sows, an essential part. Many classifications were arrived at to amplify the workings of karma. For instance, if a crime was

Two figures in Chinese porcelain. *left*: A Lohan, 14th century. *right*: An Arhat—the embodiment of wisdom, 17th–18th century.

committed unwittingly, even murder, there was no bad karma attached and there would be no suffering in future lives. A rule of thumb was devised by which one could immediately determine whether one should perform a deed or not— if it led to the harm of oneself, or of others, then one must not do it.

But the basic Theravadin teaching was concerned with cleansing the mind of its impurities, such as hatred, lust and discontent, and replacing these negative emotions by the positive ones of tranquillity, joy and confidence. The main practice for this goal was Mindfulness, an extension of the Buddha's teaching in the Eightfold Path.

To Theravadins, Mindfulness is a continuous alertness to all the activities of the person. It is extreme self-examination and the exercises begin with the body. As well as sessions of watching the breath, one must become aware of every action during the day, however tiny. People rarely attend to *all* they are doing and all that is happening to them, their minds are usually too engaged in the dream-life of future plans and past events to pay sharp attention to this moment *now*. A man can drive for an hour and not notice the country he is passing through or the actions of his hands on the controls because his consciousness is somewhere else. But bringing one's attention constantly back to what one is doing at this moment is not only a therapeutic worry-reliever—for one's mind becomes trained not to wander into speculation—but can also bring a heightened perception of sights and sounds.

A number of exercises were devised to bring about body awareness, such as becoming aware of the muscles in your foot (each one individually as far as possible) as you slowly lift it while taking a step. Or the muscles in your mouth and throat while you swallow. Examining your sensations while moving is called *vipassana* and the secret is to do everything very slowly. This can lead to comic results, as when you want the salt for your boiled egg and it takes ten minutes to reach for it.

Body mindfulness becomes emotion mindfulness when it is turned inwards and here the right way is to clearly watch a sensation or an emotion as it arises without regarding it as 'my' feeling. One should look on it as 'a' feeling, as though it were an object being studied scientifically, and then it is easier to notice exactly how it arises. In this way, events in the outside world which supposedly trigger off one's feelings are of less importance than the feeling itself; for instance, when we become angry with our neighbour who likes loud music, it is more important to watch the course of our anger than to shout at the neighbour.

Other exercises are designed to make one aware of one's fears and aversions and to observe them in the same way. This is done by imagining as vividly as one can such things as decay, stench, death and other—perhaps more personal— horrors, until they are faced fully, without reaction.

A layman must practise these methods whenever he can but a monk can devote his life to them. The other great practice for the monk is meditation. Theravada monks will spend much of their day sitting in the lotus posture and watching their breath as it comes into the body and leaves it. As thoughts arise, they too are noted but not held in the mind. Always the attention must come

Thai Buddhist monks at the London Bihara engaged in a ritual.

back to the breath until there is nothing but the breath and one's whole mind is surrendered to it.

MAHAYANA BUDDHISM

But many people saw Buddhism quite differently. They disagreed with the Theravada emphasis on scholarship, monks and world-denying asceticism. The Buddhism which travelled north to Tibet and China (and eventually Japan) based itself less on the Buddha's knowledge and intellectual powers than on his compassionate heart; less on his actual words than on the intuitive insight which is able to grasp at his meaning, at the living power behind the words.

There are two sorts of people, said Mahayana Buddhism, the enlightened and the ignorant. All enlightened people are Buddhas. All Buddhist teachings arise from the nature of Buddhahood—they tell us what the nature of a Buddha is. What is that nature?

The Buddha showed himself to be the embodiment of transcendental knowledge and wisdom (*prajna*) and also to be endowed with true compassion (*karuna*). With wisdom, he penetrated the real condition of the world, its impermanent and ever-changing state; also with wisdom he saw into man's greatest delusion, the one that is the source of all others—the belief that he has absolute reality—the belief that being a person makes him separate from the rest of the world. These two profound insights of wisdom arise from one side of a Buddha's nature; but the other side, compassion, is equally important, for it was because of his pity for man's ignorance and his unsentimental but tender care for suffering, that the Buddha came back to the world in order to dispel that ignorance with his teaching.

Figure of Kuan-Yin, the female Bodhisattva, on the waves. Carved rhinoceros horn, China, 17th–18th century.

This compassion, which regards every living being with the tenderness of a parent to an only child, expresses the true nature of Buddhahood, said the Mahayana Buddhists and this caring aspect of Buddha-nature came to be personified as a *Bodhisattva*—one who turns back at the door of Nirvana, refusing to enter until every single soul on earth is enlightened. This great and noble ideal of the Bodhisattva became the embodiment of Mahayana Buddhism, as the wise Arhat was of Theravada.

Love finds its own way to the truth, and its characteristics are flexibility and creativeness. The Buddha's return to the world after his enlightenment under the Bodhi Tree was to enable each man to follow his own path; for a man can only think of the Buddha in terms of his own experience and background, he can only follow the teachings by virtue of his own desires and circumstances. Thus, in Mahayana Buddhism, no path which leads to Buddhahood can be wrong. All that is required is that it should take its practitioner away from the narrow confines of the individual ego to the liberation and bliss which is Buddhahood. For the state of Buddhahood is for everybody, not just the monks, said Mahayana. The Buddha came back to enlighten the whole world, not just a select few.

To this day, the two schools of Theravada and Mahayana have remained spiritually apart, but it has been separation of the most amiable sort. It is frequent for monks of one school to stay in monasteries of the other. The bonds between them are much stronger than those which cause them to differ, and there has never been a Buddhist war.

'Just as, brethren, the mighty ocean hath but one savour, the savour of salt, even so, brethren, hath the Dhamma-Discipline but one savour, the savour of release.' [9]

A lotus, the Buddhist symbol of divine perfection and purity.

THE BUDDHA'S WORDS

The root cause of our journey from birth to death is, said the Buddha, Dependent Origination. By this he meant the dependence of one circumstance upon another, so that in the end a whole web has been woven of factors and circumstances, all intertwined with each other. He said:

'Deep indeed is this Dependent Origination and deep it appears to be. It is through not knowing, not understanding, not penetrating that Law that this world of men has become entangled like a ball of string and, covered with blight, resembles muñja grass and rushes, . . .'

'In him, Ānanda, who contemplates the enjoyment of all things that make for clinging, craving arises (he longs for the objects of his desire); through craving, clinging is conditioned (because he longs for things, his mind becomes conditioned to desiring, and is thus always in a state of clinging to objects); through clinging, the process of becoming is conditioned (because of his clinging, he is always adding to the delusions by which he lives); through the process of becoming, rebirth is conditioned (the more a man struggles to gain what he desires, the more karma he creates and the more he is entangled with the deluded world); through rebirth are conditioned, old age and death, sorrow, lamentation, pain, grief and despair. Thus arises the whole mass of suffering again in the future.' [10]

To cut through this mass to the Truth, and thus to be delivered of suffering was the tireless teaching of the Buddha. To help his disciples do this, he was continually exhorting them to recognize the nature of their senses—what it is that actually sees and hears and speaks. He wanted to help them discover that what we call the 'mind' is really a dim shadow of the One Mind and that there is, in existence, *only* the One Mind. This can be seen, he pointed out, when we drop all clinging to judgment and discrimination for our own ends, when we cease attributing names and value judgments to what we see.

To illustrate this, '. . . the Buddha lowered His golden hued arm with the fingers pointing downward and asked Ānanda: "As you now see my hand, is it in a correct or inverted (position)?"

The Buddha seated on a serpent. Bronze, Ceylon, 14th century.

The Buddha with two disciples. Tempera on cloth, Thailand, early 19th century.

'Ānanda replied: "All worldly men regard this as inverted but I myself do not know which position is correct or inverted."

'The Buddha asked: "If they hold that it is inverted, which position do they consider to be upright?"

'Ānanda replied: "If the Buddha holds up His hand pointing to the sky, it will be upright."

'The Buddha then held up His hand and said, "If worldly men so discriminate between an upright and inverted hand, they will in the same way differentiate between your body and the Buddha's pure . . . (one) and will say that the Tathāgata's body is completely enlightened whereas yours is upside down. If you look closely into your body and the Buddha's, where is this so called inversion?"

'After hearing this, Ānanda and the assembly were bewildered and gazed fixedly at the Buddha without knowing whether their bodies and minds were really inverted.

'The Buddha was moved with compassion and, out of pity for Ānanda and the assembly, said in His voice as steady as the ocean-tide: "Virtuous men, I have always declared that Form and Mind and all causes arising therefrom, all mental conditions and all causal phenomena are but manifestations of the mind. Your bodies and minds are just appearances within the wonderful, bright and pure Profound Mind. Why do you stray from the precious, bright and subtle nature of fundamentally Enlightened Mind and so recognize delusion. . . ?

' "(Mind's) dimness creates (dull) emptiness and both, in the darkness, unite with it to become form. The mingling of form with false thinking causes the latter to take the shape of a body, stirred by accumulated causes within and drawn to externals without. Such inner disturbance is mistaken for the nature of mind, hence the false view of a mind dwelling in the physical body and the failure to realize that this body as well as external mountains, rivers, space and the great earth are but phenomena within the wondrous bright True Mind. Like an ignorant man who overlooks the great ocean but grasps at a floating bubble and regards it as the whole body of water in its immense expanse, you are doubly deluded amongst the deluded. This is exactly the same delusion as when I hold my hand down; and so the Tathāgata says that you are the most pitiable people".' [11]

Ānanda asked the Buddha to enlighten him more about the 'wondrous bright True Mind.'

The Buddha said:

'Ānanda, the doors and windows of this hall are wide open and face east. There is light when the sun rises in the sky and there is darkness at midnight when the moon wanes or is hidden by fog or clouds. Your seeing is unimpeded through open doors and windows but is obstructed where there are walls or houses. Where there is discrimination [of objects] you perceive the stirring causes [of it] and in the dull void, you only see emptiness. . . . Ānanda, see now how I return each of these changing states to its causal origin. What are these original causes? Ānanda, of these changing conditions, light can be returned to the sun. Why? Because there is no light without the sun and since light comes from the sun, it can be returned to it (i.e. its origin). Darkness can be returned to the waning moon, clearness to open doors and windows, obstruction to walls and houses,

Buddha and the sixteen great Arhats. Painted cotton, Tibet, 18th–19th century.

causes to differentiation, emptiness to relative voidness, confused externals to unconsciousness and clear perception to the awakened state. Nothing in the world goes beyond these conditions. Now when the Essence of your Perception confronts these eight states, where can it be returned to? If to brightness you will not see darkness when there is no light. Although these states such as light, darkness, etc., differ from one another, your seeing does not differ, your seeing remains unchanged.

'All states that can be returned to external causes are obviously not YOU, but that which cannot be returned to anywhere, if it is not YOU, what is it? Therefore, you should know that your mind is fundamentally wonderful, bright and pure and that because of your delusion and stupidity, you have missed it and so are caught on the wheel of transmigration, sinking and floating in the samsaric sea (the sea of endless becoming). This is why the Tathāgata says that you are the most pitiable of men.' [12]

The Buddha constantly exhorted his monks not to cling to his teaching, but to try to understand it so well that they could let go of it. In a famous parable, he explains this to them.

' "Monks, I will teach you Dhamma [the doctrine]—the parable of the raft—for getting across, not for retaining. Listen to it, pay careful attention, and I will speak. It is like a man, monks, who going on a journey should see a great stretch of water, the hither bank with dangers and fears, the farther bank secure and without fears, but there may be neither a boat for crossing over, nor a bridge across for going from the not-beyond to the beyond. It occurs to him that in order to cross over from the perils of this bank to the security of the farther bank, he should fashion a raft out of grass and sticks, branches and foliage, so that he could, striving with his hands and feet and depending on the raft, cross over to the beyond in safety. When he has done this and has crossed over to the beyond, it occurs to him that the raft has been very useful and he wonders if he ought to proceed taking it with him packed on his head or shoulders. What do you think, monks? That the man, in doing this would be doing what should be done to the raft?"

"No, Lord."

"What should that man do, monks, in order to do what should be done to that raft? In this case, monks, that man, when he has crossed over to the beyond and realizes how useful the raft has been to him, may think: 'Suppose that I, having beached this raft on dry ground, or having immersed it in the water, should proceed on my journey?' Monks, a man doing this would be doing what should be done to the raft. In this way, monks, I have taught you Dhamma —the parable of the raft—for getting across, not for retaining. You monks, by understanding the parable of the raft, must discard even right states of mind and, all the more, wrong states of mind".' *[13]*

The compassionate insight of the Buddha enabled him to see and satisfy the true needs of anyone who presented him with a problem, and he was thus able to ease pain in a deep and lasting way. The following story shows his intuitive understanding of need:

left: Dhamek stupa. *right:* The Bodhisattva Kannon on the rock. Painting on silk, Japan, 1906.

Kisagotami *[14]* gave birth to a son but when the boy was able to walk by himself he died. The young girl, in her love for it, carried the dead child clasped to her bosom and went from house to house asking if anyone would give her some medicine for it. At last she was directed to Gautama the Buddha and doing homage to him, said: 'Lord and master, do you know any medicine that will be good for my boy?' The Buddha replied, 'I know of some.'

She asked, 'What is the medicine you require?'

He said, 'I want a handful of mustard seed.'

The girl promised to procure it for him but the Buddha continued, 'I require some mustard seed taken from a house where no son, husband, parent or slave has died.'

The girl said, 'Very good,' and went to ask for some at the different houses, carrying the dead body of her son astride on her hip.

The people said, 'Here is some mustard seed, take it.'

Then she asked, 'In your house has there died a son, husband, parent or slave?'

They replied, 'Lady, what is this that you say! The living are few but the dead are many.'

Then she went to other houses, but one said, 'I have lost a son'; another, 'I have lost my parents'; another, 'I have lost my slave.'

At last, not being able to find a single house where no one had died, from which to procure the mustard seed, she began to think, 'This is a heavy task that I am engaged in. I am not the only one whose son is dead. In the whole of the Savatthi country, everywhere children are dying, parents are dying.' Thinking thus, she put away her affection for her child, summoned up her resolution and left the dead body in a forest; then she went to the Buddha and paid him homage.

He said to her, 'Have you procured the handful of mustard seed?'

'I have not,' she replied; 'the people of the village told me that the living are few, but the dead are many.'

The Buddha said to her, 'You thought that you alone had lost a son; the law of death is that among all living creatures there is no permanence.'

When the Buddha had finished preaching the law, Kisagotami was established in her reward of intuitive knowledge, and so also were all the assembly who heard the law.

On inner stillness, the Buddha said:

'As in the ocean's midmost depth no wave is born, but all is still, so let the monk be still, be motionless, and nowhere should he stir.' *[15]*

MODERN BUDDHISM

The characteristics of Theravada Buddhism are its adherence to scriptures translated from the Indian language of Pali; and its organization, called the *Sangha*, which is composed of monks who teach the lay people, and are supported by them. The Sangha today has sent monks from Burma, Thailand and Ceylon to carry the teaching to most western countries. The monks usually live in small communities called *viharas*. There are few Theravadin monks in America, where Zen has proved to be the most popular form of Buddhism, but in Germany, Holland, France and England, there are well-established viharas in the capital cities, and meditation centres in the country. One of these meditation centres, at

The Shwe Daggon Pagoda in Rangoon.

Hindhead in England, was started by a Thai meditation master, V. R. Dhiravamsa. His lucid expositions in ever more perfect English have won him much popularity, both in England and in the United States, where he is now. He first came to England as a monk, called the Chao Khun Sobhana Dhammasudhi. Chao Khun is an office bestowed on certain monks for a period of time, and is roughly equivalent to that of an abbot. After the period of this office was over the Chao

Khun, although still a meditation master, became a layman, taking back his name of Dhiravamsa. As his confidence in the language grew, so did his ability to present teaching which was full of insight. He published a number of books and began to address audiences everywhere.

The central teaching of the Buddha, as we have seen, is a unique understanding of egolessness; 'emptiness' as it is often called. The modern teaching of Dhiravamsa has this to say about it:

'... feelings are very important if we are to bring about clear understanding of truth. Whenever there is contact there arises a feeling, and we have contact with things all the time. Even when we sit silent quietly in the room we contact something and then feeling must arise. Now if we say "I am this," or "this is mine," or "this is my feeling," then how can we be permanently happy? It is not possible because if something you grasp (which you think belongs to you) goes wrong, you feel unhappy. This can be seen in daily life very easily. But, if you are free from the "I," what is there to suffer? Who can suffer? Suffering will be unable to arise and at the same time there is nobody to suffer. So when you

A standing Buddha. Bronze, Cambodia, 12th century.

Buddhist monks at a meal.

understand or when you realise this sentence "Nothing can be taken as self or as belonging to self", then should any feeling arise whether agreeable, disagreeable or neutral, you can abide viewing impermanence, viewing dispassion, viewing stopping, and viewing the renunciation of feeling, and so come to the realization of Nirvana. This is the short way, the quicker way, and it is possible to realize this at any time when the mind is still and becomes purified. . . .

'How can we be free from sense-desires or sense pleasures? By being free from sense-desires I do not mean that you must not see, or must not hear, or must not think about anything. You must do things according to the natural state of being, or natural law. You cannot avoid seeing, or hearing, or thinking, or touching, because that is quite natural for all beings. You are fully equipped with all the sense-faculties in order to have experience, and it is through full development of these sense-faculties that you can realize the truth of Nirvana. We have six sense-faculties, five physical and one mental. We are quite fortunate beings and in many Sutras the Buddha teaches us how to keep these sense-faculties under control through the practice of *awareness*. When you are aware of sense-faculties, and when you are aware of sense-objects or sense-desires, you can use them but you are not under their control. You are master of the sense-desires or the sense-objects. When you are highly developed you can be free from all these sense-desires completely. . . . But the first step, or we can say both the first and the last, is the practice of awareness, because through this practice we can come step by step to the realization of ultimate truth, which is the fulfilment of the goal of life.

'Now what about attachment to views or ideas? Ideas are mental creations. So what is the uncreated? The word uncreated points to not creating and not thinking out. . . . Where there is thought or thinking, we are creating something, but where thought ceases completely and the feelings or experiences become cool or silent, that is the end of all *conditioned* things, the approach to the uncreated, outside time. Look at our experiences in daily life. When a person is not attached to any thing common to life he or she has no fear. Attachment is the main cause

Adoration of the Buddha. Marble, India, end 2nd century.

of fear. Untroubled and fearless, one may come to perfect peace.' [16]

In England, the first western Buddhist Society came into existence in 1907. The London Buddhist Society developed from this early beginning, its founder and President, Christmas Humphreys. Now simply called The Buddhist Society, it has become an international centre with members and affiliations all over the world. The stated aim of the Society is 'To publish and make known the principles of Buddhism and to encourage the study and application of these principles.' All schools of Buddhism are represented in the teaching at the Society. Among the many Buddhist books published by them, Christmas Humphreys has himself written fourteen, ranging from *Concentration and Meditation* to *Teach Yourself Zen* and *The Wisdom of Buddhism*. The Society also publishes *The Middle Way*, a quarterly journal. About Buddhism, Christmas Humphreys has this to say:

'The Noble Eightfold Path of Buddhism, acknowledged by all Schools, is the noblest course of spiritual training yet presented to man. It is far more than a

The death of the Buddha. Part of a bas-relief from Gandhara, India, 2nd or early 3rd century.

The Paranirvana of the Buddha, entering the state of Nirvana. Body colour on prepared cotton cloth, Tibet, 18th century.

code of morality. If the first five steps on the Way may be classed as ethics, the last three are concerned with the mind's development. "Cease to do evil, learn to do good; cleanse your own heart; this is the teaching of the Buddha. There is here no word of faith, save that which a man has in a guide who tells him of a journey and a goal and a way to it; no word of a Saviour who will make that journey for him. Each must develop his own mind, first by creating the instruments with which to develop its inner powers, and then by using them. The East has always set great store on the inner powers of the mind, knowing that its resources are infinite, and there is no instrument yet invented which can do more than the mind of a man can do when its powers are fully developed. And this is but common sense. If there is Mind-Only, there exists in Mind all the power and knowledge of the Universe. . . .

'The process of becoming is a circle; the process of becoming more, of growth, is a spiral, either up or down according as the growth is towards or away from wholeness. Buddhism begins with the Buddha's Enlightenment and ends with man's. And the final Goal? We know not, nor is it yet, or likely to be for aeons to come, our immediate concern. The faint of heart will ever seek some resting-place, some weak finality; for the strong, the first and last word is and ever more will be—Walk On!' [17]

The flexibility of Mahayana Buddhism means that it takes its character from the country of its adoption. For instance, in China the Buddhist teachings were translated into Chinese and acquired a new interpretation which, later, developed into Zen Buddhism. In Mahayana, each country will interpret the Buddha's words according to its own understanding and beliefs. This means that it is quite possible to have an English or an American or a French Mahayana school of teaching based on the Buddha's words—perhaps with a totally new understanding. In England, a western Mahayana school called The Friends of the Western Buddhist Order has begun to develop under the guidance of the Venerable Stavhira Sangharakshita. The growing need among the young for a personal journey of self-discovery has attracted many to this Buddhist group which practises meditation, yoga, karate, the *Tai Chi Ch'uan* and creates music and poetry. It now has branches in France, America, and New Zealand.

On Mindfulness, Stavhira Sangharakshita says:

'Our actions are generally impulsive. Desires are immediately translated into deeds, without a thought being given to the question of whether they are fit for the change or not. When we act with mindfulness, however, analysing motives before allowing them to influence conduct, there accrues not only the negative gain of abstention from unskilful courses of action but positively the acquisition of an undisturbed and tranquil state of mind. By carrying on even the common-place activities of life in a clearly conscious manner we introduce as it were an interval of inactivity between thought and deed, intention and execution. In the gulf of this interval, . . . our unwholesome impulses expend their force. The tempo of existence slackens. Behaviour becomes smoother, slower and more deliberate. Life proceeds at a pace like that of a mild and majestic elephant. . . .

'Bodily composure, though itself the product of a certain mental attitude, turns round as it were and, reacting on the mind, produces an even deeper quietude of spirit than before. It should moreover be noted that through the practice of mindfulness and self-possession, the most trivial occasions of life are invested with a halo of sanctity. Eating, drinking and dressing, the processes of excretion and urination even, are transformed from hindrances into helps for concentration; from interruptions of the spiritual life they become its continuation under another form. Obliterated is the distinction between things sacred and things profane. When Morality is pure and clear consciousness in all activities firmly established, from morning to night not a minute is wasted; uninterrupted from dawk till dusk flows the current of spiritual life, the stream of constant striving after holiness; and even in sleep, if the practice be intense enough, that clear consciousness is still shining, even as shines the moon amidst the darkness of the night.'[18]

TIBETAN BUDDHISM

*O nobly-born, listen. Now thou art
experiencing the Radiance of the Clear Light of
Pure Reality. Recognize it. O nobly-born, thy
present intellect, in real nature void, not formed
into anything as regards characteristics, or
colour, naturally void, is the very Reality, the
All-Good.*
*Thine own intellect, which is now voidness,
yet not to be regarded as of the voidness of
nothingness, but as being the intellect itself,
unobstructed, shining, thrilling, and blissful,
is the very consciousness, the All-Good Buddha.*

(Tibetan Book of the Dead) *[1]*

Yama, the god of death. Bronze, Tibet, 18th century.

THE TANTRIC PATH

Tibet is a country of splendour and terror. An intensely brilliant blue sky roofs the blinding whiteness of the snow-covered peaks. Range upon range of mountains contain great plateaux where icy winds howl and fearful thunderstorms rage. Here the hailstones are heavy enough to kill. But here also the glitter of the sun and the pure high air produce a radiance of colour unequalled anywhere in the world. In the valleys, the grass is unimaginably green and the lakes flash with turquoise. Everywhere, there is the feeling of limitless space.

Many Tibetans live in homesteads and in wandering nomadic villages of tents. Cut into the mountains, hewn out of the very rock, stand the monasteries. Hundreds of steps lead up the mountainsides to these monasteries, whose roofs are a blaze of red and gold. Tall poles lead the way into all the villages, and from them flutter coloured pennants on which are printed sacred messages. As the wind blows them, it 'utters' their message and thus fills the air with goodness.

But there is terror, too, in the shape of horrific temple guardians, statues with bulging eyeballs and huge powerful bodies, festooned with skulls. Some have the face of a horned beast with lolling red tongue and gleaming fangs. These are the guardians of the Dharma, the Way of the Buddha, ready to trample upon all its enemies. For the people of Tibet are always close to death and destruction by icy winds and torrential rains. They have a more intense awareness of the fleetingness of life, and of its great contrasts of sun and storm, than city dwellers. Their courage and endurance is strong and they have developed a simple, spontaneous

Tsongkapa, a Buddhist reformer and founder of the Tibetan Ge-lug-pa sect. Painted cotton, Tibet, 18th–19th century.

Mahakala, the Great Black One, a protector. Plaque of composition painted in tempera, Tibet, probably 18th century.

gaiety; but there is no shrinking from the recognition that life can be hard and bitter.

Mahayana Buddhism was introduced into Tibet in about 500 A.D. (although this date is very approximate). It was the start of a magnificent new development in Buddhism, a development which is based on the belief that each one of us is capable of responding to higher powers of Supreme Compassion according to his or her level of realization—which depends on previous lives as well as this one. We are all the embodiment of energies, from the coarsest to the finest, and

The Dalai Lama.

while we are ruled by our lusts and our fears, we are embodying raw and impure forces, of a lower quality than those of a more spiritually realized man. But each of us has the full range of universal energies within him, and each of us is capable of changing the level of his realization to that of a higher spiritual station in life. To help people accomplish this, there exist the *tulkus*, who are reincarnated spiritual leaders. The whole of Tibetan society is a living expression of the belief in the realization of the noblest form of spirituality—the compassion of the Buddha.

At the top of this great 'spiritual ladder' is the Dalai Lama, the highest personage and the ruler of the country. But to call him a personage does not indicate the way in which Tibetans think of him, for he is seen more as a lofty station of spirituality, a power-house through which the forces of compassion pass to the people. He is a tulku and in his case, his spiritual descendency comes from the principle of compassion itself, expressed in the form of a god, Avalokitesvara. It is believed that when a Dalai Lama dies, Avalokitesvara simply takes on a new

Avalokitesvara, the personification of intuitive knowledge. Gilded bronze, China, 18th century.

Lhasa, the capital city of Tibet.

body, so that he is reincarnated with every new Dalai Lama.

Tibetan Buddhism, perhaps more than any other Buddhist school, regards reincarnation as immensely important. When an ordinary man dies, his rebirth is determined by his unexhausted karma—his unfinished actions and incomplete understanding—but when a saint dies, he has no such ties to bind him and if he re-enters the world, it is a voluntary act. He chooses to be born again in order that his spiritual benevolence will remain in the world. He is then a tulku and, in Tibet, there were some two to three hundred tulkus before the Chinese invasion of 1950. One of them, Chogyam Trungpa, came to England. He tells of the way in which the monks discovered him, the child of humble village people, through a telepathic vision.

'During the New Year festival on the day of the full moon, in the Earth Hare year according to the Tibetan calendar (February 1939) I was born in the cattle byre; the birth came easily. On that day a rainbow was seen in the village, a pail supposed to contain water was unaccountably found full of milk, while several of my mother's relations dreamt that a lama (a monk) was visiting their tents. Soon afterwards, a lama from Trashi Lhaphug Monastery came to Geje; as he was giving his blessing to the people, he saw me, who at that time was a few months old; he put his hand over my head to give me a special blessing, saying that he wanted me for his monastery and that I must be kept very clean and always be carefully looked after. Both my parents agreed to this, and decided that when I grew older I should be sent to his monastery, where my mother's uncle was a monk.

'After the death in 1938 of the tenth Trungpa Tulku, the supreme abbot of Surmang, the monks at once sent a representative to His Holiness, Gyalwa Karmapa, the head of the Karma-ka-gyu school whose monastery lay near

Lhasa. Their envoy had to inform him of the death of the last abbot and to ask him if he had had any indication where his reincarnation would be found. They begged him to let them know at once should he obtain a vision. . . .

'A vision had in fact come to Gyalwa Karmapa, who dictated a letter to his private secretary, saying that the reincarnation of the tenth Trungpa Tulku has been born in a village five days' journey northwards from Surmang. Its name sounds like two words, *Ge* and *De*; there is a family there with two children; the son is the reincarnation. It all sounded rather vague; however, the secretary and monks of the Düdtsi-til Monastery at Surmang were preparing to go in search of the new abbot when a second sealed letter was received at the monastery. Rölpa-dorje, the regent abbot of Düdtsi-til, called a meeting, opened the letter and read it to the assembled monks. It said that Gyalwa Karmapa had had a second and much clearer vision: "The door of the family's dwelling faces south; they own a big red dog. The father's name is Yeshe-dargye and the mother's Chung and Tzo; the son who is nearly a year old is Trungpa Tulku." One senior monk and two others set off immediately to find me.

'After five days' journey they reached the village of Geje, and called on all the more important families; they made a list of the names of those parents who had children of a year old, and returned to Düdtsi-til. The list was sent to Gyalwa

A tanka showing Padma Sambhava, a learned Indian guru, who is said to have brought Buddhism to Tibet. Colour on prepared cloth, Tibet, early 19th century.

Karmapa, who was still at Pepung. He found that the monks had merely taken names belonging to important families and said they must go again and make further enquiries. On receipt of this message a second party of monks was sent to the village, which in the interval had removed to higher ground and changed its name to Dekyil: this time they called on every family and made a thorough search. In one tent they found a baby boy who had a sister and, as had been written in Gyalwa Karmapa's letter, the entrance faced south and there was a red dog. Also, the mother's name was Bo-Chung, though her family called her Tungtso-drölma; thus her name confirmed Gyalwa Karmapa's vision, but the father's name was different from that in the letter, and this caused a great deal of confusion; yet they looked closely at the baby, for as soon as he had seen them in the distance he waved his little hand and broke into smiles as they came in. So the monks felt that this must be the child and gave him the gifts which Gyalwa Karmapa had sent, the sacred protective cord (*sungdü*) and the traditional scarf (*khata*); this latter the baby took and hung round the monk's neck in the prescribed way, as if he had already been taught what was the right thing to do: delighted, the monks picked me up, for that baby was myself, and I tried to talk.

'The following day the monks made a further search in another part of the village, then returned to say goodbye. As they made prostration before me, I placed my hand on their heads as if I knew that I should give them my blessing, then the monks were certain that I was the incarnation of the tenth Trungpa. They spoke to my mother asking her to tell them in confidence who had been my father. She told them that I was the son of her first husband Yeshe-dargye, but that I had always been known as the son of my stepfather. This made everything clear to the monks, who immediately returned to Düdtsi-til. The news was taken to Gyalwa Karmapa who was sure that I, the child of Tungtso-drölma, was the eleventh Trungpa Tulku.' [2]

Lama Dhardo Rinpoche, a guru, Tibet.

THE WAY FOR REACHING NIRVANA

It is said that lamas, the monks of Tibet, have great powers, both magical and spiritual. Perhaps some have. The rigours of their training would leave most of us considerably changed from our ordinary workaday selves. For their aim is 'the turning about in the deepest seat of consciousness' (Lankavatara Sutra). Most spend several years in isolated hermitages, in almost unbroken solitude. Before this, there are years of deep meditation and of ritual chanting. There are initiations, none of which can be given until the aspirant has made a hundred thousand prostrations (each prostration is made by raising the hands above the head, palms slightly apart, as a salutation to the Buddha; then they are brought down to the throat, where it is a salutation to the Dharma, the teaching; then down to the heart as a salutation to the Sangha, the Buddhist monks and community. In a continuous movement, the hands are taken on down to the ground, which five parts of the body have to touch, i.e. the knees, the palms and the forehead. While this is done, a mantra is recited and a complex Buddhist scene visualized. Techniques of intense visualization are taught in which every detail of a *tanka* (a symbolic holy picture) must be brought into the mind, for in the end the tantric adept should be able to visualize a world, to create it in all its details, and then to dissolve it again, thus understanding in experience the transitory nature of all phenomena and the mistakenness of clinging to them.

Much has been written in the West about the psychic powers which some lamas acquire incidentally, during the course of this training. Such powers are not regarded as ends in themselves but if they do occur, it is proper to make use of then for the benefit of mankind. John Blofeld (*The Way of Power*) records that the most common is telepathy. Another is the knowledge of the day and place of one's own death and of one's rebirth. But there are others which seem equally astonishing. Some lamas, in a state of trance, are said to be able to cover distances at great speed, moving somewhat like a hovercraft over obstacles. They are able to shrink or enlarge their own body at will, to have it appear elsewhere, to pass through solid objects and through fire unscathed. They can leave their bodies asleep and look down on them; and they can send forth 'ghosts' of themselves, semblances which move and speak, to any part of the world.

The word *tantra* means 'to weave' and it particularly emphasizes the techniques and activities for discovering the Origin, the Source of oneself. The goal is the same as in all other forms of Buddhism—it is to be one with the Source; to know Suchness (as many Buddhists call it) as oneself. To help the student achieve this state of liberation and bliss, Tantra has devised a number of roads to follow, some of which are secret and not divulged to any but the fully-trained, as their misuse might have bad effects. Another safeguard is that a would-be student must find a lama who will accept him as a disciple, for unless he does so, he will not be given the essential initiations to take him on to further stages of training.

The emphasis in Tantra is on the *direct* experience of who one really is, beyond all words and thoughts. The main way to discover this is through the use of symbols to reach the unconscious forces in us. For a symbol, in Tantra, stands for something of which we are yet unconscious, something which cannot be known in any other way except through itself. It is believed that while we are still unconscious of dormant forces we cannot master ourselves, for we cannot reach

A mandala—a square within a circle. Colour on prepared cloth, Tibet, 18th century.

Tanka showing the four-petalled lotus, centre, which has the gods Akshobia, Ratnasambhava, Amitabha, and Amoghasiddhi with Vairocana in the middle. Colour on prepared cloth, Tibet, 18th century.

them. To become purified and master of oneself, it is necessary to bring every-thing into the light of day that it may be recognized. Thus the different *yanas* or ways, are for different levels of recognition. If we are unaware of how we function, we will not use the energies of which we are composed for anything but the satisfaction of immediate desires—for the building up of the 'I', the small self. The yana given by the guru is *precisely* designed to make us aware of what we are doing, to show to us our own functioning, and how to alter it.

The way of visualization is one of the great yanas, and it involves the use of the *mandala*. The mandala is a catalyst: through it the student sees himself, for the images it contains correspond to actual states of being, they *are* what they portray. The word mandala means, in Sanskrit, circle and centre, and a mandala is usually composed of a number of concentric circles, sometimes with a square in the middle, which represents the earth. It is not meant to be flat, but is always intended to be visualized in three dimensions.

In the brilliantly-coloured world of mandalas and Tantra, it is easy to get lost if one goes by intellect alone, for intellect cannot account for the way in which symbols stir us. Mandalas represent a bridge between our ordinary world of sense-perception and the eternal and limitless state of Suchness; they enable us to see that our human qualities, such as goodness, wisdom and compassion are like the seeds which contain the potential flower—all that we do and are has its fulfil-ment in a higher realm. The mandala contains images of all the many aspects of the Buddha's compassion. As the student meditates upon these by the practice of visualizing them, he begins to recognize himself in relationship to them and then, he and they become one. It is not that they were ever separate from him; poten-tially he was always that aspect of compassion which he was visualizing. But as his visualization grows deeper, his realization of that force of compassion within himself grows until he *is* it.

To begin with, the student must build up his visualizing powers by using a simple image. This is usually the four-petalled lotus, representing the unfoldment of the perfect mind.

The lotus is the Buddhist symbol of enlightenment, for its roots (our bodily existence) are buried in the nourishing earth and mud, while its flower (the enlightened mind) rises above the water and opens out into immensity. It is also symbolic of the act of spiritual unfolding. The urge in the seed is always to grow and within the human mind, it is always to transcend itself. The fully-opened lotus blossom is the symbol of the unfoldment of Buddha-mind.

In this mandala, the nature of the Buddha is expressed in five ways. In the very centre is the colour of deep blue. Perhaps because of the Tibetan sky, blue stands for vastness, infinity, the Absolute. It is the colour of unclouded truth, shining and eternal, and it is the light of transcendental wisdom. This blue radiance issues forth from the heart of Vairocana, whose body is white, and who sits cross-legged, the potentially flowering seed, in the middle of the lotus. He embodies the ideal of the illuminated mind and his *mudra* (gesture) is turning the wheel of the teaching. He sits on the lion-throne, roaring the truth without fear.

In the eastern right-hand quarter of the mandala is the white light of water and here sits dark blue Akshobia, the pure embodiment of form. He radiates the white of mirror-like wisdom and his mudra is that of touching the earth.

In the south, like a blazing sun, is Ratnasambhava, golden-yellow in colour.

left: Twirling the prayer wheels in a hilltop temple, Nepal and *right:* close-up of a prayer wheel. The prayer is inside the cover, which rotates on the centre pin as it is twirled. Silver cap and mountings, 19th century, ivory parts probably earlier, Tibet.

His mudra is that of supreme giving (the open hand) and from his heart shines the golden light of the Equality of all beings. He represents the principle of Feeling which, through him, becomes love and compassion for all that lives. He is seated on a horse for speed and energy.

To the west, surrounded by fire, is Amitabha, whose name means infinite light and spiritual rebirth. He radiates red for the setting sun and his mudra is that of meditation—one hand over the other. He is Perception and his red is changing to the darkness of meditation, out of which spiritual life is born.

Lastly, in the north, is Amoghasiddhi, whose colour is green and who represents the divine will. His mudra is fearlessness with the hand held up. In his female form, he is known as Tara, the all-accomplishing Wisdom.

THE YOGA OF SOUND AND THE MANY-COLOURED UNIVERSE

A mandala is incomplete and ineffective as a symbol to transform the consciousness, if the mantra accompanying each of its figures is not repeated at the same time as the mandala is visualized. A mantra, to Tibetans, is a symbolic sound—an internal vibration—and its meaning is 'that which protects the mind beyond words and thoughts'.

In the five-petalled lotus, each figure has a syllable inscribed in its centre and this syllable is the *sound* of the figure and thus of that state of consciousness itself.

OM, as in Hinduism, is the greatest sound possible. In Tibet, it is usually linked to three other words—*Om Mani Padme Hum*, which means the Jewel in the Lotus, the truth in the heart of the doctrine, the mysterious spiritual force which impels us to move towards it and transforms us as we do so.

Om Mani Padme Hum is repeated all day long and everywhere. Monks intone it to the accompaniment of great horns; it is twirled in prayer wheels and

A lotus charm containing the divine sound of AUM. Tibet, 16th–17th century.

repeated by people shopping and working. It is said that *Om* and *Hum* have great power and can awaken an intuitive understanding in a way that no mere words can ever do.

The six syllables of *Om Mani Padme Hum* are said to correspond to the six worlds of Tibetan Buddhism. Each of these worlds represents a state of the human mind, and in order that we should bring these states into our present-day consciousness, the worlds are painted in great detail so that, visualizing them, we recognize ourselves. As the world is visualized the mantra is repeated in such a way that compassion is radiated to it. As the syllables of *Om Mani Padme Hum* are intoned slowly, the written form of each syllable is visualized as emitting shining rays of comfort to the beings in each of the six worlds.

Om: gods
Ma: *asuras* (anti-gods)
Ni: humans
Pad: animals
Me: *pretas* (hungry ghosts)
Hum: hell

It is believed that the concentration of visual image and sound together, when directed outwards generates, as well as compassion, great cosmic power. It not only helps all the inhabitants of those worlds (the people in those states of mind) but it also identifies the practitioner with the embodiment of compassion itself, Avalokitesvara.

Just as the mantra vibrates to the unconscious depths of man, so the colours of the mandalas are chosen to enable him to have a direct visual experience, beyond words, of love, compassion and wisdom—the aspects of the Buddha's nature.

There is a deep pyschological truth here. Almost everything in the universe, as

Manjusri, Bodhisattva of Wisdom; with his sword he severs the bonds of ignorance. Colour on prepared cloth, Tibet, late 18th century.

perceived by us, has colour. The spectrum of colours available to us as human beings affects us emotionally far more than we consciously realize. The Tibetans make use of colours so that their effect penetrates to the very heart of man. The colours used for the concentrated meditations on compassion become spiritualized so that when the colour is seen again, its spiritual aspect is re-experienced. For instance, the green Tara, who is the female consort of Amoghasiddhi of the four-petalled lotus, is there at our birth and again at our death, helping us into the new state. The colour of green, already associated with grass, tender shoots, the forest and Nature, now becomes also the colour of rest and repose, of safety, succour, freedom from distress and refuge. The activity of Tara is to restore disturbed equilibrium. Thus green also becomes harmony and balance and the colour of justice in its healing aspect.

In Tantra, all that is mundane is to be transmuted into its corresponding divine nature. Red, the colour of warmth, means 'life'. Blood is red and also hot, so red means emotional warmth and all positive feelings. It is the colour of passion but in Tantra it is passion purified by Emptiness, an emotion which has become wholly spiritualized into Love itself.

Yellow is sunshine and ripened grain—it is growth and maturity. It is also riches and abundance in the spiritual sense. It is the colour of gold and therefore of whatever is rare and precious and gives delight. In this way, it becomes the inexhaustible creativity of the enlightened mind.

Black is night, and it is the charred wood of the cremation ground. It is death and destruction—but it is also the death of the ego and the destruction of ignorance.

Visualization of Manjusri, the Bodhisattva of Wisdom, is believed to enable one to apprehend wisdom in a way that is beyond words. The visualization is built up as follows:

First, a vast blue sky must be visualized, with rainbow-tinted clouds. Then the student must see a pale blue lotus throne. On it is spread a white mat and cross-legged on this, sits Manjusri. He is seen as a youth, a deep rich yellow figure, luminous and transparent. There is a garland round his head of five blue lotus blossoms. His face has a smiling and compassionate expression and he is the embodiment of transcendental wisdom. His right arm is uplifted and his right hand holds the flaming sword of Knowledge while his left hand holds the book of Wisdom. At his heart is a mantra, with the sound *Dha* and from it comes a ray of amber-coloured light which falls onto the head of the visualizer and then passes down into his heart, carrying the sound of the mantra, which must then be constantly repeated in the heart.

THE WHEEL OF LIFE

This most famous mandala of all depicts the six worlds of the human mind. It is a wheel, the ever-turning wheel of existence, and the hub of the wheel is occupied by three creatures: a cock, who represents craving and passionate desire for life; a snake, the embodiment of hatred and enmity; and a pig, who symbolizes deluded ignorance. Each bites the tail of the animal in front, in a perpetual round.

Encircling the hub is a narrow space, half of which is white with peaceful, happy-looking humans moving upwards and carrying prayer-wheels and

The Wheel of Life. Colour on prepared cloth, Tibet, 19th century.

rosaries; while the other half is black, and has a succession of miserable people plunging downwards, naked and chained, their attitudes showing fear and horror.

Revolving around this circle are the six segments of the wheel. At the top is the world of the gods. It is a world in which people have arrived by virtue of good deeds and purity of character and in this world, all wishes are gratified. Moving clockwise (in different order to *Om Mani Padme Hum*) next comes the world of the asuras, the anti-gods who, jealous of the serenity and happiness of their neighbours, are always at war with them. They mirror the qualities of aggression and materialism. In the third section are the hungry ghosts, people who are obsessed with irrational desires and compulsions, perpetually seeking more than the object of their desire can give. They are shown as naked and deformed, with a ravenous hunger which can never be satisfied for their mouths are too small to take in food. In the bottom section are tormented beings in hell, representing madness and acute mental suffering. In the fifth section are pairs of animals, peacefully moving about. These are people who have not developed their minds and are dominated by the demands of their bodies. When they are satisfied with life they are easy to live with, but when things go wrong for them they can be dangerously brutal. The last section depicts ordinary, intelligent human consciousness—men are buying and selling, reading, talking, meditating and being carried as corpses to be buried.

The Compassionate Buddha appears in each of the segments. His presence symbolizes the belief that, whatever state of mind we are in, there is always help from our own essential Emptiness, if we are willing to accept it. In each segment the Buddha appears in a different colour, offering what is needed. To the gods he appears in white, playing a lute, the melody of which is that their world of happiness is impermanent and they must not become attached to it but must look for the timeless and eternal. To the asuras he comes in green, holding the sword of transcendental wisdom. The sword is their own weapon, and this they must turn on themselves and cut through aggressive ambition until it becomes the will to find the Void. To the hungry ghosts the Buddha appears in red, showering them with food which they *can* eat—sanity and wisdom to replace neurotic compulsions. In hell, he comes in a smoke colour, giving refreshment—a respite from suffering which, if accepted, can lead directly to Enlightenment—for the hell of the tortured mind is sometimes the other side of the coin from the realization of Void-nature. To the animals he comes in blue, giving them a book that they may develop their minds and become more sensitive. And to the humans he comes in yellow, with a begging bowl and a staff, that they may develop compassion and detachment from their busy occupations.

Around all the six sections is the rim and here there are twelve figures, each of which represents one of the twelve chains which bind humans to this life.

These are:

1. A blind man, representing primordial ignorance.
2. A potter, fashioning the first impulses that arise out of that ignorance.
3. A monkey playing with a peach. He has become conscious of his impulses as he tastes good and evil.
4. Two men in a boat. The consciousness of personality has arisen, and this has led to name and form.
5. Six empty houses show the six sense perceptions of consciousness (Budd-

hists include the mind as a sense of perception.

6. A man and a woman in an embrace of love. The senses are now desiring contact with their objects.

7. A man with arrows in both eyes, which are the blind feeling of pleasure and pain.

8. An offering of drink, representing the thirst for more existence.

9. A monkey stealing fruit. This is the thirst for existence leading to grasping.

10. A pregnant woman. The greed for life leads to more and more becoming.

11. Childbirth, which represents rebirth.

12. A corpse, which is rebirth giving rise to decay and death and more rebirth in a perpetual round.

The whole wheel is in the grasp of a monster, Yama, the Lord of Death, who represents ignorant delusion, with the whole universe in his clutch. He wears a crown of five human skulls. Outside the wheel, the Buddha floats on clouds, pointing with his finger to the spiritual path as the way to liberation.

Many lessons can be learnt from this mirror-image of existence. Perhaps one of the more important is that even the gods can tumble to a lesser state, and that good works alone are not enough. A new consciousness must arise, the consciousness of the Ground of Being itself, if the six states of perpetual becoming are to be left behind.

left: Kalacakra, supreme Buddha with Vishvamata, the 'mother of all'. Bronze, Tibet, 17th century. *right*: A green Tara, the benefactress who represents divine purity. Copper partly gilded, Nepal, 16th–17th century.

left: Scroll depicting Marici, the goddess of the dawn, seated in a chariot drawn by pigs. Tempera on coloured paper, China, 16th–17th century. *right:* Yama, the god of death, one of the eight fearful ones. Tanka, Tibet, 15th century.

THE TANTRIC YOGA OF LOVE

Tantra is the yoga of sacramental action. It aims to bring about a transformation of consciousness by means of spiritually significant sights, sounds and movements. Mandalas are the visual means; mantras are the sacramental sounds; and movements are made by various parts of the body, such as the mudras and prostrations, which involve the whole body. Because sacramental actions necessarily involve the body, Tantra believes the body to be the vessel of enlightenment and extols its wonders. Not only is the body part of the material world in which we live, but so too are the many other material objects which are used by Tibetans for sacramental purposes, such as the prayer wheel and the *dorje*, an emblem of spiritual power. Tantra sees the whole world as expressly designed to help man towards enlightenment. The Theravadin Buddhists deny the virtues of the world, but Tibetan Buddhists believe that one should live in such a way that the whole of worldly life itself is transmuted into a transcendental sphere.

Thus the body, as the vehicle of enlightenment, is regarded as sacred, for it provides the means by which the mind can be altered. Movements of the limbs and control of the breath can change the mind; so too, for a man, can the command of the seminal fluid.

Kundalini, the yoga of psychic forces, has been described in Hinduism, where it is visualized as a serpent. The same yoga, in Tibetan Tantra, teaches how the sacramental performance of the sexual act can be a means to enlightenment. It teaches that the energy of desire, particularly of sexual desire, can be transmuted in such a way that it is freed from its usual channels and can be concentrated on sublime realization. Under the guidance of a guru, the student can be taught control over his seminal output, and the ability to re-direct it within himself so that it energizes and invigorates the *chakras* (the nerve-centres of the body).

For it is believed that as a way to enlightenment, the sexual feeling should be experienced for what it is in itself, beyond all concepts about it. Thus one rite prescribes that a man and woman, facing each other and seated in the lotus posture of meditation, should allow their sensations to be aroused while they adorn each other with flowers, light incense to each other, and offer each other wine. At a moment of perfect accord, they change their positions so that the woman is seated in the man's lap, her arms about his neck and his hands supporting her back. Gazing into each other's eyes they remain motionless, allowing the consciousness of their breathing, their bodily and genital contact, and the meeting of their eyes, to intensify their sensations to the point where words vanish and there are no longer any notions of 'sexual desire' or 'satisfaction'. When verbal thinking is transcended they are then in perfect harmony with 'what is'.

In this position, the male and female symbolize the noblest aspects of religious understanding. The man embodies *karuna*, active compassion, and the woman is

Vajradhara, the indestructible, bearer of a thunderbolt and master of all secrets. Bronze, Tibet, 18th century.

prajna, perfect wisdom. He also represents form (*rupa*) and she the void (*sunya*). As carved images, these two intertwined figures are found in all the shrines of Tibet, where they are regarded with the utmost reverence as symbolizing the highest understanding known to man, the unity of Nirvana and the world.

DEATH AND THE AFTER-LIFE

'O nobly born, the time has now come for thee to seek the Path. Thy breathing is about to cease. In the past thy teacher hath set thee face to face with the Clear Light; and now thou art about to experience it in its Reality in the *Bardo* state (the 'intermediate state' immediately following death, in which the soul is judged—or rather judges itself by choosing, in accord with the character formed during its life on earth, what sort of an after-life it shall have). In this Bardo state all things are like the cloudless sky, and the naked, immaculate Intellect is like unto a translucent void without circumference or centre. At this moment know thou thyself and abide in that state. I, too, at this time, am setting thee face to face.' (Tibetan Book of the Dead) *[3]*

Practices concerned with death and instructions about them are contained in a book of initiation into the mysteries of death, called the *Bardo Thodol*, or the *Tibetan Book of the Dead*. The rites begin before a man's death and continue afterwards, for it is believed that there is a period of some four days when the person is in a trance state, unaware that death has occurred and that he is now separated from the human body. This period is called the First Bardo and, during it, words from a lama can penetrate to the person, thus helping him to face the Clear Light which dawns in brilliant purity at this time. The Clear Light is no other than the light of the Void, Reality itself in its undifferentiated and fundamental state.

If the radiance of the Clear Light does not terrify the dead man, and he can recognize and welcome it, he will enter the transcendental state of purity and will be liberated and never reborn. But very few achieve this recognition. Most flee in terror from the Light, and it fades. The person then becomes conscious of the fact that death has occurred. At this point, the Second Bardo begins, during which he sees symbolically all that he has ever done and thought passing in front of him—a great cinema-screen showing the film of his entire life. While he watches, he feels he still has a body; but when he realizes this is not so, he develops a great desire to possess one again. Then he enters the Third Bardo, which is the state of seeking rebirth. His Karma, the net result of all his previous actions and thoughts, determines the new person and, now scared beyond endurance by his bodiless condition, the after-death state ends with his finding a comforting womb once more.

For Tibetans, therefore, it is essential to prepare for death during one's lifetime, so that the Clear Light may be encountered without flinching, especially as there may be no lama there to guide one. For Tibetans believe that the human state is hard to achieve and, once lost, is very difficult to regain. The remarkable occurrence of being a human in a land where the Buddhist doctrine is practised may take aeons of lifetimes as an animal before it happens again.

Therefore, preparation for death plays a large part in Tibetans' lives. There are various rites to be practised. One consists of sitting in a graveyard where the bodies lie unburied, compassionately offered as food for animals and birds. Here the practitioner will meditate on the transitory nature of life and on the sameness of all things. Surrounded by the stench of rotting flesh, he will reflect that there is no intrinsic difference between an attractive object and a repellent one. All are pure manifestation, and it is only the mind which discriminates and produces feelings of desire and repulsion. To be undisturbed by *all* sights leads to a tranquil fearlessness and the breaking of the Samsaric (worldly) chains.

Another, more popular practice is the pilgrimage. There are many sacred lakes and mountains and shrines to which pilgrims flock. They frequently walk many miles and some follow a practice of kneeling down every three paces and touching their foreheads to the ground in the direction of the sacred place which they are approaching. Often, when the pilgrims reach their destination, they walk round it 108 or 1080 or even 10,800 times (the number 108 comes from ancient Hindu metaphysics and is regarded as having a special importance). As they do this, they hold the mind still and repeat a mantra while they walk, some-times prostrating themselves at every three paces as well.

The more secret and highly developed practices for encountering death are yogic ones:

The Yoga of the Clear Light. The yogi tries, during his lifetime, to see the Clear Light, believing that if he can accomplish this, he will feel no terror when he gazes on it after death. To succeed in this, he must understand that birth and death are not occurrences which only happen once to him but that every moment of his life is a continuous, unbroken process of births and deaths. Science tells us that the cells of the body are continually reproducing themselves and dying; so also, Buddhists believe, are thoughts and feelings. As Alan Watts remarks: 'The beginning of the universe is now, for all things are at this moment being created,

left: A vajra—a symbol of a wisdom so hard that it can cut through all erroneous concepts. Bronze, Nepal, 15th century. *right:* One of a pair of dancing figures taken from the apron of an exorcist. Human bone, Tibet, 18th century.

and the end of the universe is now, for all things are at this moment passing away'.[4] To renounce what attaches one to all this process is to gain liberation, and the Clear Light dawns unobscured in a man once he has relinquished that which fetters him.

> When the bright radiances of Five Wisdoms shine upon me now,
> Let it come that I, neither awed nor terrified, may recognize them to be of myself;
> When the apparitions of the Peaceful and Wrathful forms are dawning upon me here,
> Let it come that I, obtaining the assurance of fearlessness, may recognize the Bardo. (Tibetan Book of the Dead) [5]

The Yoga of Consciousness Transference. The details of this practice are secret and it should not be attempted without a lama. The adept must be proficient in Kundalini. It is said that with the help of visualizations, the Kundalini moon-fluid rises upwards as a psychic force through the chakras to the top of the head, at the sagittal suture where the two parietal bones come together. In the head the Kundalini meets another force, which has been generated there, and the two together, in divine bliss of union, feed all the centres of the body. The success of the union results, so it is said, in a small hole in the top of the head spontaneously appearing, through which the practitioner's consciousness can be transferred. The yogi can then, at death, transfer himself to the realm of the Clear Light, or he can transfer himself to another body which, unlike the ordinary man, he is able to choose. During his lifetime, he can transfer himself back and forth in space and can take the form of an apparition anywhere (there are many stories of yogis taking the form of animals, and also of yogis being seen in two places at the same time, the second body being an apparition). These ghostly appearances are said to be frequent in Tibet, and might hold terror but for the fact that in such an advanced state of yoga, the yogi is only concerned with compassion and the good of all.

Other yogas lead, through meditation and trance, to the *experience* of the origin of the mind. The human mind and the knowledge it contains is knowable. For Buddhists believe that all that can be perceived and known is created by the mind, and there is nothing else knowable besides the mind. But the origin of human mind, the *nature* of Mind itself, its Suchness, is unknowable and can only be experienced.

TIBET IN THE WEST

The Chinese assumed government control in Tibet in 1950. The rights and wrongs of their case for doing so do not fall within the province of this book. But, however justified they felt their actions to be, the effect was devastating on many Tibetans. A gradually tightening grip on individuals with the introduction of identity cards and food rationing resulted in a revolt by the Tibetans in 1959. This was subdued, and there followed even tighter control, enforced by the burning of monasteries and the interrogation and torturing of lamas. The Dalai Lama escaped to India, where he remains to this day. Three young tulkus, Chogyam Trungpa Rinpoche, Lama Chime Rinpoche and Lama Akong Rinpoche (*Rinpoche* means 'precious master') also escaped to India and then came to England. In due course, they established a meditation centre in Scotland,

An 18th-century tanka from Tibet.

called Samye-Ling, which is now one of the best-known Tibetan centres in the western world.

Samye-Ling is fifteen miles away from the nearest town, Lockerbie: fifteen miles of heather-covered lowland hills and rocky streams. A salmon river flows through its grounds but fishing is forbidden, for it is believed that bad karma will

Two Tibetan bronzes. *left:* Jambala, a form of Kuvera, the god of wealth, is seen here riding on a dragon; 19th century. *right:* The female goddess of supreme wisdom, Devata Usmisavijaya, 'she who is born from the crown of the head'; 18th century.

be created if life is taken. Akong Rinpoche, who now runs Samye-Ling, will not keep pigs or sheep for the same reason—they must not be killed. So the fish swim undisturbed in the river and in the small lake which contains an island with Buddha-images, a *stupa* (shrine) and a peacock.

Meditation goes on most of the time at Samye-Ling and there are isolated huts to which one may retreat for months at a time. But as well as meditation, there is much active, practical work for students in the garden and kitchen, and facilities for pottery and metal-work; for Samye-Ling hopes eventually to support itself through its sale of Buddha *rupas* (images) and of tankas and other paintings. A Tibetan artist, Sherapalden, paints and teaches there.

A second community called Kham Tibetan House has now been started near Saffron Waldon in Essex under the direct authority of Lama Chime Rinpoche, who was the former Abbot of Benchen Monastery in eastern Tibet. There is a more formal atmosphere at Kham House than at Samye-Ling, the emphasis being on the teaching of the Six Doctrines of the School of Milarepa. These Doctrines, which were originally expounded by Tilopa, Naropa, Marpa and Milarepa, comprise the Doctrine of the Inner Fire; the Doctrine of the Illusory Body; the Doctrine of the Dream State; the Doctrine of the Clear Light; the Doctrine of the Intermediate State; and the Doctrine of the Transference of Consciousness. The School teaches the undifferentiated unity of subject and object, which rests complete in itself. It has developed a special system of meditation, Mahamudra, which is practised at Kham House.

After Samye-Ling was established, Chogyam Trungpa went to America where he has founded meditation centres in both Vermont and Colorado. His published works include *Born in Tibet*, *Meditation in Action*, and *Mudra*. About the cultivation of patience in spiritual work, he says:

'There is usually a neurotic aspect [in ourselves] which causes us in some way or another to react to a given situation and develop a neurotic way of dealing with it, which is not at all the true way. That is acting according to one's conditioning rather than according to what *is*. So in this case the person would not have the ability to develop freedom because freedom is not properly presented to him. Freedom must be presented properly. In fact the word "Freedom" itself is a relative term: freedom *from* something, otherwise there is no freedom. And since it is freedom from something, one must first create the right situation, which is patience.

'This kind of freedom cannot be created by an outsider or some superior authority. One must develop the ability to know the situation. In other words one has to develop a panoramic awareness, an all-pervading awareness, knowing the situation *at that very moment*. It is a question of knowing the situation and opening one's eyes to that very moment of nowness, and this is not particularly a mystical experience or anything mysterious at all, but just direct, open and clear perception of what *is now*. And when a person is able to see what *is now* without being influenced by the past or any expectation of the future, but just seeing the very moment of now, then at that moment there is no barrier at all. For a barrier could only arise from association with the past or expectation of the future. So the present moment has no barriers at all. And then he finds there is a tremendous energy in him, a tremendous strength to practise patience. He becomes like a warrior. When a warrior goes to war he does not think of the past or his previous experience of war, nor does he think of the consequences for the future; he just sails through it and fights, and that is the right way to be a warrior. Similarly, when there is a tremendous conflict going on, one has to develop this energy combined with patience. And this is what is known as right patience with the all-seeing eye, patience with clarity. . . .

'the whole point is that one should not expect anything from outside, one should not try to change the other person or try to put across one's opinions. One should not try to convince a person at the wrong moment, when one knows he already has a very clear idea of his own, or it is simply not the right moment for your words to get through to him. There is an analogy of two people walking barefoot along a very rough road, and one thought it would be very good to cover the whole road with leather so it would be very soft, but the other one, who was wiser, said, "No, I think if we covered our feet with leather that would be the same." So that is patience, which is not being distrustful, but is a matter of not expecting anything and not trying to change the situation outside oneself. And that is the only way to create peace in the world. If you yourself are prepared to step into it and to accept, then somebody else makes the same contribution. So if a hundred people did the same the whole thing would become right.' *[6]*

DRUGS AND THE RELIGIOUS EXPERIENCE

The 'journey to India' taken by so many young people today, has usually been to North India, to Katmandu and the borders of Tibet. If the frontier of Tibet had been open to the world, that small, remote country might well have been inundated with Europeans and Americans searching for an experience which they feel unable to find in the West—self-transcendence. Both India and Tibet, but particularly Tibet, have come to symbolize (even if falsely) a new life, a new understanding, a new beginning.

'I have to find, among other things, a new word for the universe, I'm tired of the old one,' [7] says Alan Ginsberg.

What are the young looking for, really? Aldous Huxley, in his book on mescalin, says: 'The urge to transcend self-conscious selfhood is a principle appetite of the soul. When, for whatever reason, men and women fail to transcend themselves by means of worship, good works and spiritual exercises, they are apt to resort to religion's chemical surrogates—alcohol and 'goof-pills' in the modern West, alcohol and opium in the East, hashish in the Mohammedan world, alcohol and marijuana in Central America.' . . . [8]

Is this the whole story? In his book, *Psychedelic Prayer*, Timothy Leary says:

> During the session
> Observe your body
> Mandala of the universe
> Observe your body
> Of ancient design
> Holy temple of consciousness
> Central stage of the oldest drama. [9]

The sense that life in itself is extraordinary, and that all its aspects are infinitely wonderful, is not easily found in civilizations which regard the making of money and the spending of it as most important. But a feeling of integration with life, a feeling of wholeness (in fact, just that feeling that life itself is precious) is what many people really want. Alan Watts here points out some reasons why not only modern civilizations but mankind itself seems to have lost its direction:

'We believe, then, that the mind controls the body, not that the body controls itself through the mind. . . . At the same time there has always been at least an obscure awareness that in feeling oneself to be a separate mind, [or controller] soul, or ego, there is something wrong. Naturally, for a person who finds his identity in something other than his full organism is less than half a man. He is cut off from complete participation in nature. Instead of being a body, he "has" a body. Instead of living and loving he "has" instincts for survival and copulation. Disowned, they drive him as if they were blind furies or demons that possessed him.' . . . [10]

'Is it possible, then, that Western science could provide a medicine which would at least give the human organism a start in releasing itself from its chronic self-contradiction? The medicine might indeed have to be supported by other procedures—psychotherapy, "spiritual" disciplines, and basic changes in one's pattern of life—but every diseased person seems to need some kind of initial lift to set him on the way to health. The question is by no means absurd if it is true that what afflicts us is a sickness not just of the mind but of the organism, of the very functioning of the nervous system and the brain. Is there, in short, a medicine which can give us temporarily the sensation of being integrated, of being fully one with ourselves and with nature as the biologist knows us, theoretically, to be? If so, the experience might offer clues to whatever else must be done to bring about full and continuous integration. It might be at least the tip of an Ariadne's thread to lead us out of the maze in which all of us are lost from our infancy.' [11]

The Wheel of Life painted by Sherapalden Beru in 1970.

Traditionally, man has looked towards religion to help him discover that sense of integration, of being one with himself and with the eternal Ground of his ephemeral life. But to really discover this Ground, he must *be* it, for anything which is 'not him' is liable to disappear at any moment. This is fully recognized in the East, where to be one's Self is the purpose of one's life. In the West, however, modern religion relies on faith rather than Self-discovery, and faith necessarily means believing in something outside oneself. Many of the young seem to have found this way of faith unsatisfying to their spiritual needs and have turned instead to the 'initial lift' Alan Watts talks of, the taking of drugs such as LSD and cannabis (drugs such as opium and heroin result in escape rather than transcendence).

The reaction of most reasonable people to the idea that spiritual illumination can be found through a drug is that this is much too superficial and simple a way, and that a transcendental experience which can be 'turned on' like a tap is an insult to man's soul, making him seem to be merely a bundle of chemical reactions. But, as Alan Watts points out, 'mystical insight is no more in the chemical itself than biological knowledge is in the microscope.' [12]

Charles Baudelaire declared about the effects of drugs: 'A final, supreme thought bursts forth from the dreamer's brain: "I have become God!" ' [13]. And Aldous Huxley, one of the first people in the post-war drug era to write about experiences with mescalin, describes them in such a way that one can almost share them with him:

'I took my pill at eleven. An hour and half later I was sitting in my study, looking intently at a small glass vase. The vase contained only three flowers—a full-blown Belle of Portugal rose, shell pink with a hint at every petal's base of a hotter, flamier hue; a large magenta and cream-coloured carnation; and, pale purple at the end of its broken stalk, the bold heraldic blossom of an iris. . . . At breakfast that morning I had been struck by the lively dissonance of its colours. But that was no longer the point. I was not looking now at an unusual flower arrangement. I was seeing what Adam had seen on the morning of his creation—the miracle, moment by moment, of naked existence.

' "Is it agreeable?" somebody asked. (During this part of the experiment, all conversations were recorded on a dictating machine, and it has been possible for me to refresh my memory of what was said.)

' "Neither agreeable nor disagreeable," I answered. "It just *is*." . . .

'I continued to look at the flowers, and in their living light I seemed to detect the qualitative equivalent of breathing—but of a breathing without returns to a starting-point, with no recurrent ebbs but only a repeated flow from beauty to heightened beauty, from deeper to ever deeper meaning. Words like Grace and Transfiguration came to my mind, and this of course was what, among other things, they stood for. . . . *Sat Chit Ananda*, Being-Awareness-Bliss—for the first time I understood, not on the verbal level, not by inchoate hints or at a distance, but precisely and completely what those prodigious syllables referred to. And then I remembered a passage I had read in one of Suzuki's essays. "What is the Dharma-Body of the Buddha?" (The Dharma-Body of the Buddha is another way of saying Mind, Suchness, the Void, the Godhead.) The question is asked in a Zen monastery by an earnest and bewildered novice. And with the prompt irrelevance of one of the Marx Brothers, the Master answers, "The hedge at the bottom of the garden." "And the man who realizes this truth," the novice dubiously enquires, "what, may I ask, is he?" Groucho gives him a whack over the shoulders with his staff and answers, "A golden-haired lion."

'It had been, when I read it, only a vaguely pregnant piece of nonsense. Now it was all as clear as day, as evident as Euclid. Of course the Dharma–Body of the Buddha was the hedge at the bottom of the garden. At the same time, and no less obviously, it was these flowers, it was anything that I—or rather the blessed Not-I released for a moment from my throttling embrace—cared to look at.' . . . [14]

The above experience of taking mescalin gave Aldous Huxley what he termed a 'cleansed perception.' He then had to reconcile it with ordinary life. This brought to the fore a conflict in him which many people feel—the desire to retreat from the world and be still and contemplative, like the Buddhist 'Arhat', as against the feeling that one should also be like the active, compassionate Bodhisattva, who is completely of the world, seeing that 'Suchness and the world of contingencies are one, and for whose boundless compassion every one of those contingencies is an occasion not only for transfiguring insight, but also for the most practical charity'. [15] Huxley decided that mescalin could not resolve that particular conflict, it could only pose it to those who had not been aware of it before.

The misuse of drugs leads to tragedy, as does the misuse of any discovery from nuclear energy to aspirins. The use of drugs *may* lead to deeper insight into the meaning of life. It is not the purpose of this book to make a case for or against drug-taking, but to note it as a possible means for obtaining the sort of self-transcendency which has come to be connected in the minds of many with experiences in eastern religions.

ZEN BUDDHISM

On Believing in Mind

The Perfect Way knows no difficulties
Except that it refuses to make preferences;
Only when freed from hate and love
It reveals itself fully and without disguise;
A tenth of an inch's difference,
And heaven and earth are set apart.
If you wish to see it before your own eyes
Have no fixed thoughts either for or against it.

To set up what you like against what you dislike—
That is the disease of the mind:
When the deep meaning of the Way is not understood,
Peace of mind is disturbed to no purpose.

The Way is perfect like unto vast space,
With nothing wanting, nothing superfluous.
It is indeed due to making choice
That its Suchness is lost sight of. (Seng Ts'an) *[1]*

DIRECT POINTING

Mahayana Buddhism entered China during the first two centuries A.D. It blended with the native Chinese religion of Taoism (a religion of simple spontaneity and natural mysticism) and a unique form of Buddhism was forged which is now known to the world by its Japanese name of Zen. The basis of Zen lay in its penetrating understanding of the Buddha's teaching; its uniqueness came through the down-to-earth practicality with which the Chinese masters demonstrated that teaching.

It was 'direct pointing' not only to the Buddha's words, but to the actual experience of what the Buddha himself experienced. It aimed to push aside tangles of intellectual concepts and definitions and to point, with uncompromising straightforwardness, to first-hand, concrete knowing.

Traditionally, Zen started with the arrival in China during the sixth century of Bodhidharma, a fierce-looking Indian Buddhist with a sharply piercing gaze. The first great personage he went to see was the Emperor Wu of Liang, an eminent Buddhist.

The Emperor was proud of all he had done for the Buddhist way of life, how he had built temples and supported monks and provided scribes to copy sacred books. He believed that doing all this would eventually take him to Nirvana—on a sort of first-class ticket. He asked Bodhidharma:

' "We have built temples, copied holy scriptures, ordered monks and nuns to be converted. Is there any merit, Reverend Sir, in our conduct?"

"No merit at all."

'The Emperor, somewhat taken aback, thought that such an answer was

Bodhidharma.

Zen monks with hands together in salute to the Buddha before eating.

upsetting the whole teaching, and enquired again:

"What, then, is the holy truth, the first principle?"

"In vast emptiness there is nothing holy."

"Who, then, are you to stand before me?"

"I know not, your Majesty," *[2]*

This reply was too simple for the learned Emperor and Bodhidharma stayed no longer in the court. He went to a monastery in Wei where he spent nine years. Then the monk, Hui-k'e, who was to become Bodhidharma's successor and the Second Patriarch of Zen, came to Bodhidharma for instruction. He was refused. Again and again he asked, sitting in deep snow outside the monastery and meditating patiently while he waited for each answer. It was always 'no'. At last, in desperation, he cut off his left arm as a token of complete sincerity, and presented it to Bodhidharma. At this Bodhidharma gave in and admitted him.

Hui-k'e said: ' "I have no peace of mind. Might I ask you, Sir, to pacify my mind?"

"Bring out your mind here before me," replied Bodhidharma. "I shall pacify it!"

"But it is impossible for me to bring out my mind."

"Then I have pacified your mind!" ' *[3]*

At that, Hui-k'e woke up to the true nature of his mind and this awakening, termed *satori*, is said to be the first instance of the famous Zen method of *mondo*—a question and answer exchange between master and pupil. This exchange, when the pupil becomes enlightened, is sometimes called a transmission, for it can only take place between two people. The truth which is conveyed from one to the other cannot be learnt from books. (The very first transmission is said to have taken place when the Buddha came to preach to a large congregation, and instead of entering into a lengthy discourse, silently held up a flower. Nobody understood the meaning of this except one monk, who smiled. Seeing his smile, the Buddha gave him the flower, saying 'I hand over to you the greatest treasure.'

After another nine years, Bodhidharma wished to return to India. He called his disciples and asked each one to state his understanding.

Daruna (Bodhidharma) painted by Sengai.

'Dofuku said: "As I see it, it is not employing words nor abandoning them, but directly using the Way."

'Bodhidharma said: "You have my skin."

'The nun Soji said: "As I understand it, it is as when Ananda had a vision of the paradise of the Buddha of the East; it appeared and then vanished."

'Bodhidharma said: "You have my flesh."

'Doiku said: "The four great elements are empty, and the five aggregates non-existent. According to my view, there is nothing to be obtained; words and phrases are cut off and the working of the mind disappears."

'Bodhidharma said: "You have my bones."

'Last came Hui-k'e, who just stood before the master, made a reverence, and went back to his place without a word of discussion or any phrase presenting his view. . . .

'Bodhidharma said: "You have my marrow." With these words he invested him with the succession as the Second Patriarch in China.' [4]

WHAT ZEN IS ALL ABOUT

In the no-mind of Hui-k'e we saw the essence of Zen. For him, no statement about the Way was possible, for to try to explain it was to try to explain life itself. The following story illustrates this further.

'A Confucian poet once came to the Zen master Hui t'ang to inquire the secret

left: Self-portrait by Sesson, a Zen master. Painted on paper, Japan, 16th century. *right:* The floating torii at Hsukushima Shrine, Miyajina, Japan.

of his teaching, whereupon the master quoted to him one of the sayings of Confucius: "Do you think I am hiding things from you, O my disciples? Indeed, I have nothing to hide from you." Since Hui t'ang would not allow him to ask any more questions, the poet went away deeply puzzled, but a short time after the two of them went for a walk together in the mountains. As they were passing a bush of wild laurel the master turned to his companion and asked, "Do you smell it?" Then to the answer "Yes", he remarked "There, I have nothing to hide from you!" At once the poet was enlightened.' [5]

It is the realization of the numinous nature of the everyday and here-and-now world that is the end result of *satori*, the Japanese word for enlightenment. Satori is the moment of waking up to the Suchness of life. Essentially it is seeing into Void-Nature and it results in an extraordinary, timeless insight when the everyday world is suddenly experienced *as it is in itself*. In this phenomenal clarity and perception, the duality of subject-object vanishes. Where the subject—oneself—is, there seems to be no self, but only a wonderful clarity and peacefulness. It is as though a barrier has been lifted and all the weighty baggage of one's mental processes—judgments on the state of the world and on neighbours and friends, fears as to position in life and personal success—all suddenly fall away,

A lakeside village. Painted by Hokusai, Japan, late 18th century.

leaving one free to experience the world as though for the first time.

Satori, Zen would say, is a flash of undreamt-of truth, the 'new birth' spoken of in Christianity. It is the essence of Zen; without it there is no Zen. It is entirely independent of scripture and ritual, and although these are made use of in Zen monasteries, the essential teaching is expressed in four lines:

A special transmission outside the Scriptures;
No dependence on words and letters;
Direct pointing to the mind of man;
Seeing into one's own nature. [6]

Thus Zen is self-reliant and has no patience with leaning on spiritual authority, not even that of the Buddha himself. 'If you come across a Buddha in your path, kill him!' is an old Zen saying. In other words let *nothing*, however wise and wonderful, come between you and the direct experience of Self-nature. A Zen monk, Doken, once despairingly implored his friend to help him to find the solution to the mystery of life:

'The friend said, "I am willing to help you in every way I can, but there are some things in which I cannot be of any help to you; these you must look after for yourself." Doken expressed the desire to know what these things were. Said his friend: "For instance, when you are hungry or thirsty, my eating of food or drinking will not fill your stomach; you must eat and drink for yourself. When you want to respond to the calls of nature you must take care of yourself, for I cannot be of any use to you. And then it will be nobody else but yourself that will carry your body along this highway." This friendly counsel at once opened the mind of the truth-seeking monk, who was so transported with his discovery that he did not know how to express his joy.' [7]

In its very down-to-earth quality, its lack of dogma and ritual, lies its true spirituality, Zen would say. For man is often too conceited to see the value of what lies close to him. He prefers to think that only when the truth is a far distant and nearly unattainable ideal is it worthy to be sought. 'What is Zen?' asked a student. 'A bag of rice,' was the answer. Zen is in existence itself, in the flow of ordinary humdrum events which occur every day. It is 'in the moment'—in the cooking of a meal or the catching of a bus—that all the marvel and mystery of the Suchness of life lies. Experience the moment before it passes; throw away the coloured spectacles of thought and opinion, the tawdry baggage of self, and know the moment *as it is*—the uninterrupted flow of life, the ten thousand things in their Suchness. This is Zen, an unfettered existence because the bonds of self have been broken. Zen is awareness, direct and immediate, of life as it is, in its being, as distinct from mere ideas and feelings *about* it.

How wondrously supernatural
And how miraculous this!
I draw water and I carry fuel. [8]

To grab at life is to attempt to hold on to it for one's own benefit. But life is really indefinable, ungraspable. It is never still for a moment. It is said that if the wind were to stop for us to catch hold of it, it would cease being the wind. The harder we cling to delights, the more they elude us. The present always slips through our hands and when we try to live in memories we are faced with unhappiness and frustration because the past is no longer alive—it is its ghost we try to imprison.

Therefore, says Zen, 'Let go.' Stop trying to grasp the ungraspable and instead just look—and see the amazing unfolding of the present moment where everything is every instant new. Forget worthy purposes and future goals; realize existence solely for the sake of itself *now*, and see how wonderful it is. True understanding begins here, when it is seen that there is no *need* for the world to exist at all—but there it all is—the 'ten thousand things'.

Sitting quietly, doing nothing,

Spring comes and the grass grows by itself. *[9]*

There are many descriptions of satori, or sudden illumination, in Zen literature. The sixteenth-century master, Han Shan, says of the enlightened man that his body and mind are entirely non-existent: they are the same as the absolute Void. Of his own experience, he writes '. . . I took a walk. Suddenly I stood still, filled with the realisation that I had no body or mind. All I could see was one great illuminating Whole—omnipresent, perfect, lucid, and serene. It was like an all-embracing mirror from which the mountains and rivers of the earth were projected . . . I felt as "clear and transparent" as though my body and mind did not exist at all.' . . . *[10]* 'Mind and body dropped off!' exclaims Dogen, in an ecstasy of release, 'Dropped off! Dropped off! This state must be experienced by you all; it is like piling fruit into a basket without a bottom, it is like pouring water into a bowl with a hole in it'. *[11]* 'All of a sudden you find your mind and body wiped out of existence' *[12]*, says Hakuin, 'This is what is known as letting go your hold. As you regain your breath, it is like drinking water and knowing it is cold. It is joy inexpressible.' Hakuin, at the moment of his satori, also said, "How wondrous! How wondrous! There is no birth and death from

Head and profile of the Buddha. Wood, Japan, 12th century.

which one has to escape, nor is there any supreme knowledge after which one has to strive".' [13] And Hsiang-yen put the same experience in this way:

At one stroke I forgot all my knowledge!
There's no use for artificial discipline,
For, move as I will, I manifest the ancient Way. [14]

Descriptions of modern western satori perhaps sound a little more self-conscious, but still have the authentic ring of jubilation. A Canadian housewife records, 'The least expression of weather variation, a soft rain or gentle breeze, touches me as a—what can I say?—miracle of unmatched wonder, beauty and goodness. There is nothing to do: just to be is a total act.'

And an English teacher says: 'There was a blackbird in the garden, and it was as though there had never been a blackbird before. All my inner turmoil melted away and I felt full of clarity and indescribable peace. I seemed at one with everything around me and saw people with all judgment suspended, so that they seemed perfect in themselves.'

Although the experience of satori is a turning-point, this does not mean that the person at once becomes a saint and ceases to live an ordinary life. The whole intention of Zen awakening is to encourage living in the 'market-place.' To be properly human, to be happy when others are happy and to feel sympathy when they are sad, is good Zen. A new shift of inner balance takes place with satori so that after it, the experiencer relates to other people with an awareness and awakened insight which is free of self-interest. This may take years to reach full growth, but satori is the stick which sounds the gong and shatters the silence of ignorance. To the one who has experienced this turnabout in his nature, life becomes ever more 'empty and marvellous.'

He who holds that nothingness
Is formless, flowers are visions,
Let him enter boldly! [15]   An inscription over Rinzai's door.

THE PRACTICE OF ZEN

Zen was practised in two ways, by meditation and by the sharp question and answer exchange between master and pupil, and these methods have not changed greatly to this day. But in the time of the Sixth Patriarch, there came a crucial development of Zen. It occurred in this way.

Hui-Neng, the future Sixth Patriarch, was no scholar; he was a simple, southern peasant boy who, one day, overheard a Buddhist scripture, the Diamond Sutra, being recited. When the words 'the mind abideth nowhere' were chanted, Hui-Neng was enlightened. He went immediately to the monastery on Yellow Plum Mountain where the Fifth Patriarch presided. The Patriarch recognized his satori but was afraid Hui-Neng would be persecuted for his humble origins by the scholarly monks from the north, so he was put to work pounding rice in the kitchen. A few months later, the Patriarch announced that he wished to appoint a successor to whom he could pass on his office; whoever wrote the most enlightened poem would be the next Patriarch. Shin Hsiu, the head monk, was considered by everybody to be the most learned and thus the most certain to win the honour, and nobody attempted to compete with him. Shin Hsiu composed a verse which he placed on the wall of the meditation hall. It read:

The body is the Bodhi-Tree;
The mind like a bright mirror standing.
Take care to wipe it all the time,
And allow no dust to cling. *[16]*

Everyone was very impressed by this, but next morning, when they all arrived to meditate, another verse had been placed beside it. It read:

There never was a Bodhi Tree,
Nor bright mirror standing.
Fundamentally, not one thing exists,
So where is the dust to cling? *[17]*

When Hui-Neng acknowledged himself to be the author of the second verse, the Patriarch saw that here was a truly enlightened man. But because he was only a humble rice-pounder, the Patriarch dared not publicly acclaim him. Instead,

The garden of Sesshu, a Zen master, at Tofukuji Temple, Kyoto, Japan.

he called Hui-Neng to him during the night and conferred the Patriarchy on him, giving him the robe which was the emblem of the office. Hui-Neng left the monastery that same night. Three days later, a party of furious monks went after him. They caught up with him in a mountain pass. He laid down the robe and said to the leading monk, Ming: 'This robe symbolizes our patriarchal faith and is not to be carried away by force. Take this along with you, however, if you so desire.'

'Ming tried to lift it but it was as heavy as a mountain. He halted, hesitated, and trembled with awe. At last he said; "I come here to obtain the faith and not the robe. O brother monk, pray dispel my ignorance."

'Said the sixth patriarch, "If you come for the faith, stop all your hankerings.

A Buddhist monk. Porcelain, China, late 17th century.

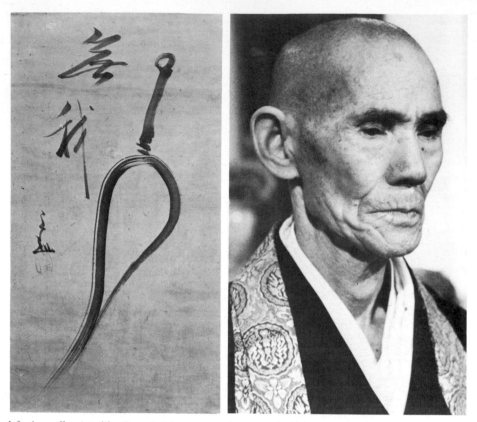

left: A scroll painted by Sengai. Ink on paper, Japan, early 19th century. *right*: Yasotani Roshi, a 20th-century Japanese master.

Think not of good, think not of evil, but see what at this moment your own original face does look like, which you had even prior to your own birth".' *[18]* Then the monk was enlightened.

What was crucial for Zen was the difference between the two verses, for this difference affected its whole future, emphasizing the real nature of Zen to be independent of learning and intellectual thought. For the true nature of Zen is a direct grasp of life itself, *not* a psychological experience to be attained by mental purification (mirror-wiping).

What is the difference between the verses? Shin Hsiu's poem tells us that when one no longer clings to the thoughts and feelings which enter the mind—when one has purified oneself so much that thoughts flow in and out of one's mind without leaving a trace—then, like a mirror, the mind reflects all that is presented to it without itself being identified with any of its contents.

But Hui-Neng's poem points out that to think of one's mind as an object, such as a mirror, which must be purified and carefully wiped all the time, is to imagine that one can grasp it and manipulate it. To believe that it can be *made* pure is to be under the spell of purity.

Shin Hsiu's method for achieving his mirror-state was to sit in meditation emptying the mind until all thoughts and feelings ceased and only consciousness was left, an effect similar to the yogi's pure consciousness of samadhi. And, as for the yogi, a great many years of concentration and meditation were needed before this could be accomplished.

But to concentrate on purifying the mind was a confusing and unnecessary idea to Hui-Neng. For him the mind was not a separate thing to receive treatment, either to be purified or to be emptied. Instead of compelling thoughts to cease, he advised simply letting go of them—not interfering with them in any way but just simply letting them come and go as they wished. Instead of 'wiping the mirror clean' he suggested letting go of the idea that there is a mind to be wiped.

As in the outer world, he said, we can see that space contains the sun and the moon and the stars, so true awakening is to realize that the essence of the mind is empty, like space, and contains thoughts and sensations which come and go of their own accord. He believed that to attempt to 'still' the mind, in the way practised by Zen at that time, was to produce an artificial 'stillness'. He thought that real meditation meant letting go of all one's barriers to direct experience, so that in the ultimate and completely open experience of ordinary life is the realization of its true nature. Thus, for Hui-Neng, and for those who followed him in the Rinzai school, the concrete objects and everyday events of life, when woken up to in their Suchness, were themselves the ultimate nature of existence. The ordinary mind, when experienced as space within which life lives itself, was the enlightened mind, and Hui-Neng saw that they were intrinsically the same.

Yasotani Roshi meditating at the Buddhist Society, London.

THE KOAN

Hui-Neng's method was the abrupt one of drawing the student's attention always to the present moment and to his no-mind. His insight was later developed by Rinzai, a master of the ninth century (after Hui-Neng there were no more Patriarchs).

Rinzai introduced a new way of coming to the direct experience of no-mind. It occurred when a monk Jō, came to him and asked, 'What is the ultimate principle of Buddhism?'

Instead of giving him a verbal answer, Rinzai left his chair, seized Jō, and then slapped him hard before letting him go. Jō stood without moving. Another monk said, 'Why don't you make a bow?' Jō was about to bow when full awakening came to him. [19]

What had occurred was that his logical mind was pushed aside altogether. He was suddenly adrift in a world without reason, adrift from the usual sequence of thoughts to which he had believed himself bound. This resulted in a forgetting of self. His feeling of 'I' was overlooked and forgotten in the immense abandon-

Part of the garden at Daitokuji Temple, Kyoto, Japan.

Statue of Masushige Kasanumi, a Samurai warrior. In the grounds of the Imperial Palace, Tokyo, Japan.

ment of all his former thinking, and his mind was thus opened to the direct experience of his own nature.

If, however, there had not been a great doubt within his mind, so that his whole heart was in his question, this would not have occurred. He had to be ready for that final push, his entire being intent on knowing the answer. Someone who asked the question out of mere curiosity, from an unaware mind, would not have been enlightened by Rinzai's actions. Thus the sincerity and single-minded purpose of the questioner is as vital to the experience as the blow (verbal or otherwise) which knocks him off his usual course and awakens him to life itself.

A student coming to a monastery of the Rinzai school was encouraged to develop his longing for insight to the extent where the master, in a flash, could help him to see the truth. The training is the same today as it was then. It consists of meditation, practical work in the kitchens and garden, and interviews with the master. At these interviews the student, according to the level of his awareness, is given a *koan*. A koan is a question which must be answered (or the student will have to leave the monastery) but which has no answer—at least no logical answer. Koans are frequently taken from records of the old masters and one of the most famous is Hui-Neng's 'What was your original face before your parents were born?' They can also take the form of mondos to be elucidated. Here are some well-known koans:

'A monk asked Joshu, "What is the meaning of Bodhidharma's coming to China?"'

Buddha-possessed, painted by Sengai. Possessed in his dreams by thoughts of Nirvana and Samsara, Sengai feels he has been made captive by the Buddha.

Guardian statue outside Asakusa Kannon Temple in Tokyo, Japan.

The laughing sages at Kokei painted by Sengai.

"The cypress tree in the courtyard." '
'Chao-Chou asked, "What is the Tao [the Way]?"
'The master replied, "Your ordinary (i.e. natural) mind is the Tao."
' "How can one return into accord with it?"
' "By intending to accord you immediately deviate".' *[20]*

A monk asked, 'All things are said to be reducible to the One, but what is the One reduced to?'

The answer was, 'When I lived in Ch'ing I had a robe that weighed seven pounds!' *[21]*

Sitting in *zazen* (meditation) came to be practised a great deal in Zen monasteries, but records show that early Chinese masters did not rate it highly. Ma-tsu, a monk, practised sitting in meditation and was tackled about it by a master, Huai-jang.

'Your reverence,' asked Huai-jang, 'what is the objective of sitting in meditation?'

'The objective,' answered Ma-tsu, 'is to become a Buddha.'

Thereupon Huai-jang picked up a floor-tile and began to polish it on a rock.

'What are you doing, master?' asked Ma-tsu.

'I am polishing it for a mirror,' said Huai-jang.

'How could polishing a tile make a mirror?'

'How could sitting in meditation make a Buddha?' *[22]*

Some masters thought that to believe that sitting has some particular virtue, and is better than standing or lying down, is to be attached to form. On another occasion Huai-jang said:

'To train yourself in sitting meditation (*zazen*) is to train yourself to be a sitting Buddha. If you train yourself in *zazen* you should know that Zen is neither sitting nor lying. If you train yourself to be a sitting Buddha, (you should know that) the Buddha is not a fixed form. Since the Dharma has no (fixed) abode, it is not a matter of making choices. If you (make yourself) a sitting Buddha this is precisely killing the Buddha. If you adhere to the sitting position you will not attain the principle (of Zen).' *[23]*

And Hui-Neng puts it succinctly:

A living man who sits and does not lie down;
A dead man who lies down and does not sit!
After all these are just dirty skeletons. *[24]*

Nevertheless, despite this criticism, many westerners brought up in an over-aggressive culture find zazen an essential practice for a peaceful and receptive mind.

THREE ZEN MASTERS
HAKUIN (1685)

In 1191, Zen began to lose its popularity in China and came to prominence in Japan, where it became the religion of the *Samurai*, the warriors. Among the great Japanese masters who influenced its development was Hakuin, of the Rinzai school. His awakening is typical of the Rinzai tradition:

' "When I was twenty-four years old, I stayed at the Yegan Monastery, of Echigo. ('Jōshus's Mu' being my theme at the time) I assiduously applied myself to it. I did not sleep days and nights, forgot both eating and lying down, when quite abruptly a great mental fixation . . . took place. I felt as if freezing in an ice-field extending thousands of miles, and within myself there was a sense of utmost transparency. There was no going forward, no slipping backward; I was like an idiot, like an imbecile, and there was nothing but 'Jōshu's Mu'. Though I attended the lectures by the master, they sounded like a discussion going on somewhere in a distant hall, many yards away. Sometimes my sensation was that of one flying in the air. Several days passed in this state, when one evening a temple-bell struck which upset the whole thing. It was like smashing an ice-basin, or pulling down a house made of jade. When I suddenly awoke again, I found that all through the shifting changes of time not a bit (of my personality) was lost. Whatever doubts and indecisions I had before were completely dissolved like a piece of thawing ice".' *[25]*

Hakuin finally laid down a firm basis for Rinzai Zen (which had degenerated into a pointless form of trick questions and gimmicks). He organized koans into six systematic stages, which meant that a master had to be fully cognizant of a pupil's development. These graded koans also acted as a sieve, separating the really dedicated from those of weaker spirit.

One of the most famous of Hakuin's koans is: 'What is the sound of one hand?' The sound of two hands put together is clapping, but what is the sound of one hand? This is not meant to be a riddle—it cannot be tackled intellectually at all. The student, who has been brought to a point of intense mental struggle becomes confused beyond endurance by this koan for he cannot make sense out of such a ridiculous question. There is nothing in the words which his mind can

left: A prunus tree by an anonymous artist. Brush and ink on silk, China, 18th century. *right:* The monkeys and the moon by Sengai. Life is like a monkey trying to reach the moon's reflection in the water.

grip at all and he cannot make it surrender its meaning to him. It is only when he finally accepts that there is *nothing* to grasp that he lets go his hold. This letting go is the supreme moment when he sees that life itself is ungraspable, unobtainable, eternally free and spontaneous and without boundry. The living truth cannot be held for a moment; the illogical koan which he tried to subjugate, and to kill by analysis, is as indefinable as life itself, and when he lets go of all his great efforts to capture it, he suddenly realizes how foolish he has been to imagine he could ever grasp anything. This realization is an immense release. 'Nothing is left for you at this moment,' writes a master, 'but to burst into a loud laugh.' And Chao-pien says:

> A sudden clash of thunder, the mind-doors burst open,
> And lo, there sitteth the old man (the Buddha-nature) in all his
> homeliness. *[26]*

DOGEN (1200)

Dogen was the founder in Japan of Soto Zen, a school of Zen which had already flourished in China. Dogen went to China and sat in meditation under a master for five years. When he returned to Japan, he was convinced that the true way of enlightenment is through sitting in zazen only.

To the followers of Soto, the mind-shattering koans and arousing of great doubt seemed a false and artificial method. The followers of Rinzai seemed to be training themselves for some unreal future state. Dogen insisted that his pupils should think of themselves as Buddhas in the present moment. They must concentrate on sitting, not as a means to an end, but as the actual realization of their Buddha-nature in the sitting. He reminded them that the future, even the next day, was unfixed and difficult to know, therefore they must think only of the present day and the present hour.

In zazen, they must sit without thought of becoming anything or avoiding anything; only realizing their Buddhahood in the sitting. Dogen emphasizes, as do the Theravadin Buddhists, that the mind should be wholly given to whatever makes up the present activity. If you walk, you give yourself up to walking; sitting, you give yourself up to sitting. In this way the mind loses its propensity to jump about and becomes still and deep. Dogen believed that every moment is really self-contained, and he used the illustration of firewood to explain this. He pointed out that firewood does not 'become' ashes; that is to say there is no intention on the part of the wood to become ash; by the time it has become it, it is no longer firewood. The two states are clear-cut and self-contained. In the same way, his pupils must not have the intention of 'becoming' Buddhas. They must sit only to sit, knowing this action to its fullest extent. In this way, spontaneously, automatically, and effortlessly, they would 'be' (not 'become') Buddhas, as the firewood at one moment is 'being' wood, and the next moment 'being' ash.

Dogen particularly applied this understanding to life and death. He said:

'It is fallacious to think that you simply move from birth to death. Birth, from the Buddhist point of view, is a temporary point between the preceding and the succeeding; hence it can be called birthlessness. The same holds for death and deathlessness. In life there is nothing more than life, in death nothing more than death: we are being born and are dying at every moment.

'Now, to conduct: in life identify yourself with life, at death with death. Abstain from yielding and craving. Life and death constitute the very being of Buddha. Thus, should you renounce life and death, you will lose; and you can expect no more if you cling to either. You must neither loathe, then, nor covet, neither think nor speak of these things. Forgetting body and mind, by placing them together in Buddha's hands and letting him lead you on, you will without design or effort gain freedom, attain Buddhahood.' [27]

BANKEI (1622)

Of all the Zen masters, Bankei was perhaps the simplest and the most intuitive. His great awakening came after many years of intense effort, and it brought to him a unique understanding of the birthless Buddha-mind. He spent the rest of his life preaching about this, in language which was uncompromisingly direct. He became a great teacher, unfailingly giving his knowledge in the plainest of words, so that all could understand. He was impatient with generalizations and preferred to come to grips with concrete experience. Thus, although realization of the Birthless was with him all the time, so that he felt that every moment of

The head of the Amida Buddha in Byodoin Temple, Japan.

his life was an expression of it, he would not have abstract ideas about it. A priest once said to him:

' "Once in the Buddha-mind, I am absent-minded."

'*Bankei:* "Well, suppose you are absent-minded as you say. If someone pricked you in the back with a gimlet, would you feel the pain?"

'*Priest:* "Naturally!"

'*Bankei:* "Then you are not absent-minded. Feeling the pain, your mind would show itself to be alert. Follow my exhortation: remain in the Buddha-mind".' *[28]*

To Bankei, the Birthless (the Buddha-mind) is our natural state which we ignorantly exchange, as it were, for other states to which we become attached. He said:

'Those who make light of the Buddha-mind transform it when angry into a demon's, into a hungry ghost's when greedy, into an animal's when acting stupidly. I tell you my teaching is far from frivolous! Nothing can be so weighty as the Buddha-mind. But perhaps you feel that to remain in it is too tough a job? If so, listen, and try to grasp the meaning of what I say. Stop piling up evil deeds, stop being a demon, a hungry ghost, an animal. Keep your distance from those things that transform you in that way, and you'll attain the Buddha-mind once and for all.'

He expands this, on another occasion, in a typically direct way:

'*Priest:* "I was born with a quick temper and, in spite of my master's constant admonitions, I haven't been able to rid myself of it. I know it's a vice, but, as I said, I was born with it. Can you help me?"

'*Bankei:* "My, what an interesting thing you were born with! Tell me, is your temper quick at this very moment? If so, show me right off, and I'll cure you of it."

'*Priest:* "But I don't have it at this moment."

'*Bankei:* "Then you weren't born with it. If you were, you'd have it at all times. You lose your temper as occasion arises. Else where can this hot temper possibly be? Your mistake is one of self-love, which makes you concern yourself with others and insists that you have your own way. To say you were born a hothead is to tax your parents with something that is no fault of theirs. From them you received the Buddha-mind, nothing else.

' "This is equally true of other types of illusion. If you don't fabricate illusions, none will disturb you. Certainly you were born with none. Only your selfishness and deplorable mental habits bring them into being. Yet you think of them as inborn, and in everything you do, you continue to stray. To appreciate the pricelessness of the Buddha-mind, and to steer clear of illusion, is the one path to satori and Buddhahood".' *[29]*

Bankei was impatient of both the Rinzai and Soto sects, particularly the Rinzai. Buddha-mind was to be realized in ordinary life, not under specially-devised conditions, and his constant advice was to cease from turning Buddha-mind into something else. If people could be aware of their birthless Buddha-mind for thirty days, he said, they would never wish to change it again. He considered birthlessness an instantly practical doctrine, needing only the experience of the clear Buddha-mind to show us immediately that we have never really strayed from it.

THE SPIRIT OF ZEN

Of all the schools of Buddhism, Zen takes itself the least seriously. The great release of satori is also a great roar of mirth at the foolish illusions people labour under. Many stories are recorded to show up these illusions. They usually have a sharp Zen cut in them somewhere—but the cut is made with compassion, as the surgeon operates to remove a cancer.

'When Banzan was walking through a market he overheard a conversation between a butcher and his customer.

"Give me the best piece of meat you have," said the customer.

"Everything in my shop is the best." replied the butcher. "You cannot find here any piece of meat that is not the best."

At these words Banzan became enlightened.' [30]

He became enlightened because he saw that when he looked without any sensation of body-centred self, each piece of meat was uniquely right in itself and could not be compared to any other.

This way of looking at things is brought out in another manner in the following story about Bankei, who saw that *everything*, even the most taken-for-granted habit, is a miracle to the enlightened:

Daibatsu Buddha at Kamakura, Japan.

'When Bankei was preaching at Ryumon temple, a Shinshu priest, who believed in salvation through the repetition of the name of the Buddha of Love, was jealous of his large audience and wanted to debate with him.

'Bankei was in the midst of a talk when the priest appeared, but the fellow made such a disturbance that Bankei stopped his discourse and asked about the noise.

' "The founder of our sect," boasted the priest, "had such miraculous powers that he held a brush in his hand on one bank of the river, his attendant held up a paper on the other bank, and the teacher wrote the holy name of Asida through the air. Can you do such a wonderful thing?"

'Bankei replied lightly: "Perhaps your fox can perform that trick, but that is not the manner of Zen. My miracle is that when I feel hungry I eat, and when I feel thirsty I drink".' *[31]*

Good Zen masters were renowned for their ability to make use of everyday, immediate happenings to bring home the truth to their pupils. A monk once came to the master, Joshu, and said:

' "I have just entered the monastery. Please teach me."

'Joshu asked: "Have you eaten your rice porridge?"

'The monk replied: "I have eaten."

'Joshu said: "Then you had better wash your bowl."

'At that moment the monk was enlightened.' *[32]*

Joshu saw that Truth is not other than life itself, and that the most insignificant event can be seen in its Absoluteness when there are no value-judgments between oneself and what is.

Intellectual concepts in the form of labels are the subjects of the following story:

'A monk asked Nansen: "Is there a teaching no master ever preached before?"

'Nansen said: "Yes, there is."

"What is it?" asked the monk.

'Nansen replied: "It is not mind, it is not Buddha, it is not things".' *[33]*

Nansen, the master, knew quite well that the Origin cannot be classified and put into words such as 'mind' or 'Buddha' or 'things'. It can only be experienced. How, then, can it be taught? The answer is that it can't—experience can't be taught any more than the colour red can be taught, or the sound of the wind. It can be spoken *about* but this is not experiencing it. So the teaching that no master ever preached before was the real teaching because it was experience itself—but no one ever preached it.

Death was not taken very seriously by those masters who were enlightened. But their monks, still in the relative condition of ideas and imagination, tried to find some great meaning in the event of death. An enlightened master would find no more significance in the relative occurrence of death than in the relative occurrence of a branch falling from a tree, or a horse biting at flies, or a frog jumping onto a lily-leaf, or a man going to sleep when he is tired. A master would know that, seen Absolutely, no one action anywhere is more important than any other. But the monks sometimes could not understand this. In the following story, a monk is determined to make some pattern—a pattern which could only be of human design—out of the incomprehensible and marvellous Void:

A Japanese Maitreya Buddha, a future Compassionate One.

'Master Hofuku called his monks together and said, "During the last week my energy has been draining—certainly no cause for worry. It's just that death is near."

'A monk asked, "You are about to die! What meaning does it have? We will continue living. And what meaning does that have?"

"They are both the Way," the master replied.

"But how can I reconcile the two?" asked the monk.

'Hofuku answered, "When it rains it pours," and wrapping his legs in the full lotus position, calmly died.' [34]

A ZEN MONASTERY TODAY

Many westerners have been attracted by Zen and have made the long journey to Japan in order to study under a master. First, they must find a master who will accept them. Then as beginners, they must spend time working in the monastery garden, cleaning rooms and preparing food. While they do this they are covertly being assessed by the master or his head monk, not only for their skill in performing tasks but for the state of mind in which these are done. Some pupils secretly consider such work a waste of time. They want to get on with meditation or the study of koans as 'the real thing'. Others may do the work willingly but show, by their insensitivity to it, that their minds are elsewhere. Inattentiveness tells the master a great deal, and the way in which a pupil sets about his jobs is often more informative than what he accomplishes.

After some months of domestic chores, the master may consider the pupil ready for instruction. Eugen Herrigel tells us that at this point 'The specifically spiritual training starts with *purification of the power of vision*. First, one is required to perceive everything that is present, in all its sensuous fullness, including everything that is displeasing or repellent, and to hold it permanently in the mind. Again and again, one must immerse oneself in the contents of perception, until one knows them by heart and can, at will, call them to mind in such a way that they present themselves without loss of clarity.

'When you can do this, you must learn to rise above it, to apprehend what you are looking at as if from the inside, to look through it and grasp its essence, just as the painter does with a few concentrated strokes. From this we can see how much art owes to Zen.

'Then, when that has been fully mastered, an intensification can be aimed at: holding the landscape, the fields with trees, flowers, cattle, and people, so intently in your gaze that in spite of the wood you still see the trees, and then thinning out the reality of the detail until you can grasp the unchanging character of the whole and retain it in its most concentrated form. Finally, even this vision of pure essence must be transcended; you must be able to picture the world itself, the cosmos and—ultimately—infinite space, thereby expanding the power of vision still further.' [35]

As well as visual exercises, there is instruction in sitting in the meditation posture, and in breathing. The sitting is on a hard cushion. The right leg is put on the left thigh and the left on the right thigh in the lotus posture or, if this is not possible, the left leg may be put on top of the right thigh. In Chinese thought, the left symbolizes quietness, and the right, activity.

The body must be balanced comfortably over the base of the spine, with the shoulders relaxed. The spine should be straight and the head resting on it in a straight line, chin down (one device is to imagine that you are suspended from the ceiling by the top of your head). The eyes remain open, looking about six feet ahead. The hands are in the lap, the right hand supporting the left, palms upwards and the thumbs together.

Breathing is from the abdomen rather than the chest, and at first each breath is counted, up to ten, and then up to ten again. This makes the mind one-pointed, concentrated only on counting the breath. Hence breathing begins to fill the mind until there is only the consciousness of breathing. Then, relaxed, the

The stone garden of Ryoanji Temple, Kyoto, Japan.

breathing finds its own rhythm, and the pupil is sitting.

Hours of sitting, sometimes ten a day, are interspersed with walks round the garden, work in the kitchen, and interviews with the master. In the *zendo*—the long meditation hall—the monks sit facing each other in Rinzai temples, or facing outwards in Soto monasteries. Sometimes monks nearly fall asleep; for them, and for those who have aching backs, or are in a bad frame of mind, there is the *kyosaku*. The kyosaku is a long flat stick wielded by the monk in charge of meditation, who whacks it down onto the shoulders of those in need of it— whether they are conscious of their need or not. It may hurt—but it relieves muscular tension and is said to be better than any words of advice.

Some westerners do not become monks, but live outside the monastery and attend it every day. But twice a year, there are great *sesshins* (a week of concen- trated meditation and interviews) which they must attend. These are occasions to be both feared for the enormous effort which will take place, and looked forward to for the comments of the master, which may be favourable.

Although, to outsiders, this austere and strict way of life, with its periodic times of strain and turmoil, may sound hard and grim, yet a Zen monastery is the opposite of a dreary place. There is much laughter and gaiety as the monks go about their work. The building itself is composed of rooms which are austerely beautiful in their simplicity, unadorned except, perhaps, for a single flower. Zen gardens are renowned for their calm, sculptured beauty—they have an indefin- able *satisfactoriness* about them, so that as one gazes, one feels fulfilled and content. Margaret Hooper, a visitor to Japan, who knew nothing of Buddhism, discovered a great truth when she looked at a Zen garden at Ryoanji Monastery:

'I went to Kyoto on my own, urged by a friend to have a look at the famous old city. Although I was emotionally involved and reluctant to spend part of my short stay in Japan away from him, I went and stayed at an hotel and collected some tourist brochures. On the second day I went by bus to Ryoanji. It was a very cold November day and I walked up a path by a lake. There was a notice that said "There used to be many duck on this lake, but about four hundred years ago they went away." Such a long time spoken of as yesterday.

'I went up some steps and came upon a walled garden with rocks and sand. Immediately something happened, and I was looking at the inside of my mind. I don't know why I instantly recognised it as the core of me, since it had no land- marks, was unemotional and impersonal, nor why it should have caused me to weep since the emotion it produced was one of immense relief. Relief that all is well and within oneself and that this still true core of oneself is not bound by the limitations of personality, but part of a continuum with no separate boundaries.

'A Buddhist monk spoke to me, and I was sitting down seeing the garden again, wishing he would go away so that I could think and try and recapture what I had seen. But he was telling me about the history of the garden, and about Zen—the first time I had ever heard the word. He kept on talking so I had to go away—sure that if I did not think about it quickly it would fade. But I need not have feared as three years after it is just as clear to recall.' *[36]*

left: A mountain landscape painted by Mokubei. Ink and colour on paper, Japan, late 18th century. *right:* Peacock and peonies painted by Ichiryusai Hiroshige, Japan, 1832.

ZEN IN THE ARTS

To the Zen painter, space is as real and vivid as any of the objects in his composition. In both China and Japan, Zen was felt as a deep inner Emptiness from which came all that exists—the flow and dance of creation. Painting shared with poetry the wonder and reverence felt by the person who is one with what he sees. The artist expressed not himself, but life. His brush strokes sprang from an inner aliveness. But although spontaneous, his art was never undisciplined. The watchful eye of a master held the student, perhaps for years, to the understanding that there was no hurry, there was nothing to be accomplished. For Zen believes that each thing exists in relation to everything else, and therefore there are no ends to be attained. The very idea of some particular goal to be achieved would have meant a division between the artist's work and life itself, which would not have been tolerated. To the Zen artist, a mountain painted itself; or the stream flowed across his paper; or the flower opened onto the page. Self-expression was an unknown term, for the brush-strokes were no more 'his' than the breezes which sway a bamboo are wind-expression.

To have a set goal is to hurry on, with the achievement of that goal in mind. In so doing, much of life is swept aside, not lived at all. This is grotesque to the Zen artist, for whom the essence of life is that all events should be experienced equally fully, as they chance to come along. Purposelessness, so abhorrent to the West, is felt by Zen as 'going nowhere in a timeless moment'; it is then, when there is no urgency and the mind is still, that the senses can catch the essence of the moment in, perhaps, the leap of a fish on a soft summer's evening, or the solitary pine tree leaning over a canyon, or a small boat being poled across a misty grey river.

Zen painting is full of these vivid and haunting glimpses of life in its pure Suchness. So, too, is *haiku*, a Japanese form of poetry using seventeen syllables (in Japanese). The movements of the 'ten thousand things' in their miraculous interplay can be expressed by:

On a bare branch
A rook roosts:
Autumn dusk. (Basho) *[37]*

and:

Still baking down—
The sun, not regarding
The wind of autumn. (Basho) *[38]*

and:

Painting pines
On the blue sky,
The moon tonight. (Hatteri Ransetsu) *[39]*

The Zen insight that what man regards as his individual mind (*not* awareness) exists only by what he knows and sees, and is therefore part of the world and not separate from it, is expressed in a modern haiku:

My delight
Goes stamping up the road
In a little boy's coat. (Colin Oliver) *[40]*

Zen calligraphy was regarded as highly as painting, every stroke of the sharply pointed brush conveying the artist's degree of insight. Thus, an unaccompanied poem by Sengai, who used satire in both pen and brush, shared equal place with one accompanied by a painting. Here is one he wrote on himself:

> The Buddha's congregation is said to have numbered eighty thousand;
> Confucius too had disciples, as many as three thousand.
> How fortunate that this lazy monk finds himself abandoned by his brother-
> monks!
> Accompanied only by a white cloud he sleeps away his long sleep on the
> rock. [41]

In Zen painting and in calligraphy, one holds the brush upright, without resting the wrist on the paper. Since the black Chinese ink used for both is

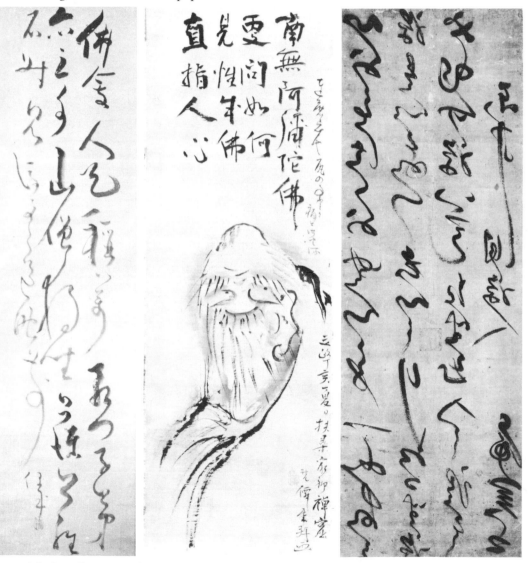

left: Sengai's poem on himself. *centre:* Daruna (Bodhidharma) by Sengai. *right:* Calligraphy by the Zen priest, Kokan Shiren. Sumi on paper, Japanese, late 13th–early 14th century.

Trevor Leggett, a Judo Black Belt, in combat.

absorbed immediately by the paper, the movement of the hand and arm must be both free and assured.

This confident spontaneity of movement arises both from complete mastery of the medium, and from an inner harmony of understanding. It is expressed in the martial arts of *judo*, *karate*, *kendo* and archery as an inner balance of personality and an outer mastery of the body so complete that all movements arise without the intervention of thought. Many people have had the experience of their body moving instinctively, before their mind has had time to consciously weigh up the situation. This intuitive movement is usually effortless because no emotion has had time to cloud the mind with fear or aggression, and to tense the muscles. In judo, the student is required to develop the dynamic purposelessness of the artist in movements directed towards attack and defence. All depends on

Osensei Nagaboshi Tomio demonstrating a karate leap.

balance, and judo is the nearest of the arts to life itself. From his inner balance, the judo student will know without knowing when it is time to act, when it is time to use his opponent's strength against him, and when it is time to be still.

The 'artless art' of archery has the same principle of unselfconscious mastery. Eugen Herrigel studied archery for several years under Japanese masters and he tells us that it was only after four years that he was allowed to aim at a target. He asked his teacher why he had never been taught to take aim. His teacher replied: 'If you hit the target with nearly every shot you are nothing more than a trick archer who likes to show off. For the professional who counts his hits, the target is only a miserable piece of paper which he shoots to bits. The "Great Doctrine" holds this to be sheer devilry. It knows nothing of a target which is set up at a definite distance from the archer. It only knows of the goal, which cannot be aimed at technically, and it names this goal, if it names it at all, the Buddha.' They went on practising and at first Eugen Herrigel was unmoved by where his arrows fell. But after a while he began to worry again and at last reached the end of his tether. He said to his teacher:

'I think I understand what you mean by the real, inner goal which ought to be hit. But how it happens that the outer goal, the disc of paper, is hit without the archer's taking aim, and that the hits are only outward confirmations of inner events—that correspondence is beyond me."

'You are under an illusion,' said the Master after a while, 'if you imagine that even a rough understanding of these dark connections would help you. These are processes which are beyond the reach of understanding. Do not forget that even in Nature there are correspondences which cannot be understood, and yet are so real that we have grown accustomed to them, just as if they could not be any different. I will give you an example which I have often puzzled over. The spider dances her web without knowing that there are flies who will get caught in it. The fly, dancing nonchalantly on a sunbeam, gets caught in the net without knowing what lies in store. But through both of them "It" dances, and inside and outside are united in this dance. So, too, the archer hits the target without having aimed—more I cannot say.' [42]

WESTERN ZEN

When Zen came west, it first struck root in England and America. The writings of Dr Daisetz Suzuki, an original and inspired Japanese thinker, who translated a large quantity of the literature of Zen, revolutionized the religious thinking of many people on both continents. Here was a down-to-earth spirituality, unself-conscious and human, which did not preach or moralize, and in which there was no anxiety to be right. For the western concept of God as good, against bad, often creates guilt and worry and confusion. Zen showed a whole region which is beyond both, about which there could be no guilt and where, at last, there was a merging of the self with Suchness. Zen denied nothing; it merely advised people to disentangle themselves from the ways of conventional thought, and to cease trying to justify themselves. Live life as it comes along, it said, and experience it for itself alone, not for what can be got out of it. Give to each moment what belongs to it, but live free from the moment, unattached to it, your inner self at one with the Way, empty and marvellous.

The Zen way of looking at religion liberated the minds of many westerners. Some Americans, however, ignored the basis of Zen, which is the inward-looking to one's no-self; rather, they took up the individual features of Zen—the koans and haikus, the famous stories of blows and enlightenments, the uninhibited attitudes towards painting and poetry. Zen was adopted as a protest against 'plastic' America and this understanding of it came to be called Beat Zen. It was described by Jack Kerouac in his famous book, *Dharma Bums*.

Unattached to this movement, in fact unattached to any, Alan Watts wrote movingly and brilliantly on the real nature of Zen. His books showed to America the profound essence of this strange religion whose monks laughed with irreverence and derision at the intellect, and whose image was quite unlike that of the Christian ascetic, or the trance-bound yogi.

The Phoenix Hall of the Byodoin Temple, Nara, Japan, built in 1053.

A more dedicated attitude to Zen emerged than the Beat one, and during the last thirty years or so, many Zen centres have been founded. Among them is the First Zen Institute of America, in New York, started by a Rinzai master, Sasaki, now dead. The Institute continued after his death, inspired by his widow, Ruth Sasaki, who also worked in Japan, helping many western students with their training there. They issue a publication containing Sasakai Roshi's comments, called *Zen Notes*. Travelling northward from New York, there is another well-known centre founded by Philip Kapleau, called the Zen Meditation Centre of Rochester. Philip Kapleau studied in Japan under both Rinzai and Soto masters and he has established a dynamic merging of both schools at Rochester, the empasis always being on experience rather than an intellectual approach. His publication is *Zen Bow*. In California, the home of so many fringe cults, a sane and strong Zen movement resulted in the Zen Centre in San Francisco. In 1966, Zen Centre bought some five hundred acres at Tassajara, in the mountains south of San Francisco. Here they established Zen Mountain Centre, a group of buildings in a beautiful area of ravines and rugged mountains, where Suzuki Roshi, a Soto master, was installed. Zen Mountain Centre is perhaps the best-

A print of a plum tree and rising sun signed Gakutei. Colour print from woodblocks, Japan.

known and largest Zen retreat in America and is the hub of Zen activity. Its publication is *Windbell*.

In France, Soto Zen has become well established in Paris under a master, Taisen Deshimaru; while in England, Christmas Humphreys, the founder of the Buddhist Society, has conducted classes and written many excellent books to popularize Zen. Two developments have recently taken place in England which promise a renewed understanding of Zen. One is the establishment of the first English Zen monastery at Throssel Hole in Cumberland. It is under the guidance of Jiyu Kennett Roshi, an Englishwoman who received her Soto training and her transmission in Japan. She is also the Professor of Buddhism at UCLA at Berkeley, California and has founded a Soto monastery in America, Mount Shastra Abbey in California, from which the monks come to England. Throssel Hole is an old farmhouse on a hill, overlooking a lovely Cumberland valley. The routine of meditation and work in these pleasant surroundings is interspersed with interviews and practical advice on problems; Jiyu Kennett Roshi is becoming known for her intuitive, almost telepathic, grasp of her students' states of mind. She always spends the summer at Throssel Hole.

Zen masters of old were able to help their pupils experience Void-nature by the original and creative use of whatever was at hand, however humble, which would by-pass the pupil's analytical and concept-ridden mind. The second development in modern Zen is in line with those masters. Douglas Harding, who has now established a workshop at Nacton in Suffolk, discovered one day that Void-nature was himself—he was Void—because, in his experience, he was without a head.

'What actually happened was something absurdly simple and unspectacular: I stopped thinking. A peculiar quiet, an odd kind of alert limpness or numbness, came over me. Reason and imagination and all mental chatter died down. For once, words really failed me. Past and future dropped away. I forgot who and what I was, my name, manhood, animalhood, all that could be called mine. It was as if I had been born that instant, brand new, mindless, innocent of all memories. There existed only the Now, that present moment and what was clearly given in it. To look was enough. And what I found was khaki trouserlegs terminating downwards in a pair of brown shoes, khaki sleeves terminating sideways in a pair of pink hands, and a khaki shirtfront terminating upwards in —absolutely nothing whatever! Certainly not in a head.

'It took me no time at all to notice that this nothing, this hole where a head should have been, was no ordinary vacancy, no mere nothing. On the contrary, it was very much occupied. It was a vast emptiness vastly filled, a nothing that found room for everything—room for grass, trees, shadowy distant hills, . . . I had lost a head and gained a world.' [43]

Since that experience, thirty years ago, the 'Headless Way' of seeing into one's nature has been developing in a truly contemporary and western style at Nacton, and in other parts of England and the United States, where Douglas Harding demonstrates it. This way proceeds in an unusually down-to-earth fashion. It claims that modern man is more likely to see Who he really is in a minute of active experimentation than in years of reading, lecture–attending, thinking, ritual observances, and passive meditation of the traditional sort. Instead of these it uses a variety of simple, non-verbal, fact-finding tests. Douglas Harding says: 'These tests are asking: *how do I look to myself?* They direct my attention to my blind spot—to the space I occupy, to what's given right here at the Centre of my universe, to what it's like being 1st-person singular, present tense.'

Many of us have unconsciously acquired a view of ourselves from outside, as other people think of us, which obliterates our native view of ourselves from inside, as we really are. The cure for this, says Douglas Harding, is to take a fresh look at oneself-as-one-is-for-oneself and discover who one really is. He recommends a number of pointers to this Self-realization (some of which use other senses than vision) but he emphasizes that they must be carried out in practice and not just constructed in the mind from reading about them. Here is a selection of such pointers:

a. *Pointing here.* Point to your friend's feet, then yours; to his legs, then yours; to his torso, then yours; to his head, then. . . . What, *on present evidence*, is your finger now pointing at?

b. *Putting on a no-face.* Cut a head-sized hole in a card. Hold the card out at arm's length, noting the hole's boundaries. See how they vanish into your boundlessness as you bring the card forward and put it right on—to your face?

c. *In the body?* By stroking and pinching and pummelling, try to build up here on your shoulders the sort of thing you see over there on your friend's shoulders. Now try to get inside it, and describe its contents. Aren't you still out-of-doors, as much at large as ever? Look at your hand. Are you in it, or is it in you?

d. *This paper bag will show you!* Get an ordinary bag (preferably white) about twelve inches square, and cut the bottom off. Fit your face into one end while

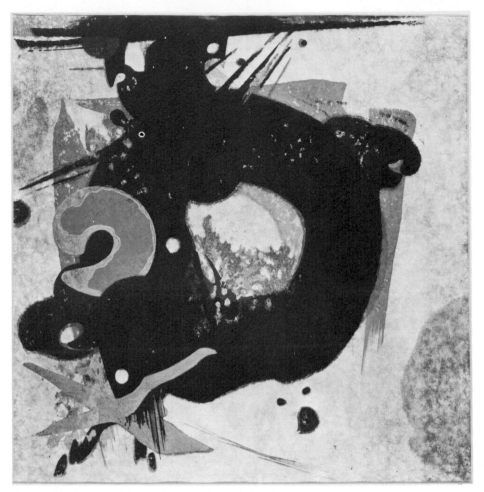

A woodblock print of 'Space' by Hokada Yoshida. 20th century, Japan.

your friend fits his into the other. While you and your friend (we'll call you A and B) do this, another friend, C, slowly puts the following questions to you:

1. Going by what's given now (not by what you remember or imagine) how many faces are there in the bag?
2. Is your end closed, or open?
3. Are you face-to-face, or face-to-no-face?

Come out for air, A and B, and then go back for more questions from C:

1. A or B, could that face register as form   if you weren't void?
2. A or B, could that face register as anything   if you weren't no-thing?
3. A or B, could that face register as coloured if you weren't colourless?
4. A or B, could that face register as opaque   if you weren't transparent?
5. A or B, could that face register as moving   if you weren't still?
6. A or B, could that face register as complex if you weren't simple?
7. A or B, could that face register as limited   if you weren't boundless?
8. A or B, could that face register as changing if you weren't changeless?

After another interval, into the bag again for more questions:

1. Are you now (as 1st person singular, present tense) the sort of thing that could grow old or decay, begin or end?
2. Unable to say 'I am this, or that', aren't you still able to say 'I AM'?
3. Who or What is this unborn, undying 'I AM'?

Interval

1. Can you make yourself out to be here (at a distance of 0 inches) *anything* like your partner there (at ten inches)?
2. Can you find any 'matter' (head, face, eyes . . .) your end?
3. Can you find any 'spirit' or 'consciousness' the other end?
4. Have you been living a double lie—awarding consciousness to that face, and a face to this consciousness?
5. Could this double pretence underlie your personal-relationship problems, all your problems?

Pagoda of Kiyomizu Temple, Kyoto, Japan.

Interval

1. Do you see that face more clearly, fearlessly, penetratingly, now it's only a coloured, moving shape?
2. Do you find that face any less lovable, now it's unhaunted, part of the décor?
3. Is 'spirit' divisible, and any less your partner's now it isn't peeping through those eyes?
4. Can you now say to your partner: 'Your face is no more than your temporary appearance; I am no less than your everlasting Reality'?
5. Can you now say to all beings everywhere: '*Here*, I am you'?
6. And to your *self*: 'Congratulations!'?

   For further investigation: Is what you discovered in the bag true outside the bag always?

'You have seen (says Douglas Harding) by carrying out such exercises in basic attention, what it is to be 1st-person singular—the No-thing that is nevertheless keenly aware of Itself as the Container or Ground of the whole display. This seeing is believing. Altogether unmystical (in the popular sense) it is a precise, total, all-or-nothing experience admitting of no degrees—so long as it lasts. Now your task is to go on seeing your Absence/Presence in all situations, till the seeing becomes quite natural and continuous. This is neither to lose yourself in your Emptiness nor in what fills it, but *simultaneously* to view the thing you are looking at and the No-thing you are looking out of. There will be found no times when this two-way attention is out of place or can safely be dispensed with.

'The initial seeing into your Nature is simplicity itself: once noticed, Nothing is so obvious! But it is operative only in so far as it is practised. The results— freedom from greed and hate and fear and delusion—are assured only while the One they belong to isn't overlooked.'

TAOISM

Action and Non-Action
The non-action of the wise man is not inaction.
It is not studied. It is not shaken by anything.
The sage is quiet because he is not moved,
Not because he wills to be quiet.
Still water is like glass.
You can look in it and see the bristles on your chin.
It is a perfect level;
A carpenter could use it.
If water is so clear, so level,
How much more the spirit of man?
The heart of the wise man is tranquil.
It is the mirror of heaven and earth
The glass of everything.
Emptiness, stillness, tranquillity, tastelessness,
Silence, non-action: this is the level of heaven and earth.
This is perfect Tao. Wise men find here
Their resting place.
Resting, they are empty. (Chuang Tzu) *[1]*

The Universe, by Sengai. The circle represents the Infinite, the triangle the Beginning of all forms, the square (the triangle doubled) the First form.

THE WAY

Existence is beyond the power of words
To define:
Terms may be used
But are none of them absolute.
In the beginning of heaven and earth there were no words,
Words came out of the womb of matter;
And whether a man dispassionately
Sees to the core of life
Or passionately
Sees the surface,
The core and the surface
Are essentially the same,
Words making them seem different
Only to express appearance.
If name be needed, wonder names them both:
From wonder into wonder
Existence opens. (Lao Tzu) *[2]*

Existence—the Way—the Nameless—Ultimate Reality—the Void—Emptiness—the Absolute—all of these are Tao and yet none of them are, for the Tao is beyond description by the human mind. It is like the Hindu 'THAT' and the Buddhist 'Suchness', it can only be described by negatives, 'not this thing, not that thing'. For this reason it is usually left untranslated as it is thought of as undefinable. 'He who knows does not speak and he who speaks does not know.' But since it must be referred to, it is usually termed the Way.

The Way is the way of life itself and it must be discovered intuitively, for it cannot be found through the application of the intellect; it is revealed in actual living, in the seeing of the Way in each unique moment of life. Thus Taoism has no dogma, for the ever-changing flow and growth of life itself cannot be bound by rules nor by man-made intellectual categories. Life, when it is stripped to its bare essence, is free, unknowable, and undifferentiated. It is One, the Tao, whole and unbound. Its power becomes manifest as all its myriad forms, each one unique; and each man must find his own relationship to the Tao, his own understanding of the truth, the fulfilment of the Way within his own life.

This is the adventure of the spirit presented to all men. For every man knows, deep within himself, that there is more than he has yet discovered. Zen says: Let go of all your fixed ideas and self-imposed boundaries and *see* what life really is. Taoism says: Flow into it and with it. Accept what comes along with a joyful awareness. See the universe as the creative dance of the Tao and move in step with it. The realm of Tao is the realm of man's inner essence, his Reality; to live in accord with the Tao is to live at one with one's being. Thus the Tao is both the Way and the Goal.

Nobody knows when Taoism really began in China, although it is believed that it might have taken its form under the Yellow Emperor (possibly mythical) in 2000 B.C. But in the sixth century B.C., the *Tao Te Ching* (the Book of the Virtuous Way) was written by Lao Tzu, the first recorded Taoist sage, although he, too, is considered by some to be a legendary figure. Indeed, he is said to have

Shou-lao, the god of long life. Jade plaque, China, probably Ming Dynasty. (See p. 192 for the reverse of this plaque.)

lived in his mother's womb for seventy years and to have been born white-haired. Historic validity has little place in eastern religions, where it is the doctrine that matters and not its origin.

According to some evidence, Lao Tzu was a historian in charge of the archives of the State of Ch'u. Observing that the State was falling into a period of decline, he left it to retire to the mountains in the West. At the frontier, the keeper begged him to write down his teachings, whereupon Lao Tzu wrote the *Tao Te Ching* and then departed, never to be seen again.

Although 'Te' is usually translated as 'virtue', the whole message of the *Tao Te Ching* is that conventional virtue, as we understand it, already belongs to a corrupt society. For true, untainted virtue arises from an inner balance which gives to the Taoist such a harmonious interaction with his surroundings that all actions are performed with perfect spontaneity and without thought of 'virtue'.

When people lost sight of the way to live
Came codes of love and honesty,
Learning came, charity came,
Hypocrisy took charge;

When differences weakened family ties
Came benevolent fathers and dutiful sons;
And when lands were disrupted and misgoverned
Came ministers commended as loyal. (Lao Tzu) *[3]*

Hence, there is no doctrine of sin in Taoism (and indeed no word for it, equivalent to our western concept) for, to the Taoist ethics emerge from the inner condition of man and are not to be imposed from outside. Bad behaviour was regarded as stupidity and ignorance, for no one would knowingly violate the natural Way:

Those who would take over the earth
And shape it to their will
Never, I notice, succeed.
The earth is like a vessel so sacred
That at the mere approach of the profane
It is marred
And when they reach out their fingers it is gone.
For a time in the world some force themselves ahead
And some are left behind,
For a time in the world some make a great noise
And some are held silent,
For a time in the world some are puffed fat
And some are kept hungry,
For a time in the world some push aboard
And some are tipped out:
At no time in the world will a man who is sane
Over-reach himself,
Over-spend himself,
Over-rate himself. (Lao Tzu) *[4]*

A deer, the symbol of peace. Black marble with green and white intrusions, China, 19th century.

The Haunt of the Sage. China, 13th century.

Living in tune with the laws of the universe makes for serenity of mind and this was regarded as a prerequisite for ordinary life by Taoists, whereas living by rules was seen as a form of false security. If rules are followed, there may be a superficial feeling that all is well, but really life cannot be structured in a rigid way and volcanoes will inevitably erupt from underneath. True morality arises from wisdom, and Taoism considered it better that people should learn to be wise than try to conform to an ethical code.

    It is better not to make merit a matter of reward

    Lest people conspire and contend,

    Not to pile up rich belongings

Lest they rob,
Not to excite by display
Lest they covet.
A sound leader's aim
Is to open people's hearts,
Fill their stomachs,
Calm their wills,
Brace their bones
And so to clarify their thoughts and cleanse their needs
That no cunning meddler could touch them:
Without being forced, without strain or constraint,
Good government comes of itself. (Lao Tzu) [5]

Confucius, who lived at about the same time as Lao Tzu, and whose ethical code of right living made such an impression on the Chinese that it, if anything, survives today, was the constant target of the Taoists. But their arrows were more witty than painful because they could respect a morality, such as that taught by Confucius, which was based on a profound sense of good manners, a feeling for decorum, and for the right way of doing things. Although Confucianism was never at ease with the subtle, elusive Taoism, yet they were at one in seeing the universe as basically good and man's place in it as a naturally happy one. There is no hell in the Taoist religion, nor any concept of man as 'fallen' and in need of redemption. In the same way, because the true Taoist did not desire anything which was out of harmony with his intrinsic nature, there was no feeling of special holiness either. The Taoist did not seek any special illumination which was different in kind from his other experiences. He wanted only to be so sensitive to the Way, and so aware of perfect stillness within movement, that he would become the flawless response to a situation. In any case, to a Taoist, all things are interdependent and he could not conceive of a separation between the holy and the everyday.

The surest test if a man be sane
Is if he accepts life whole, as it is,
Without needing by measure or touch to understand
The measureless untouchable source
Of its images,
The measureless untouchable source
Of its substances,
The source which, while it appears dark emptiness,
Brims with a quick force
Farthest away
And yet nearest at hand
From oldest times unto this day,
Charging its images with origin:
What more need I know of the origin
Than this? [6]

The *Tao Te Ching* has come to be one of the most popular books in the world, the number of copies sold second only to the Bible. Perhaps this is because we see glimmers of an old Eden, a spontaneous and unselfconscious way of life which we seem to have lost. We fill our lives with ever more and more sense-satisfactions and in doing so we may be overlooking the Source of ourselves, to our peril. 'Therefore let desire be stilled while you contemplate the Mystery; when desire reigns, you behold only its outward manifestations,' says Lao Tzu. The true mystery of our existence lies at our root—at the still centre of the turning wheel.

> Thirty spokes are made by holes in a hub
> By vacancies joining them for a wheel's use;
> The use of clay in moulding pitchers
> Comes from the hollow of its absence;
> Doors, windows, in a house,
> Are used for their emptiness:
> Thus we are helped by what is not
> To use what is. (Lao Tzu) [7]

The symbol for Yin and Yang, the two opposites. The essense of one (a point) is always found in its opposite.

YIN AND YANG

Emerging from such a distant past in China that their history is unrecorded (although sometimes attributed to Fu-hsi, the first Chinese ruler, 2852 B.C.) *Yin* and *Yang*, the symbols of manifest duality, were used extensively by both Taoism and Confucianism. It was thought that from the Tao—the undifferentiated One—arose duality, all the pairs of complementary existence in nature, such as male and female, north and south, black and white; and duality as such was symbolized by Yin and Yang. They must not be thought of as entities in themselves, but as the qualities inherent in all substance. Thus they are principles, which eternally act and react upon each other.

The quality of Yin is dark, negative and feminine. Yin is the primordial chaos which gives rise to creativity and birth. Thus Yin is the state of potentiality. Since Yin is seen as dark, and symbolizes the dark womb from which the light of the intellect—Yang—is born, it is also thought of as repose and rest, while Yang is motion. Yang is the principle of light, the sun, the male, the spirit.

Yang is justice and correctness while Yin is mercy and wisdom. Yang is active and aggressive while Yin is soft and receptive.

In the diagram of Yin-Yang, the two forces of the world—negative and positive, female and male—are held in complete balance and equality, their nature manifest in everything that exists. Because they are not statically divided (or the world would come to an end) but are always interacting, the seed of one is shown as being contained in its opposite in the diagram, a black point in the

left: A gathering of the immortals painted by Tomioka Tessai. Colour on silk, Japan, 1896. *right*: Shou-lao, the god of long life, painted by Shugetsu Tokan. Colour on paper, Japan, late 15th century.

white and a white in the black. Although they are called opposites, their action is always that of co-operation in order to achieve the right balance (for instance, a strongly intellectual man should welcome some intuitive, soft Yin in himself in order to be properly integrated).

Yang is also sometimes symbolized by a circle, which represents dynamic movement; and Yin by a square, which is the womb, passive and dark as earth.

In China, everything is Yin and Yang. The house is Yang because it is built of hard stone, and the garden is Yin. Gold and jade are Yang, while silver and pearls are Yin. In our day, the macrobiotic diet, so popular with the young, is based on the qualities in food of Yin and Yang, and their proper balance.

Western society is sometimes accused of being too Yang; overbalanced towards aggressiveness and the intellect, towards the rational analytical mind which knows things by their outside nameable appearance and which fails to take cognizance of their inner intangible nature (which can only be known by the

A tomb figure of a lady. Pottery, engraved and painted, China, T'ang Dynasty.

left: A tortoise, the symbol of stability, encountering a snake. Stone rubbing after a Chinese painting by Wu Tao-tzü, China, 8th century. *right:* Geese by a stream, painted by Lin Liang. China, late 15th century.

Yin qualities of intuition and the heart). In the good society, according to Taoism, the right balance of Yin and Yang produced the Sage, or the Perfect Man (sometimes called the Superior Man) referred to frequently by both Taoists and Confucians.

The two ways of philosophy of Taoism and Confucianism themselves provided a Yin-Yang balance in China, for the Yang Confucius was a highly cultured scholar, a lover of tradition who discoursed on the rites and ceremonies of the past, and who had a gift for summing up his teachings in memorable epigrams. 'A journey of a thousand miles must start with a single step' is a saying of Confucius. He believed that man has four innate virtues, those of benevolence, justice, propriety and wisdom, and that he has only to obey the law of his own nature in order to be perfect. In this understanding, there was a similarity with Taoism, but the Yang of Confucius was very rigid in its insistence on a formal attitude to life, in which the right thing must be done in the right way. Yin-like Taoism would have said that the right thing cannot help being done in the right way if the doer is in harmony with the Tao.

Because the interactions of Yin and Yang hold the world in dynamic balance and because they exist in mutual interdependence and were recognized in China as being always in relationship, the differences between them were only regarded as apparent. Hence, the good was not concentrated on at the expense of the bad, for inevitably, if this is done, man is a prisoner of his bad side, unable to acknowledge it as part of himself, and thus not free to integrate it with the good.

Intrinsic to Yin and Yang is the principle of change. The Tao has no opposite; it is the Absolute Ground, pure, eternal and unchanging. But once it is manifest into the duality of Yin and Yang, there is no absoluteness to be found in any manifestation; all pairs of opposites can become each other and all the time do so. Happiness turns to sorrow, life becomes death, day turns into night. Lieh Tzu, the Sage, found this out when he was on a journey and, eating by the roadside, he happened to see a hundred-year-old skull. Pulling away the weeds and pointing his finger, he said, 'Only you and I know that you have never died and you have never lived. Are you really unhappy? Am I really enjoying myself?' [8]

CHUANG TZU—THE GREAT SAGE

One of the most famous teachings of Taoism is the strength of weakness. Yin, in its passivity, endures better than the head-on direct actions of Yang. This is exemplified by the humble reed which will bend in the wind while the mighty pine will break; by the low valley which receives all the waters of the high mountains; by the passive power of water itself which flows round an obstacle,

The eight Taoist immortals with their attributes. Jade plaque, China, probably Ming Dynasty. (See p. 184 for the obverse of this plaque.)

never attempting to conquer it. Chuang Tzu, considered by many to be as great a sage as Lao Tzu, discoursed on the power of weakness when he told the story of Tzu-ch'i of Non-po, who 'was wandering around the hill of Shang when he saw a huge tree there, different from all the rest. A thousand teams of horses could have taken shelter under it and its shade would have covered them all. Tzu-ch'i said, "What tree is this? It must certainly have some extraordinary usefulness!" But, looking up, he saw that the smaller limbs were gnarled and twisted, unfit for beams or rafters, and looking down, he saw that the trunk was pitted and rotten and could not be used for coffins. He licked one of the leaves and it blistered his mouth and made it sore. He sniffed the odor and it was enough to make a man drunk for three days. "It turns out to be a completely unusuable tree," said Tzu-ch'i, "and so it has been able to grow this big. Aha!—it is this unusableness that the Holy Man makes use of!" ' *[9]*

Chuang Tzu lived after Lao Tzu. His gift was a direct grasp of reality in itself. He was thus a forerunner of the Chinese Zen masters who were to do as he did—to take the everyday and the concrete and show it in its undifferentiated essential Truth. He said:

'Men of the world who value the Way all turn to books. But books are nothing more than words. Words have value; what is of value in words is meaning. Meaning has something it is pursuing, but the thing that it is pursuing cannot be

Kuan Yu, a general, later deified as god of War. Porcelain, China, 17th–18th century.

put into words and handed down. The world values words and hands down books but, though the world values them, I do not think them worth valuing. What the world takes to be value is not real value.

'What you can look at and see are forms and colors; what you can listen to and hear are names and sounds. What a pity!—that the men of the world should suppose that form and color, name and sound are sufficient to convey the truth of a thing. It is because in the end they are not sufficient to convey truth that "those who know do not speak, those who speak do not know." But how can the world understand this!' [10]

Chuang Tzu expounded and interpreted the compact verses of Lao Tzu in teachings which are witty and poetic. He was a scholar who refused the office of Prime Minister of the State of Chu because he preferred to wander about freely as a sage.

The story is told that he was fishing in the P'u River with his bamboo pole when two officials, sent by the Prince of Chu, arrived to tell him that the Prince wished him to become Prime Minister. Chuang Tzu remembered a certain tortoise which had been kept for three thousand years and was much venerated by Prince Chu, who had wrapped it in silk and placed it in a shrine (in Taoism the tortoise is a symbol of long life). He asked the officials whether they thought the tortoise would rather be dead, leaving its shell as a sacred object, or be alive, dragging its tail in the mud.

'It would rather be alive and dragging its tail in the mud,' they said.

'Then go home,' said Chuang Tzu, 'and leave me to drag my tail in the mud.' [11]

The underlying theme of Chuang Tzu's teachings is liberty; how to be free in a world which is dominated by injustice, poverty, suffering and greed. Many philosophers, throughout history, have proposed specific reforms of a political, social or economic nature to overcome these problems. Chuang Tzu, however, did not attempt to deal with evils on their own level. Instead, he proposed the way of Taoism (which was later to be developed in Buddhism)—that of freeing oneself from the idea that there is a problem.

The world of Chuang Tzu was not different from our world today. People fell ill and died of dread diseases; crops failed and children starved. There were wars, and there was man-made injustice of rich and poor. To Chuang Tzu, the fundamental error seemed to be in man's value-judgments, in his actions which sprang from the labelling of things as good or bad. To Chuang Tzu, the cause of suffering was man himself who labelled suffering as suffering and thereafter tried to avoid it.

> When we look at things in the light of Tao
> Nothing is best, nothing is worst.
> Each thing, seen in its own light,
> Stands out in its own way.
> It can seem to be 'better'
> Than what is compared with it
> On its own terms.
> But seen in terms of the whole,
> No one thing stands out as 'better'.
> If you measure differences,

What is greater than something else is 'great',
Therefore there is nothing that is not 'great';
What is smaller than something else is 'small',
Therefore there is nothing that is not 'small'.
So the whole cosmos is a grain of rice,
And the tip of a hair
Is as big as a mountain—
Such is the relative view.

You can break down walls with battering rams,
But you cannot stop holes with them.
All things have different uses.
Fine horses can travel a hundred miles a day,
But they cannot catch mice
Like terriers or weasels:
All creatures have gifts of their own.
The white horned owl can catch fleas at midnight
And distinguish the tip of a hair,
But in bright day it stares, helpless,
And cannot even see a mountain.
All things have varying capacities.

Consequently: he who wants to have right without wrong,
Order without disorder,
Does not understand the principles
Of heaven and earth.
He does not know how
Things hang together.
Can a man cling only to heaven
And know nothing of earth?
They are correlative: to know one
Is to know the other.
To refuse one
Is to refuse both.
Can a man cling to the positive
Without any negative
In contrast to which it is seen
To be positive?
If he claims to do so
He is a rogue or a madman. *[12]*

It is practical wisdom to live in the Tao, to place oneself at the still centre of the moving world. Suffering is then seen to be relative, less to be rejected than to be experienced, like any other experience. For it is man's unrealistic labelling of natural events—such as illness and health and death and life—as wrong or right, bad or good, which is the cause of trouble in the world, according to Chuang Tzu. While men act in the belief that the course of life can be divided into separate compartments in this way, they are moving further and further from the undifferentiated wholeness of the Tao, and binding themselves ever more strongly with ropes made from the imagination. Men suffer needlessly, failing to see the relative as relative, and tied by habits of thought and socially accepted values of right and wrong. Chuang Tzu illustrates this with the story of Nan-jung Chu who went to hear the Master Kengsang speak of the Way. 'Nan-jung Chu . . . said, "A man like myself who's already on in years—what sort of studies is he to undertake in order to attain this state you speak of?"

'Master Keng-sang said, "Keep the body whole, cling fast to life! Do not fall prey to the fidget and fuss of thoughts and scheming. If you do this for three years, then you can attain the state I have spoken of."

'Nan-jung Chu said, "The eyes are part of the body—I have never thought them anything else—yet the blind man cannot see with his. The ears are part of the body—I have never thought them anything else—yet the deaf man cannot hear with his. The mind is part of the body—I have never thought it anything else—yet the madman cannot comprehend with his. The body too must be part of the body—surely they are intimately connected. Yet—is it because something intervenes?—I try to seek my body, but I cannot find it. Now you tell me, 'Keep the body whole, cling fast to life! Do not fall prey to the fidget and fuss of thoughts and scheming.' As hard as I try to understand your explanation of the Way, I'm afraid your words penetrate no further than my ears."

"I've said all I can say," exclaimed Master Keng-sang, "The saying goes, mud daubers have no power to transform caterpillars. The little hens of Yüeh cannot hatch goose eggs, though the larger hens of Lu can do it well enough. It isn't that one kind of hen isn't just as henlike as the other. One can and the other can't because their talents just naturally differ in size. Now I'm afraid my talents are not sufficient to bring about any transformation in you. Why don't you go south and visit Lao-Tzu?"

'Nan-jung Chu packed up his provisions and journeyed for seven days and seven nights until he came to Lao Tzu's place. Lao Tzu said, "Did you come from Keng-sang Chu's place?"

"Yes Sir," said Nan-jung Chu.

"Why did you come with all this crowd of people?" asked Lao Tzu. . . .

'Nan-jung Chu, astonished, turned to look behind him.

"Don't you know what I mean?" asked Lao Tzu.' [13]

There was nobody with Nan-jung Chu. . . . 'the "crowd of people" that he came with was the baggage of old ideas, the conventional concepts of right and wrong, good and bad, life and death, that he lugged about with him wherever he went' [14]. It was this collection of concepts which had made Master Keng-sang give up teaching him. For when he was told to live life as it is, without thoughts about it, he immediately presented Master Keng-sang with a number of ideas about blindness, deafness and madness which he did not know from direct experience but only from imagination as happening to 'other people'. 'Other people' are ideas, for one isn't other people in reality, and this also was the 'crowd' Lao Tzu referred to when speaking to him. For, as long as we live in the imaginary world of other people's states and do not live simply in our own, we are accompanied everywhere by a crowd.

In all his teachings, Chuang Tzu was concerned to show the natural way as distinct from the actions men take when they are out of touch with it. He relates the story of a nobleman:

'Duke Huan was in his hall reading a book. The wheelwright, P'ien, who was in the yard below chiseling a wheel, laid down his mallet and chisel, stepped up into the hall, and said to Duke Huan, "This book Your Grace is reading—may I venture to ask whose words are in it?"

"The words of the sages," said the duke.

"Are the sages still alive?"

"Dead long ago," said the duke.

"In that case, what you are reading there is nothing but the chaff and dregs of the men of old!"

"Since when does a wheelwright have permission to comment on the books I read?" said Duke Huan. "If you have some explanation, well and good. If not, it's your life!"

'Wheelwright P'ien said, "I look at it from the point of view of my own work. When I chisel a wheel, if the blows of the mallet are too gentle, the chisel slides and won't take hold. But if they're too hard, it bites in and won't budge. Not

A hanging scroll depicting a bird and a lotus painted by Li K'u-chan. Ink and colour on paper, China, 20th century.

too gentle, not too hard—you can get it in your hand and feel it in your mind. You can't put it into words, and yet there's a knack to it somehow. I can't teach it to my son, and he can't learn it from me. So I've gone along for seventy years and at my age I'm still chiseling wheels. When the men of old died, they took with them the things that couldn't be handed down. So what you are reading there must be nothing but the chaff and dregs of the men of old".' *[15]*

In this story, Chuang Tzu shows one of the great insights of Taoism, that the intuitive feel for life is more important than intellectually-formed ideas about it, particularly when those ideas are not even one's own but are the reported words of someone long dead. When men die they take with them the things that can't be handed down, P'ien says. He means that what *can* be handed down is unimportant. What can't be handed down is each man's personal 'feel' for existence and this cannot be taught to others nor can others ever learn it—men must experience it for themselves. This truth is the tap-root of Taoism.

THE I CHING—THE BOOK OF CHANGE

The *I Ching* is popularly known as a unique book containing an ancient method for divining the future. In fact, it is one of the oldest books in the literature of the world. Its origin goes back at least three thousand years and Confucius, when he came to edit it, announced that if he had fifty years to spare, he would spend them all studying the Book of Change. The Book is common to both Taoism and Confucianism and much of the wisdom of both philosophies has sprung from it.

The theme that pervades the philosophy of the Book is the idea of change. For when the meaning of change is understood, the inimitable law of Tao—the way of things—can be seen working within it. The interplay of Yin and Yang is the change which can either transform one force into another or can alternate connected phenomena, such as day and night, and winter and summer. Change, in the meaning of the Book, is when 'The yin and yang shine on each other, maim each other, heal each other; the four seasons succeed each other, give birth to each other, slaughter each other. Desire and hatred, rejection and acceptance thereupon rise up in succession; . . . Security and danger trade places with each other, bad and good fortune give birth to each other, tense times and relaxed ones buffet one another, gathering-together and scattering bring it all to completion. These names and realities can be recorded, their details and minute parts can be noted. The principle of following one another in orderly succession, the property of moving in alternation, turning back when they have reached the limit, beginning again when they have ended—these are inherent in things.' *[16]*

Dr Carl Jung, who wrote a preface to Richard Wilhelm's translation of the *I Ching*, believed that the divinations the Book gives—the alleged extraordinarily accurate forecasts of what will occur—are based on 'synchronicity'. We usually think of events as a sequence in time, which seem to occur in a straight line—for instance, one's hands are cold and so one drops a box of matches and they spill. But synchronicity does not look at these events as a sequence so much as an arrangement, which contains the total of the universal

left: A tiger painted by Mu Ch'i. Ink on paper, China, 13th century. *right:* Shou-lao, painted by Tomioka Tessai. Sumi on paper, Japan, 1914.

situation at that moment. There is an ever-changing world situation in which everything is included, down to the merest atom. The dropping of the box is an expression of that situation; and the way the matches fall is also in accordance with the pattern of the moment. Synchronicity is the operation of Yin and Yang in the moment, and this Far Eastern way of seeing the juxtaposition of occurrences bears little resemblance to the western idea of one step following another in logical sequence.

Thus the answer to your problem, when arrived at in the Book of Change, will be the result of taking into account the forces involved in the problem at that particular time. A week later the answer might well be different.

The way the forecasts are made is by the reading of hexagrams. These hexagrams came into being through the ancient usage of linear signs as oracles. For instance, 'yes' was shown by a single unbroken line (—) and 'no' by a broken line (– –). As time went on, need was felt for more complex answers and the lines were put in pairs, to which another line was added, making eight trigrams, the maximum number able to be formed with two different lines. The broken lines are Yin, the unbroken are Yang.

```
—     – –     – –     – –     —     —     —     – –
—     – –     – –     —     – –     —     – –     —
—     – –     —     – –     – –     – –     —     —
```

The meaning of these eight trigrams was complex. They were held to be symbols of all that happens on earth, continually changing into each other just as phenomena become one another in the physical world (coal becomes ash; ice becomes water). So the reading of these trigrams was concerned less with a static situation than with the movements of change.

The trigrams were combined with each other at an early date and in this way, a total of sixty-four signs was obtained, each of six lines. Each line was Yin (negative) or Yang (positive) and each was capable of change to its opposite.

Thus, if we take the first hexagram in the Book, which is called Heaven, we have

```
—
—
—
—
—
—
```

which is the brilliant Source of All, the Creative Principle itself, and it augurs sublime success. If the lowest line changes, we then have

```
—
—
—
—
—
– –
```

which gives us a yielding line beneath Heaven; and as the bottom trigram also symbolizes the wind, there is a blowing away of total virtue, a yielding of the male to the female.

Hexagrams are arrived at by drawing sticks or throwing coins. It is considered more respectful to the authority of the *I Ching*, and of greater benefit to the petitioner, if the sticks are used, as sorting them out is a form of meditation and gives the mind time to become peaceful and humble.

The value of the *I Ching* is less, perhaps, in forecasting actual events than in showing to the questioner the aspect of himself which has caused the problem. As Jung remarks, the *I Ching* insists on self-knowledge throughout. The uncanny thing about it is that it appears to know one better than one knows oneself! For instance, one may be impatiently waiting for a letter from an employer, or a lover and, longing to know the answer in the letter, one may consider writing again, or pestering in some other way. If the *I Ching* were consulted about this, the answer might be Hexagram No. 5, Calculated Inaction, where one would be told 'Calculated inaction (or exhibiting the power to wait) and the

left: The figure of a monkey was often used as the symbol of a man in his restless, clever aspects, as in the famous Taoist-Zen story, *Monkey* byWu Ch'eng-en, translated by Arthur Waley. *right:* A hanging scroll from China.

Daikoku, the god of good fortune.

confidence of others win brilliant success. . . . To accord with the circumstances now prevailing, action must be avoided. Danger lies ahead; but, with firmness and strength, we shall avoid failure. *[17]* This answer seems to tell us that the writer of the awaited letter has confidence in us *not* to plague him, therefore he has some respect for us. Self-restraint is implied in 'firmness and strength' and as we think this over, the whole problem may begin to seem less to do with waiting for an outside change than with the need to alter ourselves in such a way that we are not so childishly dependent on the outside world. The advice to be firm and strong may show us, if we are receptive enough, how weak we are being and we may see that it was this underlying weakness which was seen by others, although hitherto not apparent to ourselves, and which has been the real cause of the hesitancy of the letter-writer.

Critics of the *I Ching* are many, the main comment being that one can read into the words of the answer anything one wants. To this, Carl Jung says: 'The Chinese standpoint does not concern itself as to the attitude one takes towards the performance of the oracle. It is only we who are puzzled, because we trip time and again over our prejudice, viz., the notion of causality. The ancient wisdom of the East lays stress upon the fact that the intelligent individual realises his own thoughts, but not in the least upon the way in which he does it. The less one thinks about the theory of the I Ching, the more soundly one sleeps.' [18]

POPULAR TAOISM

The penetrating profundity of Taoism always existed side by side with, and was eventually largely overtaken by, more superficial beliefs in magical heavens where reigned the Immortals; in Blessed Isles of the West where the drug of immortality grew; in supernatural powers gained through yoga; and in magic of all kinds. Whereas the essential nature of Taoism—spontaneous action springing from inner harmony with the Way—came to be one of the greatest influences in Zen Buddhism, the actual practice of Taoism came more and more to be identified with alchemy and yoga practices, the search for the drug of immortality, and with spells and charms to ward off demons. Nature always had a great influence on Chinese thought. The true mystics of Taoism felt the power of natural scenery and were deeply moved by moments of ineffable beauty, such as the mysterious grace of a willow tree seen against the sky, or water reeds bending in the breeze. Their scrolls show us some of the most beautiful landscapes ever painted. But many Taoists, rather more superstitious, had a different feeling for nature and endowed the mountains, trees, rocks and streams with spirits, such as water-sprites. John Blofeld [19] tells us that even in the 1930s, belief in fox-spirits existed, and he came across a factual newspaper report of a fox-spirit harrassing a policeman by daylight on one of Peking's largest thoroughfares. He also relates that he was told by a Taoist recluse, T'ang, that T'ang's brother had offended a fox-spirit by being forced to urinate (he was with a party of female pilgrims) near a fox-tower (believed to be the home of a playful fox-spirit). He was careless enough to urinate in such a manner that there was a trickle over the sun-baked earth on to the base of the tower. Warned that he should make amends to the fox by taking incense, candles and roast chicken to the tower, he neglected to do this. Among the strange events which happened to him after that was a

Autumnal scenery by the lake, attributed to Chao Ling-Jang. Colour on silk, China, late 11th century.

A tomb guardian. China, T'ang Dynasty.

mocking voice which laughed every time he went near the place, and hailed him as 'Loose-Penis Immortal'!

Taoist monasteries, usually in wild and remote country, existed in China until recent years, but nobody in the West knows whether there are any now left. Although the teachings of Lao Tzu and Chuang Tzu formed their basic philosophy, their practices included telepathy and other psychic arts, the acquiring of powers to heal and prolong life, alchemy, and the arts of painting, poetry, music and self-defence—all were regarded as ways to the Way. As in Tantric Yoga, Kundalini was practised and in recent years, there has been much written about the yoga of sex—the sexual act as a means of bodily union with the spirit so long as the semen is not ejaculated. The *Tao of Sex [20]* tells us that the Yellow Emperor 'retained his semen while having intercourse with twelve hundred women' (presumably sequentially). This made him into an Immortal

A ceremonial cup carved from a rhinoceros horn with ebonized wood stand. China, 18th century.

Seated Kuan-Yin. Porcelain, China, 17th century.

and he ascended into heaven in broad daylight. Instructions were written giving advice on every aspect of sexual behaviour including how to achieve a proper mental state beforehand, what postures to use for different conditions, what to do about a small organ (jade-stalk), how to retain the semen, how to ward off intercourse with demons, and many, many prescriptions for vigour and enjoyment.

THE T'AI CHI CH'UAN

As well as this and other yogic practices, a more serious Taoist art-form has recently become popular in the West. This is the *T'ai Chi Ch'uan*, a form of movement which is based on Yin and Yang and has links with the *I Ching*, although it is of considerably later date than that work. According to legend, Chang San-Feng, an Immortal, meditating in his house one day, heard an unusual noise in the courtyard and saw from his window a snake hissing at a crane which flew down to attack it. The snake turned its head away from the crane's sword-like beak and beat at the crane's neck with its tail. The crane defended its neck with its right wing and then the snake twined around the crane's legs. The crane lifted its left leg and lowered its left wing to help it attack the snake but although it stabbed again and again with its beak, it could never catch the snake, which always twisted out of reach. In the end they both gave up from sheer tiredness and the crane went back to its branch while the

White Rain, one of the fifty-three stations of the Tokaido. Colour print by Hiroshige, Japan, early 19th century.

snake crawled into a hole in the trunk of the same tree. The next day the fight occurred all over again.

This extraordinary scene gave Chang San-feng the understanding of the principle of the *I Ching*; that the strong becomes the yielding and the yielding turns into the strong. He studied other forms of nature, such as the movements of clouds and of water, and of trees bending in the wind. From this he developed a system of movement co-ordination which follows the principle of Change. This system, T'ai Chi Ch'uan, is regarded by many Taoists as a means of meditation.

The principles of the T'ai Chi Ch'uan are to still the mind; to breathe in harmony with the movements of the body so as to produce an inner vital force called *chi* (a combination of mind, breath and energy), which must be concentrated into an area below the navel; and to move the limbs with even smoothness, balance and relaxation. The movements (called a dance in the West) are performed slowly, each movement flowing naturally and uninterruptedly from the one before. The image is that of a flowing river. Exertion is avoided because of the balance of the body, which is alternated from one foot to the other in an effortless change, and does not call for excessive strength. The biggest difficulty for westerners is in learning 'soft knees', which means keeping the knees slightly bent all the time. Suppleness of the biceps involved in this stance is said to defeat the shrinking of old age.

The T'ai Chi Ch'uan is a uniquely Taoist exercise, still widely practised in China. Da Liu, in his book *T'ai Chi Ch'uan and I Ching* says, 'T'ai Chi Ch'uan can be considered a kind of preparatory exercise for meditation, although of course, it can be studied for a variety of other reasons. It disciplines the body, teaches relaxation and clear-headedness, accustoms the student to regulated breathing, and demonstrates the circulation of chi, the flow of psychic energy, by a method far more close to the real event of meditation than looking at diagrams or hearing oral descriptions. More than that, T'ai Chi Ch'uan gives something of the spirit of meditation, a spirit which, in our over-active, anxiety ridden lives, we seldom taste in day-to-day living—a spirit which promises a glimpse of peace beyond the scope of our present imagination or our ordinary understanding of the world.' [21]

Ivory netsuke of a cock pecking a radish. Signed Shuosai, Japan, 19th century.

SUFISM

The Worker is hidden in the workshop: enter the
workshop and behold Him!
Inasmuch as the work has woven a veil over the
Worker, you cannot see Him outside of His work.
The Worker dwells in the workshop: none who stays
outside is aware of Him.
Come, then, into the workshop of Not-being, that
you may contemplate the work and the Worker together. (Rumi) *[1]*

THE PATH OF ILLUMINATION

The quest for illumination and the rapture of realizing it, has been seen to be the base of Hinduism and Buddhism. The highest Reality of all is not, as in western religions, to be thought of as separate from us—a grand Individual whom we try to please and whose laws we obey—but is rather the undifferentiated Consciousness common to all of us, which is the divine origin of our ordinary consciousness, as it is also our ultimate Self or Spirit.

Mysticism is realizing the Self, or God, as one's inner Being, more truly oneself than one's manifest self. The eastern religions are mystical, while the three religions which have their origin in the Near East—Judaism, Christianity, and Islam—are not, for they believe that God is to be found 'out there', somewhere infinitely beyond man. But there are many mystics within these three religions and the Sufis are such a group within Islam.

Theirs is a religion of love and its doctrine is about the way of surrender to God—the ecstatic leap of the spirit into oneness with him.

> Though from my gaze profound
> Deep awe hath hid Thy face,
> In wondrous and ecstatic Grace
> I feel Thee touch my inmost ground. (Al-Junaid) [2]

'They asked (*Bistāmi*), "When does a man know that he has attained real gnosis (understanding)?" He said: "At the time when he becomes annihilated under the knowledge of God, and is made everlasting on the carpet of God, without self and without creature".' [3]

'It (Sufism) is this: that God should make thee die to thyself and should make thee live in Him.' [4]

The Sufis began their existence during the eighth and ninth centuries A.D. They had rebelled against the era of sumptuous luxury and corrupt power which followed the death of the Prophet Mohammed, and they became desert wanderers and ascetics, dressed in garments made from coarse wool—called *suf* in Arabic—from which came their name. They were described as 'travellers' and 'strangers' because of their wanderings over the deserts, and they lived a life of self-denial, silence and detachment.

They came mainly from Persia, where both Hinduism and Buddhism had penetrated deeply and where the Hindu Upanishads were widely read. But whereas to the Hindus, the ultimate sublimity was to merge with the Godhead as 'THAT art thou', to the Sufis, the supreme surrender was to God as the Beloved—the merging of the lover with the Loved—an ecstasy of union which was called 'passing away in God'.

The Sufis were Moslems and were not concerned to start a new religion. But because the truth does not belong, finally, to any religion, but transcends them all, the Sufis came to be apart from the more rigid followers of Mohammed, their mystical insight transcending Moslem dogma. Great Sufi teachers founded schools of study and guided disciples in a number of practices and beliefs, their writings passed down from one generation to the next.

The disciple's progress was by way of seven stages, each stage having to be achieved by his own effort, although it was believed that God's help was always forthcoming. The disciple's final goal was thought of in various ways: he was to

Majnun in the desert, the tragic love story of Majnun and Laila symbolizes the relationship of man to God.

The night journey of the prophet Mohammed in his ascent to heaven.

شكل ٧١٤ ـ نموذج كتابة زخرفية بخط ديواني على هيئـة دائرية واقـواس ، نصها « الرزق على الله » ، كتبها الخطاط عبدالقادر .

Decorative Diwani script reading: *ar-Rizq 'ala Allah*—'Livelihood is from God', written by the calligrapher 'Abol al-Qadir. Persia, probably late 19th century.

be consumed in the fire of God's love; or he would see God in his unveiled perfection; or he would abandon himself and be filled with the glory of God. This last way—the bliss of abandonment—was often called 'intoxication', a dying-to-self: 'God should cause thee to die from thyself and to live in Him'.

The mystical journey was concerned with discarding the self, setting the disciple free from the bondage of desires, and purifying the will. He must learn self-abandonment so that he would be wholly pliant in the hands of God. Abu Said told his disciples that to be Sufis they must give up all worries and there was no worse worry than the feeling of 'I'. When the 'I' sensation occupied them, God could not and they were separated from Him. The way to God was but one step, he told them, the step out of themselves. When a man knew himself to be non-existent, he found God as his own being. And Mahmud Shabistari said:

'Who is the traveller on the road to God? It is that one who is aware of his own origin. He is the traveller who passes on speedily: he has become pure from self as flame from smoke. Go you, sweep out the dwelling-room of your heart, prepare it to be the abode and home of the Beloved: when you go out He will come in. Within you, when you are free from self, He will show his beauty. When you and your real self become pure from all defilement, there remains no distinction among things, the known and the Knower are all one.' [5]

DIVINE GRACE

All the accomplishments of the disciple in the seven stages of his journey were 'acquired', in the sense that the effort had been his—his had been the determination to purify himself by travelling the sevenfold path of repentance, abstinence, detachment, solitude, poverty, patience, and self-surrender. But when he was stripped of self and had become empty and receptive for the Divine Love, his own efforts were needed no longer. From then on, that Love was expressed in mystical graces which swept the traveller onward into deeper and deeper states of transcendental bliss.

I am silent. Speak Thou, O Soul of Soul of Soul,

From desire of whose Face every atom grew articulate. (Rumi) [6]

The Graces given by God were thought, by the Sufis, to be manifested in three ways. One way was by the heart, which knows God. Another was by the spirit, which loves God. And the third was by the inmost ground of the soul, which contemplates God. It was this third way which was experienced when the traveller gazed on His face—which turned out to be his own.

You name His name; go, seek the reality named by it!

Look for the moon in heaven, not in the water!

If you desire to rise above mere names and letters,

Make yourself free from self at one stroke!

Like a sword be without trace of soft iron;

Like a steel mirror, scour off all rust with contrition;

Make yourself pure from all attributes of self,

That you may see your own pure bright essence! (Rumi) [7]

The strange and wonderful power which draws the traveller ever onwards was thought to be one of the greatest mystical graces, for it can never be induced.

Planispheric astrolabe of cut and incised brass. Persia, 17th century.

A specimen of decoratively structured calligraphy mainly in Thuluth script, consisting of the names: Allah, Muhammad, 'Ali, Fatmah, Hasan and Husayn, by the calligrapher Husayn Husani. Persia, 1904.

Its creation is not within human understanding. Bayazid Bistami said:

'I fancied that I loved Him, . . . but on consideration I saw that His love preceded mine.' *[8]*

It was believed that God created the world in order that he should be known and *recognized* by the world, and man was thought to be the eye with which God sees himself. Man was thought to be the end-product of a great movement, the journey forth into the world of all the flow of creation, a journey called, by the Sufis, 'No God'. But man, as the culmination, is also the turning-point—the point at which the outward journey ends and the return journey begins, and this homeward voyage to the Source was called 'But God'. To know oneself returning to God was a mystical grace, and was closely connected with the belief in the cosmic progress of the soul. Rumi described it thus:

I died as mineral and became a plant,
I died as plant and rose to animal,
I died as animal and I was Man.
Why should I fear? When was I less by dying?
Yet once more I shall die as Man, to soar
With angels blest; but even from angelhood
I must pass on: *all except God doth perish.*
When I have sacrificed my angel-soul,

I shall become what no mind e'er conceived.

Oh, let me not exist! for Non-existence

Proclaims in organ tones. 'To Him we shall return.' *[9]*

One of the greatest mystical graces was Certainty. It was Divine Knowledge beyond all tremor of doubt. It was this knowledge of God which caused Mishkat al- Masabih to utter the following words, said to be God's:

'He who approaches near to Me one span, I will approach to him one cubit; and he who approaches near to Me one cubit, I will approach near to him one fathom; and whoever approaches Me walking, I will come to him running; and he who meets Me with sins equivalent to the whole world, I will greet him with forgiveness equal to it.' *[10]*

'Understand, therefore,' (said Ibn al-'Arabi) 'that the knower's knowledge of himself is God's knowledge of Himself, because his soul is nothing but He. . . . And whoever attains to this state, . . . his existence is the existence of God, and his word the word of God, and his act the act of God, and his claim to the knowledge of God is a claim to the knowledge of himself.' . . .

I know the Lord by the Lord, without doubt or wavering.

My essence is His essence in truth, without defect or flaw.

There is no becoming between these two and my soul it is which manifests that secret.

The mausoleum of 'Ali ibn Abi Talib, first Imam of Iraq, with decorative Arabic calligraphy in Thuluth script.

Alexander watching Elias and Khizr at the Waters of Life.

> And since I knew myself without blending or mixture,
> I attained to union with my Beloved, without far or near. *[11]*

The mystic knowledge of the Sufis is generally given the name of *gnosis*. It is the light of God, an illumination so penetrating that, like a sword, it severs the disciple's feeling of 'I' for ever, and from then on he is not he, but God. The Sufi believes that a man cannot know anything unless it is already within himself—he could not know God if God were not already there to be found in himself. Gnosis is the discovery that he is 'the eye of the world whereby God sees His own works.' In knowing God, he finds that he knows himself as he really is. He finds, as in the eastern religions, that there is no separate 'I'. Indeed, Sufis say that 'I' is merely a convenience and a figure of speech. All acts, words, feelings and thoughts are not 'mine' but God's. Man is created as an image of God, and all his attributes are God's attributes. 'Niffari heard the divine voice saying to him:

"When thou regardest thyself as existent and dost not regard Me as the Cause of thy existence, I veil My face and thine own face appears to thee. Therefore consider what is displayed to thee, and what is hidden from thee!" ' *[12]*
Gnosis is the realization that there is no 'other' in the world than the Oneness of God. What we take to be 'other' is an illusion. We ignorantly believe that differentiation is difference. 'The names are many, their underlying unity is the same' says Ibn al-'Arabi. He goes on to say: 'God is known by a particular name in a particular aspect: thus one aspect is said to be sky, another earth: the reality is the same in everything . . . extensions are different. The reality appears multitudinous on account of its aspects and their relationships, e.g. man is the same as horse in reality or essence: but different from it in its aspect or temperaments.

'Do not create a partner with God in existence; for there can be no division of existence into two. . . . All faces or aspects exhibit one single reality. Sin is the identification of an aspect with reality itself. . . .

'The true gnostic is one who sees every thing worshipped as a manifestation of God; hence every worshipped thing gets the name of *ilah* (God) besides its own name of stone, tree, animal, man or angel.' . . . *[13]*

And Abu al-Antākī says: 'Act, then, as if there were no one on earth but yourself and no one in Heaven but God.' *[14]*

THE PATH TO ECSTACY

Gnosis and love, spiritually the same for the Sufis, were the greatest goal, and the path to them was marked by heightened perceptions and deepening mystical grace. As with other religions, there were practices to be followed to help the disciple reach this goal. These practices were all-important to the Sufi experience —without them there was no progress along the path. For books may contain an inkling of reality but the blazing fire of Certainty comes only when 'a man's whole being is in a state of surrender to the Truth', and this condition could only be arrived at, for a Sufi, when he had been guided by a teacher and been trained in certain practices.

It is essential to the understanding of these practices to first look at the Sufi belief in Essence. Essence is what Buddhists term Suchness and Hindus Thatness. It is the inner reality, Being, the thing in itself, which can only be seen when all concepts about it have been dropped. The Sufi's quest was to discover his own Essence—his own Reality—what he was in himself. There is a Sufi saying, 'He who knows his essential self knows his God'. Sufis believed that man's Essence was hidden from him by veils of his own making, such as desire, hypocrisy, greed and sloth. Therefore, practical exercises were devised to remove these veils so that his Essence could shine forth in all its clear light to the disciple.

A *dervish* was the name given to a Sufi disciple, and the great Sufi teachers of the past had their own schools, founded on Orders of dervishes. When the disciple had been accepted by the master of a dervish Order, he had to start his training by becoming ready for new experiences, ones which his everyday mind would not be capable of accepting. These new experiences took the form of an awakening of five centres of illumination, called the *lataif* (singular *latifa*). The method for doing this was to concentrate his consciousness on certain places in

Majnun brought in chains before Laila.

The dance of the dervishes, a form of surrender to God.

Bowl in the form of a dervish's wallet. Watered steel, chased and engraved, Persia, 19th century.

the head and the body, each place being linked with a latifa. As his concentration penetrated that area, so the latifa was activated, and brought about a change of consciousness and·an expansion of the mind towards its Essence. In this way, the chains binding the disciple to habitual attitudes of mind were broken, and the disciple grew progressively freer to apprehend his Essence. The five centres, the activation of which was essential to the Sufi path, were the Heart, which was awakened by concentration on the area round the physical heart; the Spirit, on the side opposite to the heart; the Secret, exactly between the Heart and the Spirit; the Mysterious, in the forehead; and the Deeply Hidden, in the brain.

Sometimes activation of one of these areas occurs without special preparation. While gazing at an object, *without any purpose in mind*, it is possible to feel an extraordinary sense of communication with it, seeming to emerge from one's forehead; a feeling of expansion, almost as though the bones have been moved aside. Sufi teachers were aware that 'accidental' awakenings occurred but pointed out that unless the other centres were activated too, the subject could not obtain a total awakening; this one illumination would lead to nothing on its own.

At the same time as activation of the lataif, the student also learnt to recognize the effect of this activation on all the many strands of his personality. He had to learn the difficult truth, central to other religions also, that his feeling of 'I' was not based on a real entity but on a shifting sea of sense-impressions and their accompanying thoughts, the movement of which is so rapid as to be indistinguishable to the conscious mind, as the moving sequence of stills of which a film is composed is indistinguishable to the man watching the film, and as the perpetual movement of atoms comprising a 'solid' body cannot be seen by the naked eye. He had to learn that he was not one person but many, his moods and imaginings having created all his 'veils'. As his teacher helped him to see these aspects of himself in the light of the lataif illumination, so the illumination itself was reinforced and integrated with the changes occurring to him.

Breathing techniques, such as keeping the breath in one place, varied from Order to Order; as did exercises of movement, such as the *ist* exercise, where all movement had to freeze when the teacher called 'Halt'. The effect of the continual interruptions of movement was the shattering of old habits of thought, a similar effect to that arising from the Zen master's physical shaking of his pupil.

A widespread exercise was *zikr*, the repetition of a devout incantation, or one of the Beautiful Names of God. There are ninety-nine of these names to correspond to the Sufi rosary, and the practice of zikr was not a meaningless repetition but an intense invocation, with all the student's attention centred on the spiritual meaning of the phrase or name, until all it implied took possession of him, forcing his usual thoughts away. This practice might be done by a group, or alone. Zikr is sometimes translated as 'remembrance', for it is in the act of true 'remembering' that the one who remembers is transmuted into the One remembered. For as the zikr practice becomes firmly rooted, it begins to lift the heart upwards towards God and when this happens, the tongue ceases and the heart continues until perfection is reached. The heart was considered to be the centre of the first inner perceptions as they arose.

Poetry, music and dancing were also used as means to open up the lataif, and when all five centres were illumined, the goal of the dervish training took place—

A modern dervish of the Rel Moha Order.

the ecstasy of annihilation in God, called *fana*. Although there were still three more states for the Sufi to enter, these were beyond the teaching, and thus ecstasy became the much sought after dervish goal. Jalaludin Rumi, a great thirteenth-century Sufi poet and teacher, initiated the Order of Whirling Dervishes, his dervishes coming to ecstasy by way of a dance, the exact movements of which were not known outside the Sufi world. The dance, still practised today, is based on the movements of the planets round the sun. Each dervish rotates, using certain steps and beginning slowly. The direction he takes while revolving is one of the secrets of the dance. The speed of the rotations gradually increases until the whole group, in their specially voluminous skirts, is a swirl of rapid circling movement. The dance continues, faster and faster, perhaps for hours, until the dervishes individually fall into a trance of ecstasy and 'pass away into God'.

Outwardly (says Rumi) 'we are ruled by the stars, but our inward nature has become the ruler of the skies.

Therefore, while in form thou art the microcosm, in reality thou art the macrocosm.' [15]

The dance is thus designed to transport the dervish from outer delusion to inner reality, from the misunderstanding that he is the microcosm to the moment of bliss when he realizes that in truth there is only the macrocosm.

The passion and secrecy of the dance was expressed by Rumi in his poem *The Soul of the World*:

> I have circled awhile with the Nine Fathers in each Heaven.
> For years I have revolved with the stars in their signs.
> I was invisible awhile, I was dwelling with Him.
> I was in the Kingdom of '*or nearer*', I saw what I have seen.
> I receive my nourishment from God as a child in the womb;
> Man is born once, I have been born many times.
> Clothed in a bodily mantle, I have busied myself with affairs,
> And often have I rent the mantle with my own hands.
> . . . I am both cloud and rain: I have rained on the meadows.
> Never did the dust of mortality settle on my skirt, O dervish!
> I have gathered a wealth of roses in the garden of Eternity.
> I am not of water nor fire, I am not of the froward wind,
> I am not of moulded clay: I have mocked them all.
> O son, . . . I am the Pure Light.
> If thou seest me, beware! Tell not anyone what thou hast seen! [16]

In the above poem, the use of both symbolism and a secret mystical language can be seen. Many Sufis believed that the language of a mystic could only be understood by another mystic, and many words came to have hidden meanings known only to the dervishes. Mathematics and astronomy were used in the secret language, and the number seven was thought to have special significance. R. A. Nicholson, who translated Rumi's poems, tells us that 'the *seven* Fathers' was often used to describe the planets, each of which was supposed to have a ruling intelligence, which gave it the name of 'Father'. Rumi has raised the number to nine by perhaps adding the Head and Tail of the 'Dragon' of astrology, but there may be an even deeper explanation of the number nine in the poem. 'Man is born once, I have been born many times' means that the ordinary body is born only once, but the mystic who has identified himself with the World-Spirit, is manifested over and over again, evolving upwards from plant life until he manifests finally and completely in the Perfect Man.

The Persian reed flute was the instrument mainly used for Rumi's dance of the Whirling Dervishes. In his most famous poem, Rumi uses the flute as a symbol for the soul which is now emptied of self and one with the Divine Spirit. This soul, while on earth, yearns for the return to the embrace of God and for the final and permanent loss of self into Self.

The Song of the Reed

Hearken to this Reed forlorn,
Breathing, ever since 'twas torn
From its rushy bed, a strain
Of impassioned love and pain.

'The secret of my song, though near,
None can see and none can hear.
Oh, for a friend to know the sign
And mingle all his soul with mine!

'Tis the flame of Love that fired me,
'Tis the wine of Love inspired me.
Wouldst thou learn how lovers bleed,
Hearken, hearken to the Reed!' *[17]*

After he had attained the ineffable state of fana, the dervish still had three more stages to reach. The first was the stabilization into a steady and permanent equilibrium of all his understanding. In future, he would cease being 'intoxicated' and would become the Perfect Man, a teacher and a point of magnetism towards which all might turn for help and knowledge. This development, the return to the world as a perfected human, is considered the proper result of true mystical experience in most religions.

The dervish's next stage was a refinement of the last. He was now so detached from the world and so much his own master that he was no longer bound by the framework of his own culture. With an intuitive 'feel' for all people, he was able to give the teaching necessary for anyone's potential understanding. Because of this he might appear differently to different men, as Idries Shah's story, *Three Visits to a Sage*, illustrates:

'Bahaudin Naqshband was visited by a group of seekers.

They found him in his courtyard, surrounded by disciples, in the midst of what seemed obviously to be revels.

Some of the newcomers said:

"How obnoxious—this is no way to behave, whatever the pretext." They tried to remonstrate with the master.

Others said:

"This seems to us excellent—we like this kind of teaching, and wish to take part in it."

Yet others said:

"We are partly perplexed and wish to know more about this puzzle."

The remainder said to one another:

"There may be some wisdom in this, but whether we should ask about it or not we do not know."

The teacher sent them all away.

And all these people spread, in conversation and in writing, their opinions of the occasion. Even those who did not allude to their experience directly were affected by it, and their speech and works reflected their beliefs about it.

Some time later certain members of this party again passed that way. They called upon the teacher.

Standing at his door, they noticed that within the courtyard he and his disciples now sat, decorously, deep in contemplation.

"When a man is working, he does not always explain himself to casual visitors, however interested the visitors may think themselves to be. When an action is in progress, what counts is the correct operation of that action. Under these circumstances, external evaluation becomes a secondary concern".' *[18]*

At the end of the third stage, the dervish, now the Perfect Man, was able to guide those who were dying to another stage of their development, as the lama guides the dying and the dead in Tibetan Buddhism. Rumi gave the outline of man's soul development in the following poem:

The Progress of Man
First he appeared in the realm inanimate;
Thence came into the world of plants and lived
The plant-life many a year, nor called to mind

A mosque–lamp inscribed with a dedication to the Sultan Baybars II, and around the neck three verses from the Koran. Glass enamelled and gilt, Syria, 14th century.

What he had been; then took the onward way
To animal existence, and once more
Remembers naught of the life vegetative.
Save when he feels himself moved with desire
Towards it in the season of sweet flowers,
As babes that seek the breast and know not why.

Again the wise Creator whom thou knowest
Uplifted him from animality
To Man's estate; and so from realm to realm
Advancing, he became intelligent,
Cunning and keen of wit, as he is now.
No memory of his past abides with him,
And from his present soul he shall be changed.

Though he is fallen asleep, God will not leave him
In this forgetfulness. Awakened, he
Will laugh to think what troublous dreams he had,
And wonder how his happy state of being
He could forget and not perceive that all
Those pains and sorrows were the effect of sleep
And guile and vain illusion. So this world
Seems lasting, though 'tis but the sleeper's dream;
Who, when the appointed Day shall dawn, escapes
From dark imaginings that haunted him,
And turns with laughter on his phantom griefs
When he beholds his everlasting home. [19]

A dervish bowl carved from pear-wood or box-wood by the inhabitants of Abadeh. Persia, 19th century.

Alexander the Great of Macedon visiting a hermit.

THE HIDDEN TEACHING

The dervish schools were restricted to those who had a genuine and unshakeable desire to surrender themselves to God; and the capacity and intention of a would-be disciple was well tested before he was accepted into a school. But there were many men who wished for teaching, although they were not able to undertake the dervish training. One of the outstanding gifts of the Sufis was to present the teaching in such a way that its meaning was available to all people according to their capacity, and the form they used was the short, sharp story.

Symbolic illustration of two dervishes who had been imprisoned as suspected spies: one was strong, the other weak and after some days in their walled prison, the 'stronger' had died.

Dervishes dancing outside Sa'di's tomb.

The early teachers left a rich heritage of stories and parables, to be used both for the dervish at all stages of his training, and for the ordinary man, whose enquiry would be still bound by conventional habits of thought. Thus many stories, apparently merely light and witty, contain a secret impact, the strength of which varies according to the hearer's receptivity.

One of the most famous is about four men—a Persian, a Turk, an Arab and a Greek—who were standing in a village street. They were travelling companions, making for some distant place: but at this moment they were arguing over the spending of a single piece of money which was all that they had among them.

' "I want to buy *angur*," said the Persian.

"I want *uzum*," said the Turk.

"I want *inab*," said the Arab.

"No!" said the Greek, "we should buy *stafil*."

'Another traveller passing, a linguist, said, "Give the coin to me. I undertake to satisfy the desires of all of you."

يـاسَرِیٰ'ڈه

Elegant Ta'liq script, reading *Hada min Fadl Rabbi*—'This is from the favour of my lord'. It was produced by Yasari Zadah in the late 18th century.

'At first they would not trust him. Ultimately they let him have the coin. He went to the shop of a fruit seller and bought four small bunches of grapes.

"This is my *angur*," said the Persian.

"But this is what I call *uzum*," said the Turk.

"You have brought me *inab*," said the Arab.

"No!" said the Greek, "this in my language is *stafil*".'

The grapes were shared out among them, and each realized that the disharmony had been due to his faulty understanding of the language of the others.

The true meaning, according to the teaching, is that 'the travellers are the ordinary people of the world. The linguist is the Sufi. People know that they want something, because there is an inner need existing in them. They may give it different names, but it is the same thing. Those who call it religion have different names for it, and even different ideas as to what it might be. Those who call it ambition try to find its scope in different ways. But it is only when a linguist appears, someone who knows what they really mean, that they can stop the struggling and get on with eating the grapes.'

Idries Shah tells us that 'the Sufi speaks of wine, the product of the grape, and its secret potential, as his means of attaining "inebriation". The grape is seen as the raw form of the wine. Grapes, then, mean ordinary religion; while wine is the real essence of the fruit. The travellers are therefore seen to be four ordinary people, differing in religion. The Sufi shows them that the basis of their religions is in fact the same. He does not, however, offer them wine, the essence, which is the inner doctrine waiting to be produced and used in mysticism, a field far more developed than mere organized religion. That is a further stage. But the Sufi's role as a servant of humanity is brought out by the fact that, although he is operating on a higher level, he helps the formal religionist as far as he can, by showing him the fundamental identity of religious faith. He might, of course, have gone on to a discussion of the merits of wine; but what the travellers wanted was grapes, and grapes they were given. When the wrangling over

A dervish watching a prince with his pigeons.

Infatuation of a dervish for a prince.

smaller issues subsides, according to the Sufi, the greater teaching may be imparted. Meanwhile, some sort of primary lesson has been given.' *[20]*

Another famous story is that of the elephant felt in the dark. Rumi tells it thus:

The One True Light

The lamps are different, but the Light is the same: it comes from Beyond.

If thou keep looking at the lamp, thou art lost: for thence arises the appearance of number and plurality.

Fix thy gaze upon the Light, and thou art delivered from the dualism inherent in the finite body.

O thou who art the kernel of Existence, the disagreement between Moslem, Zoroastrian and Jew depends on the standpoint.

Some Hindus brought an elephant, which they exhibited in a dark shed.

As seeing it with the eye was impossible, every one felt it with the palm of his hand.

Dervishes dancing outside Sa'di's tomb.

The hand of one fell on its trunk: he said, 'This animal is like a
   water-pipe.'
Another touched its ear: to him the creature seemed like a fan.

Another handled its leg and described the elephant as having the
   shape of a pillar.
Another stroked its back. 'Truly,' said he, 'this elephant resembles
   a throne.'
Had each of them held a lighted candle, there would have been no
   contradiction in their words. [21]

The meaning of this story suggests that the intellect, full of preconceptions
which set it to groping about in the dark, can never see the full reality of God.
Only he with a lighted candle, the mystic whose self has been replaced by the
illumination of God, can see things as they really are. Each Hindu felt one part of
the elephant and thought that his part was the whole—as we each see only part of
existence and think our part the whole. Groping in the dark, we do not realize
that God's illumination would give us light to see it in its totality.

A third teaching story is *The Indian Bird*, by Rumi, translated by Idries Shah:
' A merchant had a bird in a cage. He was going to India, the land from which
the bird came, and asked whether he could bring anything back for him. The
bird asked for his freedom, but was refused. So he asked the merchant to visit a
jungle in India and announce his captivity to the free birds who were there.

'The merchant did so, and no sooner had he spoken than a wild bird, just like
his own, fell senseless out of a tree on to the ground. The merchant thought that
this must be a relative of his own bird, and felt sad that he should have caused
this death.

'When he got home, the bird asked him whether he had brought good news
from India. "No," said the merchant. "I fear that my news is bad. One of your
relations collapsed and fell at my feet as soon as I mentioned your captivity."

'As soon as these words were spoken, the merchant's bird collapsed and fell to
the bottom of the cage.

' "The news of his kinsman's death has killed him too," thought the merchant.
Sorrowfully he picked up the bird and put it on the window-sill. At once the
bird revived and flew to a nearby tree. "Now you know," he said, "that what
you thought was disaster was in fact good news for me. And that the message,
the suggestion how to behave in order to free myself, was transmitted to me
through you, my captor." And he flew away, free at last.' [22]

At first sight, this is merely a clever story. But more deeply, it shows how the
teaching of the Sufis—the free birds—could reach one of their number in whatever country or condition. Even the most unlikely event (the merchant) could
convey the truth, if the recipient could understand its meaning. The meaning, in
this story, is that to be free one must appear to die—the death of the self.

Humour becomes a good teacher when it breaks down the barriers of social
distinction and conventional thought. A character devised by the Sufis to
penetrate all the Middle East was Mulla (Master) Nasrudin, a sometimes dis-
reputable, sometimes saintly character, immensely human, whose encounters
with the world were told in many stories which always had a twist in the tail.

For instance, to illustrate the belief that a person is not one single, independent entity but is really a multitude of 'faces' according to mood and circumstance, the following story is told:

The Mulla walked into a shop one day.

The owner came forward to serve him.

'First things first,' said Nasrudin; 'did you see me walk into your shop?'

'Of course.'

'Have you ever seen me before?'

'Never in my life.'

'Then how do you know it is *me*?' *[23]*

The theme of the interdependence of all manifestations is a vitally important one, which occurs in most religions. When the feeling of 'I' has gone, it can be seen that the personality of the whole world is one's own, rather in the way that the physical elements of the world can be found in one's body. When there is no barrier of 'I', my beauty is in another's face and my sorrow in another's desolation; all the events of the world happen to me because the world *is* me. The eminent biophysisist, Erwin Schrodinger, says something similar when he puts it thus: 'It is not possible that this unity of knowledge, feeling and choice which you call *your own* should have sprung into being from nothingness at a given moment not so long ago; rather this knowledge, feeling and choice are essentially eternal and unchangeable and numerically *one* in all men, nay in all sensitive beings. But not in *this* sense—that *you* are a part, a piece, of an eternal, infinite being, an aspect or modification of it, . . . For we should have the same baffling question: which part, which aspect are *you*? What, objectively, differentiates it from others? No, but inconceivable as it seems to ordinary reason, you —and all other conscious beings as such—are all in all. Hence this life of yours which you are living is not merely a piece of the entire existence, but is in a certain sense the *whole*; only this whole is not so constituted that it can be surveyed in one single glance.' *[24]*

'My heart has become capable of every form,' said Ibn al-'Arabi. *[25]*

Qur'anic verse on faience decoration for a window in Sultan Fatih Mosque, written in Thuluth Jali script. Persia, 1470.

The story about Nasrudin told by the Sufis to illustrate this point is deceptively simple, but speaks its message clearly when the truth is perceived.

'One day Nasrudin was walking along a deserted road. Night was falling as he spied a troop of horsemen coming towards him. His imagination began to work, and he feared that they might rob him, or impress him into the army. So strong did this fear become that he leaped over a wall and found himself in a graveyard. The other travellers, innocent of any such motive as had been assumed by Nasrudin, became curious and pursued him.

'When they came upon him lying motionless, one said, "Can we help you— why are you here in this position?"

'Nasrudin, realising his mistake, said, "It is more complicated than you assume. You see, *I* am here because of *you*; and you, *you* are here because of *me*".' *[26]*

Many dervish stories were studied in groups and were designed for that purpose, although they could also be understood in solitude. One such is

The Caravanserai

Once Khidr went to the king's palace and made his way right up to the throne. Such was the strangeness of his appearance that none dared to stop him.

The king, who was Ibrahim ben Adam, asked him what he was looking for.

The visitor said:

'I am looking for a sleeping place in this caravanserai.'

Ibrahim answered:

'This is no caravanserai, this is my palace.'

The stranger said:

'Whose was it before you?'

'My father's,' said Ibrahim.

'And before that?'

'My grandfather's.'

'And this place, where people come and go, staying and moving on, you call other than a caravanserai?' *[27]*

This illustrates the theme, common to all religions, that the world is not to be clung to as a permanent reality, in the way that the king clung to the idea of his palace. To Khidr, finding a sleeping place was the next action in his life and he was not concerned about its name, for the world of names no longer had meaning for him. He knew that the magnificence of the palace belonged only to the relative and fleeting world, and therefore its riches meant nothing to him. Nor did the title of the king. But Ibrahim, bound by ideas of past and future, and tied to concepts of rich and poor, good and bad, could not understand him.

The way in which people in search of truth sometimes limit themselves by concepts of what they expect to find, and then feel disillusioned when the truth fails to fit their idea of it, is shown in this group-study text.

The Way In Which They Bring Their Teaching

Do not expect the way in which they bring their teaching to be wholly within your ordinary way of understanding. A pearl may be carried in a leather purse. The ignorant cry out: 'This square object with a flap does not look like the necklace which has been described to me.' *[28]*

Alexander the Great and a hermit.

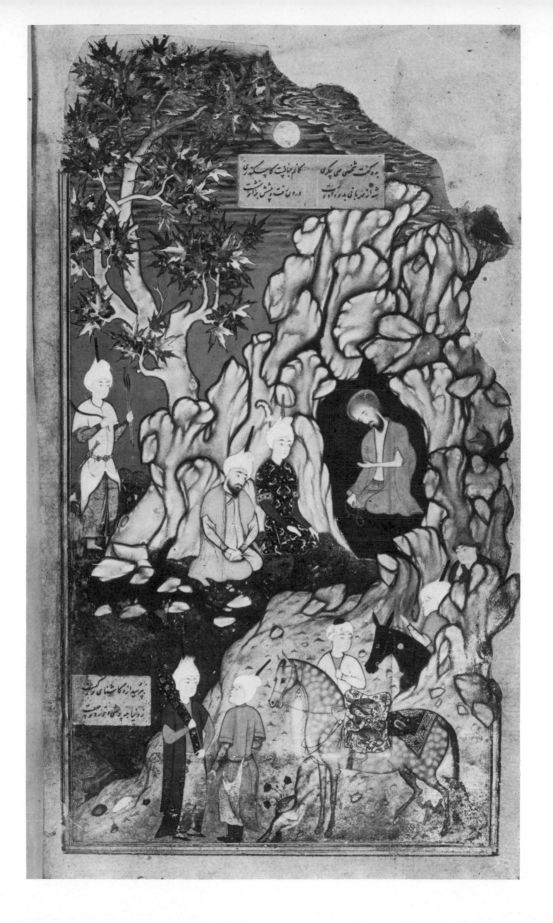

A steel panel pierced with a religious inscription, said to be from the tomb of Isma'il, the first Safavi Shah of Persia. Persia, early 16th century.

The same theme is echoed in:

Symptoms

One man has a headache, another blurred vision.

Both are caused by the wrong food.

Say: 'Your digestion is upset', and both will reply: 'Away, fool! We seek relief to head and eye, not absurdity.' *[29]*

The Sufi understanding that the whole material world is, mysteriously, the workings of God and nothing but God, was described by Ibn Arabi, when he said: 'God does not create anything. Creation means simply the coming into concrete existence of something already existing in God.' This theme is expanded by Sheikh Ismail Hakki in the following study-group advice:

Remembering

Everything is dependent upon remembering. One does not begin by learning, one starts by remembrance. The distance of eternal existence and the difficulties of life cause one to forget.

It is for this reason God has commanded us:

'Remember!' *[30]*

THE SUFIS TODAY

Sufis consider Sufism to be not so much a separate religion as the essence of all religions, expressing itself particularly through poetry, music, and healing. Because of this informal approach, Sufi groups tend to come together for a purpose, such as spiritual healing, and then to dissolve when that purpose has been fulfilled. They do not create organizations as such, and any group structure which continues to exist after the work of the group has been accomplished will be an empty shell—the Sufi life will have fled and be manifesting itself elsewhere This gives the whole Sufi movement an organic, continually creative and flexible composition, unlike the usual western organizations which follow a more formal pattern. Sufism has penetrated Europe and America widely but because it never advertises or announces itself in any way, it is an elusive movement to find.

One of the main founders of the Sufi movement in the West was Inayat Khan, who came from India in 1910. He went to the United States first and then proceeded to France and Russia before coming to England. He left disciples in all countries and the Sufi message became well established.

The followers of Inayat Khan believe that all religions are theirs. They study with equal devotion the Bible, Vedanta, the Koran, and the Kabala, as well as religious thought from many other sources. They do not consider themselves separate in any way from other people or groups. As Inayat Khan himself says:

'It should be now clear that Sufism does not add another community to the numbers of castes and creeds which already exist. Any person can study Sufism, and make use of it for guidance in daily life, without discarding his existing associations with other communities. As he perceives the underlying wisdom, he perceives also that he is related to every other community, and is at one with them in the path of love and light.' [31]

A tile from the mosque at Meshed. Decorated in relief and painted in lustre and blue, Persia, early 13th century.

To be initiated into the Inayat Khan Sufi Order, it is necessary to agree with Sufi teachings and aims; to cease attaching importance to differences between religions, and to see the embodiment of the Divine Spirit in the great masters of all creeds. One may then find a teacher (*murshid*) who will guide one towards the realization of the self, and the knowledge of God. The initiate becomes a Disciple when he has a teacher, and should adopt a way of life which is reserved, somewhat solitary, unassuming, pure, and diligent. Inayat Khan particularly warns his followers against 1. 'wonder-working'—claiming to know or possess something not common to all people; 2. communicating with spirits; 3. telling a person's character, and general fortune-telling; 4. showing oneself to be over-wise in conversation with others about spiritual things, and looking to others for approbation. One should look for and contemplate the love, harmony and beauty to be seen in the universe. Music, for many Sufis, is the finest expression of true harmony and of this Inayat Khan says:

'It is owing to our limitations that we cannot see the whole being of God; but all that we love in colour, line, form or personality belongs to the real beauty, the Beloved of all. And when we trace what attracts us in this beauty which we see in all forms, we shall find that it is the *movement* of beauty; in other words the music. All forms of nature, for instance the flowers, are perfectly formed and coloured; the planets and stars, the earth, all give the idea of harmony, of music. The whole of nature is breathing; not only the living creatures but all nature; and it is only our tendency to compare that which seems living with what to us is not so living which makes us forget that all things and beings are living one perfect life. And the sign of life given by this living beauty is music.' [32]

Music is also closely connected by Inayat Khan with the sound vibrations of the mantra, and the Sufi practice of *zikr* (see p. 222) is similar to the mantra in its opening effect. Sound and colour are the means by which we communicate with the outer world and therefore, to the followers of Inayat Khan, it is essential that there should be harmony in the colours and sounds around them. But whereas colour is connected with forms, and poetry has names and words suggestive of forms, music alone can raise the soul beyond form.

As well as Inayat Khan, there have been other Sufi leaders in the West, and prominent among these today is Idries Shah. He lives in London and is the author of many clear and authoritative books about the Sufis. On Sufism, he says:

'Sufism is engaged upon developing a line of communication with ultimate knowledge. . . . It is eastern thought only insofar as it retains beliefs which have fallen into abeyance in the west. It is occult and mystical inasmuch as it follows a path other than that which has been represented as the true one by authoritarian and dogmatic organisation. . . . Sufi mysticism differs tremendously from other cults claiming to be mystical. Formal religion is for the Sufi merely a shell, though a genuine one, which fulfils a function. When the human consciousness has penetrated beyond this social framework, the Sufi understands the real meaning of religion. The mystics of other persuasions do not think in this manner at all. They may transcend outer religious forms, but they do not emphasise the fact that outer religion is only a prelude to special experience. Most ecstatics remain attached to a rapturous symbolization of some concept derived from their religion. The Sufi uses religion and psychology to pass beyond all this. Having

Dervishes dancing.

done so, he "returns to the world", to guide others on the way.' [33]

   Several writers in the West appear to have been influenced by Sufi ideas. A recent writer, whose books are widely read, is Kahlil Gibran (1883–1931). Born on Mount Lebanon, Gibran spent much of his life in America and wrote many of his books there. He taught through verse, as is also the Sufi custom. His best-known book is *The Prophet*, in which he expounds many aspects of life. On Teaching, he says this:

> Then said a Teacher, Speak to us of Teaching.
>
> And he said:
>
> No man can reveal to you aught but that which already lies half asleep in the dawning of your knowledge.
>
> The teacher who walks in the shadow of the temple, among his followers, gives not of his wisdom but rather of his faith and lovingness. If he is indeed wise he does not bid you enter the house of his wisdom, but rather leads you to the threshold of your own mind.
>
> The astronomer may speak to you of his understanding of space, but he cannot give you his understanding.
>
> The musician may sing to you of the rhythm which is in all space, but he cannot give you the ear which arrests the rhythm nor the voice that echoes it.
>
> And he who is versed in the science of numbers can tell of the regions of weight and measure, but he cannot conduct you thither.
>
> For the vision of one man lends not its wings to another man.
>
> And even as each one of you stands alone in God's knowledge, so must each one of you be alone in his knowledge of God and in his understanding of the earth. *[34]*

A LAST LOOK

'That art thou' says Hinduism. Only *That*, the transcendent, completely other, is. Only *That* can manifest Itself as the myriad 'thous' of the world without Itself being altered by the 'thou' which It manifests. This is the great principle which underlies the religions in this book. 'According to Eastern traditions, I am' says Douglas Harding '—so to speak—an onion. The outer skin of the onion is this body, its inner skins are successive layers of mind and feeling, and its core is Nothing—Nothing but Consciousness. I *am* this core: the onion is what I *have*. I'm not what I'm aware of, but what's aware. My task is to peel the onion, skin by skin, till this core of Awareness is exposed. This alone is my Self. This alone is without qualities, unchanging, free, unaffected by anything whatsoever, indestructible, real. To *see* this is to be Enlightened.'

The ways to find the core of the onion are what this book has been about and they are as varied as the cultures and historical eras from which they sprang.

Hinduism, the oldest of all, evolved through many centuries. It has been said that in India all thought is religious thought, and for the Hindu the whole point and reason for living is to discover that his inmost self is the Self, the very heart of God. When a man says 'I am God' in India, his friends congratulate him for having discovered the truth. We have looked at the ways in which the Hindu searches for this truth—using his mind to discriminate between what is eternal and what is perishable in Jnana Yoga; giving himself up in devotion to That when he practises Bhakti Yoga; losing himself in service to others in Karma Yoga; the powerful quest for all the layers of himself in Raja Yoga; spiritualizing his body in Tantric Yoga; and the stilling of his chattering mind through the sound vibration of mantras.

How many of these practices formed the basic training for other, later religions? The Buddha, born and brought up as a Hindu, naturally meditated a great deal. It is said that he continued to do so all his life, believing that it was necessary even for the Enlightened. He discarded the ascetic practices of the yogis, however, and also refused to let his monks seek supernatural powers, pursue speculation about God or other worlds, or practise ritual. Throwing away Hindu theology, he pared religion to the bone, telling his questioners to find out for themselves by direct experience. For only through complete awareness and mindfulness would they begin to understand the relationship between cause and effect that creates what we regard as existence.

We have seen how the Theravadins, taking the Buddha's words very literally, established an austere school of practical Buddhism in the countries of South Asia, developing his teaching on mindfulness as an essential part of their training, spending many years in meditation, and having as their ideal the Arhat, the Enlightened One who, having clearly seen that there is no permanence or self anywhere and having overcome all his desires, enters Nirvana, never to return to this world of suffering.

At the same time, in the north, the followers of Mahayana were making the Bodhisattva their ideal, the Enlightened One who is so filled with compassion for the world that he returns again and again until the last person on earth is enlightened. The tantric practices of Tibetan Buddhism, with their emphasis on colour and sound and an impressive array of incarnate deities, seems much more like devotional Hinduism than the austere Buddhism of the Theravadins. And yet the strange thing is that Buddhism keeps its unity and both schools complement each other. For both have in common the Buddha's greatest teaching, his basic intuition of the Void. Theravada says that everything changes but behind all change is the Void—the unchanging. Mahayana says that all things are in themselves void, that voidness is their nature. Here, too, is Vedanta, the essence of Hinduism, which tells us of 'That which knows no differentiation or death . . . which is eternally free and indivisible'.

Zen grew out of the profound wisdom of the Tao and out of Buddhism brought by Indians to China. The merging of the two created a uniquely Chinese form of Buddhism. Indeed the Tao, or the Way, is just a Chinese word for the Void of Buddhism and the That of Hinduism: but with the difference that the Tao is *This*—here and now—the true nature of everything—and it was this immediacy that brought about the inspired insights of the Chinese Zen Masters and, later, their Japanese successors. Hui-Neng and his followers developed their koans some thousand years after the Buddha died, but to many Buddhists, Zen, with its constant admonitions to experience life directly without the intervention of thought, has more in common with the Buddha's teaching than either the Theravada of Burma, Thailand and Ceylon, or the Mahayana of Tibet. In Zen there is no speculation, there are no deities. The content of life itself is the teaching and to see life as Void and thus attain satori is the aim of the tough Zen training which, nowadays, includes much meditation as well as rigorous work on koans.

Lastly, and historically the most recent, come the Sufis—Islamic desert wanderers from a culture totally different to the Chinese or the Tibetans, but close in thought to the Hindus. What is their link? It is that of self-naughting, joyful surrender to God, the small self merged in the Self, the Beloved, so that the separate individual ego disappears. When Rumi says: 'In me there is Another by whom these eyes sparkle' he is expressing 'That art thou'. The Sufis, through the medium of Moghul India, absorbed many Hindu influences while, to the general eastern path, they added their own special understanding.

Perhaps the essential nature of all these journeys to Reality may be summed up thus:

'What is the goal of this process?'
'Realising the Real.'
'What is the nature of Reality?'
'(a) Existence without beginning or end—eternal.
 (b) Existence everywhere, endless—infinite.
 (c) Existence underlying all forms, all changes, all forces, all matter, all
     spirit.
The many change and pass away, whereas the One always endures.'
(Ramana Maharshi) *[11]*

ACKNOWLEDGEMENTS

Acknowledgements are due to the following for permission to reproduce photographs:

HINDUISM

The Philadelphia Museum of Art, Philadelphia, photographs by A. J. Wyatt Staff Photographer; pages, 12, 27, 42.
The Metropolitan Museum of Art, New York; pages, 14, 32 left, 37, 59.

The Gulbenkian Museum of Oriental Art, Durham, England; pages, 15, 20, 23, 40, 44, 60, 69.
The Victoria and Albert Museum, London; pages, 16, 26, 29, 31, 32 right, 41, 46, 52, 54, 64, 66.
Light on Yoga by B. K. S. Iyengar published by George Allen and Unwin, London; pages, 18, 35.
The Ashmolean Museum, Oxford; pages, 19, 33, 47 left, 56, 57, 67.
The Smithsonian Institution, Freer Gallery of Art, Washington, D.C.; page, 24.

The Royal Scottish Museum, Edinburgh, photographs by Tom Scott; page, 25.
The Venerable Maha Srhavira Sangharakshita; pages, 38, 40.
Jean-Claude Ciancimino, photographs by Cuming Wright Watson Associates, London; pages, 47 right, 48.
Barnabys Picture Library, London; pages, 51, 62, 70.
Ramana Maharshi and the Path of Self-Knowledge by A. Osborne published by Rider & Company, London; page, 58.

BUDDHISM

The Metropolitan Museum of Art, New York; pages, 74, 77, 82, 103.
The Smithsonian Institution, Freer Gallery of Art, Washington, D.C.; pages, 75, 84, 104.
The Philadelphia Museum of Art, Philadelphia; photographs by A. J. Wyatt Staff Photographer; page, 95.
The Ashmolean Muscum, Oxford; pages, 78, 90 left.
The Venerable Maha Srhavira Sangharakshita; pages, 79, 80, 85 right, 93, 98 left, 102.
The Victoria and Albert Museum, London; pages, 85 left, 88, 92, 97.
Barnabys Picture Library, London; pages, 87, 100.
The Royal Scottish Museum, Edinburgh; pages, 90 right, 94, 101.
Anne Vickers Associates, London; page, 91.
The Museum Yamato Bunkakan, Nara, Japan; page, 98 right.
The Gulbenkian Museum of Oriental Art, Durham, England; page, 105.

TIBETAN BUDDHISM

The Victoria and Albert Museum, London; pages, 110, 112, 121 right, 122, 128 left, 133, 134 left.
The Victoria and Albert Museum, London; photograph by Peter Wren Howard; page, 137.
Philip Goldman, photographs supplied by the Arts Council of Great Britain, London; pages, 111, 134 right.
Gallery 43, photograph supplied by the Arts Council of Great Britain, London; page, 127 left.
John Dugger and David Medalla, photograph supplied by the Arts Council of Great Britain, London; page, 131 left.
The Venerable Maha Srhavira Sangharakshita; pages, 112, 116.
The Royal Scottish Museum, Edinburgh; page, 113.
The Radio Times Hulton Picture Library, London; page, 114.
The Gulbenkian Museum of Oriental Art, Durham, England; pages, 115, 118, 119, 125.
Barnabys Picture Library, London; page, 121 left.

City of Liverpool Museums, Liverpool; page, 123.
The Ashmolean Museum, Oxford; pages, 127 right, 128 right, 129, 131 right.

ZEN BUDDHISM

Japan Information Centre, London; pages, 142, 153, 154, 161, 165, 175.
Private Collection, photograph by C. H. Cannings; page, 143.
The Idemitsu Art Gallery, Tokyo; pages, 144, 156 above, 157, 159 right, 171 left and centre.
The Museum Yamato Bunkakan, Nara, Japan; pages, 145 left, 171 right.
Barnabys Picture Library, London; pages, 145 right, 155, 156 below, 163.
The Victoria and Albert Museum, London; pages, 146, 151, 159 left, 169 right, 176.
The British Museum, London; page, 148 both pictures.
The Japanese National Tourist Organization, London; pages, 150, 167, 180.
The Gulbenkian Museum of Oriental Art, Durham, England; page, 152 left.
The Buddhist Society, London, photographs by Fred Dustin; pages, 152 right, 153.
The Ashmolean Museum, Oxford; pages, 169 left, 179.
Trevor Leggett; page, 172.
Terry Dukes; page, 173.

TAOISM

The Idemitsu Art Gallery, Tokyo; page, 182.
The Victoria and Albert Museum, London; pages, 184, 186, 192, 193, 201 left, 202, 204, 206, 208.
The Ashmolean Museum, Oxford; pages, 185, 197.
The Museum Yamato Bunkakan, Nara, Japan; page, 189 both pictures, 199 right, 203.
The British Museum, London; pages, 190, 191 both pictures, 199 left, 207.
The Gulbenkian Museum of Oriental Art, Durham, England; page, 201 right.
The Royal Scottish Museum, Edinburgh; page, 205.

SUFISM

The British Museum, London; pages, 210, 212, 213, 215, 216, 217, 218, 220, 226, 228, 229, 230, 231, 232, 233, 235, 237, 241.
The Victoria and Albert Museum, London; pages, 214, 221, 225, 227, 238, 239.
The Radio Times Hulton Picture Library, London; page, 222.

Endpapers: painted tanka in the form of four mandalas, Tibet, 15th century. The Victoria and Albert Museum, Crown Copyright, London.

GLOSSARY

AHIMSA (Jain): The practice of non-violence, resulting in an extreme form of reverence for life.

AJIVA (Jain): A term for all which is not the soul.

ALLAH (Sufi): The Moslem term for God.

ANATTA (Buddhist): The doctrine that no permanent ego or entity can be found in the human faculties; that the only permanence is in the Reality behind all appearance.

ARHAT (S. Buddhist): One who has travelled the Eightfold Path and reached Enlightenment.

ASANA (Hindu): A posture of Hatha Yoga.

ASHRAM (Hindu): A community of disciples established around a teacher.

ASURA (Hindu and N. Buddhist): The name for a demon or anti-god.

ATMAN (Hindu): That which is eternal within man and of the same nature as Brahman. Sometimes called the Self or the soul.

AVALOKITESHVARA (N. Buddhist): The Buddha who looks in all directions.

AVIDYA (Buddhist): Ignorance, in the sense of lack of enlightenment.

BHAKTI YOGA (Hindu): The way to Self-realization through devotion and worship.

BHIKKU or BHIKSHU (Buddhist): A monk.

BODHI (Buddhist): Intrinsic wisdom.

BODHISATTVA (Buddhist): An enlightened being who dedicates himself to helping others attain enlightenment.

BRAHMA (Hindu): A deity representing the creator of the universe.

BRAHMAN (Hindu): The name for 'the Immensity'—the ultimate indivisible principle beyond thought or form.

BRAHMIN (Hindu): A priest.

BUDDHA: A Sanskrit word for one who has become enlightened about the real nature of existence. The Buddha refers to Prince Siddhartha Gautama, born in Nepal in 563 B.C.

BUDDHISM: The name given to the teachings of Gautama, the Buddha.

CHAKRA (Hindu): A centre of psychic energy within the body.

CHITTA (Hindu): The constant chatter which goes on in the mind.

DERVISH (Sufi): A disciple.

DHARMA (Buddhist): The doctrine and teachings of the Buddha.

DUKKHA (Buddhist): The imperfection of relative life.

FANA (Sufi): Ecstasy.

GNOSIS (Sufi): Mystical knowledge.

GURU (Hindu): A spiritual teacher.

HAIKU (Zen): A Japanese poem of seventeen syllables.

HATHA YOGA (Hindu): A way of increasing bodily awareness through the practice of postures.

HINDUISM: The beliefs of the Hindus, who form the largest religious group in India.

I CHING (Taoist): The Book of Change. A Chinese method of divining the future.

IST (Sufi): A spiritual exercise.

JAINISM: An ancient branch of Hinduism.

JAPA (Hindu): Repetition of the name of a deity as a practice for obtaining a deeper level of consciousness.

JIVA (Hindu): That which is reincarnated—the vitalizing element sometimes called a soul. (Jain): The soul, which must always try to subdue the body, in which it is encased.

JNANA YOGA (Hindu): The way to Self-realization through discrimination between reality and illusion.

KALI-YUGA (Hindu): This present age.

KALPA (Hindu): A day of Brahma, said to be 4,320,000,000 years long.

KARMA (Hindu): The continuing process of cause and effect so that all past actions determine the present moment. (Jain): A subtle substance which obscures the light of the soul.

KARMA YOGA (Hindu): The way to Self-realization through selfless action.

KARUNA (Buddhist): Active compassion.

KOAN (Zen): A question or statement in enigmatic language which points to the direct truth.

KUNDALINI (Hindu): The female serpent power representing dormant energy, said to be coiled at the base of the spine.

LAMA (Tibetan): A monk.

LATAIF (Sufi): The five centres of illumination in the body and mind.

LATIFA (Sufi): One of the lataif.

LINGAM (Hindu): A symbol of manifest form, shaped like a human phallus.

LILA (Hindu): The dance of life.

LOTUS (Buddhist): A symbol of enlightenment—its roots are in the mud, its flower in the immensity.

MAHAYANA BUDDHISM: The northern school of Buddhism which appeals to the heart and intuitive wisdom, seeking to expand the Buddha's teaching in ways to suit every type of person.

MANDALA (Hindu): Symbolic circles and squares containing sacred Sanskrit letters. (N. Buddhist): Representations of deities, demons and Bodhisattvas around the central figure of the Buddha.

MANTRA (Hindu and N. Buddhist): A sound, in the form of one or more syllables, representing an aspect of the universe.

MARA (Buddhist): A legendary personification of temptation and evil.

MAYA (Hindu): The relative world seen as illusion or dream.

MURSHID (Sufi): A spiritual teacher.

NETI-NETI (Hindu): A description of God as 'not this, not that'—beyond human words and ideas.

NIRVANA (Buddhist): The goal of Buddhism—realization of 'being' as distinct from 'becoming'. The experience of egolessness, of Ultimate Reality in place of the separate self.

NIYAMA (Hindu): The five observances of Raja Yoga.

OM or AUM (Hindu and N. Buddhist): The greatest mantra, thought to be the sound of God.

OM MANI PADME HUM (N. Buddhist): 'The Jewel in the Lotus'; the best-known Tibetan Buddhist mantra.

PALI: An Indian language adopted by the Theravada Buddhists to convey the memorized teachings of the Buddha.

PATIVEDHA (Buddhist): Pure awareness of an object.

PRAJNA (Buddhist): Transcendental wisdom and intuition.

PRĀNA (Hindu): A power which manifests as motion, energy, gravitation and magnetism.

RAJAS (Hindu): The quality of energy and passion.

RAJA YOGA (Hindu): A way of Self-realization through insight.

RINZAI (Zen): One of the two main Zen sects in Japan, founded by the master Rinzai (867 A.D.).

RISHI (Hindu): A sage with developed powers.

RUPA (Buddhist): Form (e.g. *Buddha-rupa*—an image of the Buddha).

SAMADHI (Hindu): A state of absorption of the ordinary mind into limitless awareness.

SAMSARA (Buddhist): The relative world of phenomena; the state of present existence which is subject to 'becoming' as contrasted with the 'being' of Nirvana.

SANGHA (Buddhist): Community of monks.

SANSKRIT: An Indian language considered sacred by the Hindus.

SATORI (Zen): The Japanese term for the experience of enlightenment or awakening to the Buddha-nature.

SATTVA (Hindu): The quality of spiritual wisdom.

SESSHIN (Zen): A period of concentrated meditation.

SHAKTI (Hindu): A goddess representing the Supreme Mother, the creative energy of the world.

SHIVA (Hindu): A god known as the Lord of Sleep and personifying the change and disintegration which comes to all manifest things before they can be born again.

SKANDHAS (Buddhist): The five elements which condition the appearance of life in any form —body, feelings, perception of feelings, consciousness of perceptions and understanding of perceptions.

SOTO (Zen): One of the two main Zen sects in Japan, founded by Dogen (1200-1253 A.D.).

STUPA (Buddhist): A mound containing the relics of a holy man.

SUFI: A Moslem mystic and teacher.

SUFISM: The teachings and practices of the Sufis.

SUNYA (N. Buddhist): The Void. The doctrine which declares the phenomenal world to be without self-substance.

SUNYATA (N. Buddhist): Voidness.

SUTRA (Hindu and Buddhist): A group of statements relating to the highest truth.

SWADHARMA (Hindu): A person's innate law of development.

SWAMI (Hindu): A distinguished spiritual teacher.

TAJJALAN (Hindu): A description of Brahman as that from which all things are born, into which they dissolve and in which they breathe and move.

TAMAS (Hindu): The quality of stupidity.

TANHA (Buddhist): Thirst for existence as a human being.

TANTRA (Hindu and Buddhist): Teachings of cosmic unity.

TANTRIC YOGA (Hindu and Buddhist): The practice of Tantra.

TAO: The Way.

TAOISM: An ancient Chinese religion concerned with intuitively living by the laws of the universe.

TATHAGATA (Buddhist): A title of the Buddha used when speaking of himself, meaning 'He who has come and gone as former Buddhas'.

THERAVADA BUDDHISM: The school of southern Buddhism in which each man works for his own enlightenment.

TIRTHANKARA (Jain): A preacher of the truth who lived in the distant past.

TULKU (Tibetan) A reincarnated spiritual leader.

UPANISHAD (Hindu): Literally, 'sit near'. Discourses given to chosen pupils in the Vedic age, who were allowed to 'sit near' their teachers.

VEDANTA (Hindu): The teachings of the deepest truths of the Vedas.

VEDAS (Hindu): The oldest Indian scriptures.

VIHARA (Buddhist): A monastery or a community of monks.

VIPASSANA (S. Buddhist): A Theravada practice of insight meditation.

VISHNU (Hindu): A deity representing the inner cause of life, the power which holds the universe together.

YAMA (Hindu): The five restraints of Raja Yoga.

YANA (Buddhist): A way of progress. A vehicle of salvation from the relative world of Samsara.

YANTRA (Hindu): A geometrical figure representing the thought-form of a deity.

YIN and YANG (Taoist): Symbols of duality—female and male.

YOGA (Hindu): A system of practices for realizing man's divine nature.

YOGI (Hindu): One who practises yoga.

ZA-ZEN (Zen): The practice of sitting in meditation.

ZEN: A school of Mahayana Buddhism originating in China and Japan and directed

towards the attainment of satori.

ZENDO (Zen): A Zen meditation hall.

ZIKR (Sufi): The repetition of a holy name, or incantation.

REFERENCES

1, 20. HUXLEY, A. *The Perennial Philosophy*. Reprinted by permission of Mrs Laura Huxley, Chatto & Windus Ltd and Harper & Row, Publishers Inc. Copyright, 1944, 1945, by Aldous Huxley.

2, 3, 19. HUME, R.E. (trans.) *The Thirteen Principal Upanishads*. Reprinted by permission of Oxford University Press, London.

4, 22. PRABHAVANANDA, Swami and MANCHESTER, F. (trans.) *The Upanishads*. Reprinted by permission of Vedanta Press, Hollywood, Calif.

5, 18. EDGERTON, F. (trans.) *The Bhagavad-Gita*. Reprinted by permission of Harvard University Press.

6, 17. PRABHAVANANDA, Swami and ISHERWOOD, C. (trans.) *The Song of God Bhagavad Gita*. Reprinted by permission of Vedanta Press, Hollywood, Calif.

7, 15. SMITH, H. *Religions of Man*. Reprinted (with 7 paraphrased) by permission of Harper & Row, Publishers Inc. Copyright © 1958 by Huston Smith.

8, 9. SHASTRI, H. P. (trans.) *Ashtavakra Gita*. Reprinted by permission of Shanti Sadan, London.

10, 13, 26. OSBORNE, A. (ed.) *The Teaching of Ramana Maharshi*. Reprinted by permission of Rider and Company.

11. ISHERWOOD, C. (ed.) *Vedanta for Modern Man*. Reprinted by permission of George Allen & Unwin Ltd.

12. PRABHAVANANDA, Swami and ISHERWOOD, C. (trans.) *Shankara's Crest—Jewel of Discrimination*. Reprinted by permission of Vedanta Press, Hollywood, Calif.

14. CAMPBELL, R. (trans.) *St John of the Cross: Poems*. (Penguin Books Ltd). Reprinted by permission of the author.

16. *A Synthesis of the Bhagavad Gita*. Reprinted by permission of the Shrine of Wisdom, Godalming, England.

21. WOOD, E. *Concentration, a Practical Course*. Reprinted by permission of The Theosophical Publishing House, Madras.

23. RADHAKRISHNAN, SIR S. *The Principal Upanishads*. Reprinted by permission of George Allen & Unwin Ltd.

24. WATTS, A. *The Book*. Paraphrased here by permission of Jonathan Cape Ltd and A. M. Heath & Company Ltd (for the author).

25, 28, 29, 32. NIKHILANANDA, Swami. *Ramakrishna, Prophet of New India*. Reprinted by permission of the Ramakrishna-Vivekananda Center, New York.

27, 30, 31. ISHERWOOD, C. *Vedanta for the Western World*. Reprinted by permission of George Allen & Unwin Ltd and Vedanta Press, Hollywood, Calif.

33. *Back to Godhead,* the magazine of the Hare Krishna Movement, no. 49. Reprinted by permission of Iskcon Press, Los Angeles.

The author also wishes to acknowledge Ernest Wood's *Yoga* (Penguin Books Ltd) as an invaluable reference work on the subject of Tantric Yoga.

BUDDHISM

1. MULLER, F. M. *The Sacred Books of the Buddhists, vol. II*. Reprinted by permission of The Clarendon Press, Oxford.

2, 3. BURTT, E. A. (ed.) *The Teachings of the Compassionate Buddha*. Reprinted by permission of New American Library Inc.

4. RAHULA, W. *What the Buddha Taught*. Reprinted in abbreviated form by permission of Gordon Fraser Gallery Limited, London.

5. HUME, D. *Treatise of Human Nature, vol. I*. Reprinted by permission of J. M. Dent & Sons Ltd and E. P. Dutton & Co Inc (Everyman's Library Series).

6, 7, 9, 13, 14. HUMPHREYS, C. *The Wisdom of Buddhism*. Reprinted by permission of Rider and Company.

8. SMITH, H. *Religions of Man*. Reprinted by permission of Harper & Row, Publishers Inc. Copyright © 1958 by Huston Smith.

10. MAURICE, D. *The Lion's Roar*. Reprinted by permission of Rider and Company.

11, 12. LUK, C. *The Surangama Sutra*. Reprinted by permission of Rider and Company.

CONZE and HORNER (eds.) *Buddhist Texts*. Reprinted by permission of Bruno Cassirer (Publishers) Ltd.

16. DHAMMASUDHI, S. *Insight Meditation*. Reprinted by permission of the Committee for the Advancement of Buddhism.

17. HUMPHREYS, C. *Buddhism* (Pelican Original; 3rd edition, 1962). Reprinted by permission of Penguin Books Ltd. Copyright © Christmas Humphreys, 1951.

18. SANGHARAKSHITA, Ven. M. S. *A Survey of Buddhism*. Reprinted by permission of the author and The Indian Institute of World Culture, Bangalore.

TIBETAN BUDDHISM

1, 3, 5. WENTZ, W. Y. E.- *The Tibetan Book of the Dead*. Reprinted by permission of Oxford

University Press, London.

2. TRUNGPA, C. *Born in Tibet.* Reprinted by permission of George Allen & Unwin Ltd.

4. Reprinted by permission of Alan Watts.

6. TRUNGPA, C. *Meditation in Action.* Reprinted by permission of Robinson & Watkins Books Ltd; U.S. publisher: Shambala, Berkeley, Calif.

7, 13. EBIN, D. *The Drug Experience.* Reprinted by permission of Grove Press, Inc. Copyright © 1961 by David Ebin.

8, 14, 15. HUXLEY, A. *The Doors of Perception.* Reprinted by permission of Mrs Laura Huxley, Chatto & Windus Ltd and Harper & Row, Publishers Inc. Copyright 1954, by Aldous Huxley.

9. LEARY, T. *Psychedelic Prayer.* Reprinted by permission of Academy Editions and Lyle Stuart Inc.

10, 11, 12. WATTS, A. *The Joyous Cosmology.* Reprinted by permission of Jonathan Cape Ltd and Pantheon Books/A Division of Random House Inc. Copyright © 1962 by Alan W. Watts.

ZEN BUDDHISM

1. CONZE, E. (trans.) *Buddhist Scriptures.* Reprinted by permission of Penguin Books Ltd. Copyright © Edward Conze, 1959.

2, 3, 5, 6, 8, 26. WATTS, A. *The Spirit of Zen.* Reprinted by permission of Grove Press, Inc. Copyright © 1958 by Alan W. Watts.

4. LEGGETT, T. *A First Zen Reader.* Reprinted by permission of Charles E. Tuttle Co., Inc.

7. SOHL, R. and CARR, AUDREY (eds.) *The Gospel according to Zen.* Suzuki extract reprinted by permission of Grove Press, Inc. and Rider and Company.

9, 14, 16, 17, 21-24. WATTS, A. *The Way of Zen.* Reprinted by permission of Thames and Hudson Ltd and Pantheon Books/A Division of Random House Inc. Copyright © 1957 by Alan W. Watts.

10. CHEN-CHI, C. *The Practice of Zen.* Reprinted by permission of Rider and Company.

11. SUZUKI, D. T. *Essays in Zen Buddhism, III.* Reprinted by permission of Rider and Company.

12. SUZUKI, D. T. *Essays in Zen Buddhism, II.* Reprinted by permission of Rider and Company.

13, 18-20, 25. SUZUKI, D. T. *Essays in Zen Buddhism, I.* Reprinted by permission of Rider and Company.

15, 27-29. STRYK, L. and IKEMOTO, T. (eds.) *Zen: Poems, Prayers, Sermons, Anecdotes, Interviews.* Reprinted by permission of Doubleday and Co Inc. Copyright © 1963, 1965 by Lucien Stryk and Takashi Ikemoto.

30-33. REPS, P. *Zen Flesh, Zen Bones.* Reprinted by permission of Charles E. Tuttle Co, Inc.

34. KAPLEAU, P. (ed.) *The Wheel of Death.* Reprinted by permission of George Allen & Unwin Ltd and Harper & Row, Publishers Inc. Copyright © 1951 by Philip Kapleau.

35. HERRIGEL, E. *The Method of Zen.* Reprinted by permission of Routledge & Kegan Paul Ltd and Pantheon Books/A Division of Random House Inc.

36. *The Middle Way,* the quarterly publication of the Buddhist Society, vol. XLVII, no. 3. Reprinted by permission of the Buddhist Society, London.

37-39. BOWNAS, G. and THWAITE, A. (eds.) *The Penguin Book of Japanese Verse.* Reprinted by permission of Penguin Books Ltd. Copyright © by Geoffrey Bownas and Anthony Thwaite, 1964.

40. (Unpublished); reprinted by permission of Colin Oliver.

41. *Sengai,* a catalogue published by the Arts Council of Great Britain for an exhibition of his work. Reprinted by permission of The Japan Foundation, Tokyo.

42. HERRIGEL, E. *Zen in the Art of Archery.* Reprinted by permission of Routledge & Kegan Paul Ltd and Pantheon Books/A Division of Random House Inc.

43. HARDING, D. *On Having no Head.* Reprinted by permission of the Buddhist Society, London.

TAOISM

1, 11, 12. MERTON, T. *The Way of Chuang Tzu.* Copyright © 1965 by the Abbey of Gethsemani. Reprinted by permission of New Directions Publishing Corporation and George Allen & Unwin Ltd.

2-7. BYNNER, W. (trans.) *The Way of Life— according to Lao-Tzu.* Reprinted by permission of John Day Co, Inc. Copyright © 1944 by Witter Bynner.

8-10, 13-16. WATSON, B. (trans.) *The Complete Works of Chuang Tzu.* Reprinted by permission of Columbia University Press.

17. BLOFELD, J. *The Book of Change.* Reprinted by permission of George Allen & Unwin Ltd and E. P. Dutton & Co Inc.

18. WILHELM, R. (trans.) *The I Ching: or Book of Changes,* rendered into English by Cary F. Baynes. Reprinted by permission of Princeton University Press and Routledge & Kegan Paul Ltd. Copyright © 1950 & 1967 by Bollingen Foundation.

19. BLOFELD, J. *The Secret and Sublime.* Reprinted by permission of George Allen & Unwin Ltd.

20. ISHIHARA, A. and LEVY, H. S. *The Tao of Sex.* Reprinted by permission of the authors.

21. LIU, D. *T'ai Chi Ch'uan and I Ching.* Story paraphrased by permission of Harper & Row, Publishers Inc. Copyright © 1972 by Da Liu.

SUFISM

1, 9, 15-17, 19, 21. NICHOLSON, R. A. *Rumi, Poet and Mystic.* Reprinted by permission of

George Allen & Unwin Ltd.

2, 3, 7, 10, 11. SMITH, MARGARET. *The Sufi Path of Love*. Reprinted by permission of Luzac & Company Ltd.

4, 8, 12, 25. NICHOLSON, R. A. *Mystics of Islam*. Reprinted by permission of Routledge & Kegan Paul Ltd.

5, 14. SMITH, MARGARET. *Readings from the Mystics of Islam*. Reprinted by permission of Luzac & Company Ltd.

6. DAVIS, F. H. *The Persian Mystics*. Reprinted by permission of Sh. Muhammad Ashraf, Lahore.

13. HUSAINI, M. S. A. Q. *Ibn Al 'Arabi*. Reprinted by permission of The Theosophical Publishing House, Madras.

18, 22, 27–30. SHAH, I. *The Way of the Sufi*. Reprinted by permission of Jonathan Cape Ltd and E. P. Dutton & Co Inc. Copyright © 1968 by Idries Shah.

20, 23, 26, 33. SHAH, I. *The Sufis*. Reprinted by permission of W. H. Allen & Co Ltd and Doubleday and Co Inc. Copyright © 1964 by Idries Shah.

24. SCHRODINGER, E. *My View of the World*. Reprinted by permission of Cambridge University Press, London.

31. KHAN, I. *The Way of Illumination*. Reprinted by permission of the Sufi Movement, Geneva.

32. KHAN, I. *Music*. Reprinted by permission of the Sufi Movement, Geneva.

34. GIBRAN, K. *The Prophet*. Reprinted by permission of Alfred A. Knopf, Inc. Copyright © 1923 by Kahlil Gibran; renewal copyright 1951 by Administrators C.T.A. of Kahlil Gibran Estate, and Mary G. Gibran.

CONCLUSION

1. OSBORNE, A. (ed.) *The Teaching of Ramana Maharshi*. Reprinted by permission of Rider and Company.

FURTHER READING

BOUQUET, A. C. *Comparative Religion*. Cassell, London 1961; Penguin, Baltimore, Md. 1964.

CAMPBELL, J. *The Masks of God: Oriental Mythology*. Secker & Warburg, London and Viking, New York 1962.

ELIADE, M. *From Primitives to Zen*. Collins, London and Harper & Row, New York 1967.

GUIRAND, F. (ed.) *New Larousse Encyclopedia of Mythology*. Hamlyn, Feltham, Middx. and Putnam, New York 1969.

HARDING, D. *Religions of the World*. Heinemann Educational, London 1969.

NEEDLEMAN, J. *The New Religions*. Doubleday, Garden City, N.J. 1970.

PARRINDER, G. *The World's Living Religions*. n.e. Pan Books, London 1964.

ROSS, NANCY W. *Three Ways of Asian Wisdom: Hinduism, Buddhism, Zen*. Simon & Schuster, New York 1968; Faber, London 1973.

SMITH, H. *Religions of Man*. Harper & Row, New York 1958.

HINDUISM

BHAKTIVEDANTA, SWAMI A. C. (trans.) *The Bhagavad Gita As It Is*. Macmillan, New York 1972; Collier-Macmillan, London 1973.

BOUQUET, A. C. *Hinduism*. Hutchinson University Library, London and New York 1966.

CHAUDHURI, H. *Integral Yoga*. Allen & Unwin, London 1965.

DANIELOU, A. *Hindu Polytheism*. Routledge & Kegan Paul, London and Princeton University Press, Princeton, N.J. 1964.

HUME, R. E. (trans,) *The Thirteen Principal Upanishads*. Oxford University Press, London and New York 1931.

ISHERWOOD, C (ed.) *Vedanta for Modern Man*. Allen & Unwin, London 1952; New American Library, New York 1972. (ed.) *Vedanta for the Western World*. Allen & Unwin, London 1948.

OSBORNE, A. (ed.) *The Collected Works of Ramana Maharshi*. Rider, London and Weiser, New York 1969. *Ramana Maharshi and the Path of Self-Knowledge*. Weiser, New York 1969; Rider, London 1970. (ed.) *The Teaching of Ramana Maharshi*. Rider, London and Weiser, New York, 1971.

PANDIT, M. P. *Mystic Approach to the Veda and the Upanishad*. Ganesh and Co., Madras 1966.

PRABHAVANANDA, SWAMI and ISHERWOOD, C. *How to Know God*. Allen & Unwin, London 1953. *Shankara's Crest—Jewel of Discrimination*. New English Library, London 1970. (trans.) *The Song of God, Bhagavad-Gita*. New English Library, London 1970; Vedanta Press, Holywood, Calif. 1969. (trans.) *The Upanishads*. New English Library, London 1971.

RADHAKRISHNAN, S. and MOORE, C. A. *A Source Book in Indian Philosophy*. Princeton University Press, Princeton, N.J. and Oxford University Press, London 1957.

SEN, K. M. *Hinduism*. Penguin, Harmondsworth, Middx. and Baltimore, Md. 1962.

SHASTRI, H. P. (trans.) *Ashtavakra Gita*. Shanti Sadan, London 1961.

SWAMI, S. P. and YEATS, W. B. *The Ten Principal Upanishads*. Faber, London 1937.

TAGORE, R. T. *Gitanjali*. Macmillan, London 1913; Branden, Boston, Mass. 1971.

WALKER, B. *Hindu World*. (2 vols.) Allen &

Unwin, London and Praeger, New York, 1968.

ZAEHNER, R. C. *Hindu and Muslim Mysticism.* Schocken Books, New York 1969.
Hinduism. Oxford University Press, London and New York 1966.
(trans.) *Hindu Scriptures.* Dent, London and Dutton, New York 1966.

ZIMMER, H. *Philosophies of India.* Routledge & Kegan Paul, London 1951; Princeton University Press, Princeton, N.J. 1969.

BUDDHISM

BURTT, E. A. *The Teachings of the Compassionate Buddha.* New English Library, London and New American Library, New York 1955.

CONZE, E. *Buddhist Scriptures.* Penguin, Harmondsworth, Middx. and Baltimore, Md. 1969.

and HORNER (ed.) *Buddhist Texts through the Ages.* Bruno Cassirer, Oxford 1964; Harper & Row, New York 1965.

DHAMMASUDHI, S. *Insight Meditation.* Committee for Advancement of Buddhism, London.

HUMPHREYS, C. *Buddhism.* Cassell, London 1962; Penguin, Baltimore, Md. 1965.
A Buddhist Student's Manual. Luzac, London 1956; Finch Reprints, Ann Arbor, Mich., 1972.
The Wisdom of Buddhism. Michael Joseph, London 1960; Harper & Row, New York 1970.

LUK, C. *The Surangama Sutra.* Rider, London and Hillary House, New York 1966.

MAURICE, D. *The Lion's Roar.* Rider, London 1962.

RAHULA, W. *What the Buddha Taught.* Grove, New York 1962; Gordon Fraser Gallery, Bedford 1967.

SANGHARAKSHITA, VEN. M. S. *A Survey of Buddhism.* Indian Institute of World Culture, Bangalore 1966.

THERA, VEN. A. B. *Dhammapada.* Buddha Vacana Trust, Bangalore 1966.

WOODWARD, F. L. (trans.) *The Gradual Sayings.* (5 vols.) Luzac, London 1951–65.
(trans.) *Some Sayings of the Buddha.* Oxford University Press, London and New York 1925.

TIBETAN BUDDHISM

BLOFELD, J. *The Tantric Mysticism of Tibet.* Allen & Unwin, London and Dutton, New York 1970.

DAVID-NEEL, ALEXANDRA. *Initiation and Initiates in Tibet.* (r.e.) Rider, London 1958; Shambala, Berkeley, Calif. 1970.
Magic and Mystery in Tibet. Souvenir, London 1967; Dover, New York 1971.

and LAMA YONGDEN. *The Secret Oral Teachings in Tibetan Buddhist Sects.* City Lights Books, San Francisco, Calif. 1967.

GOVINDA, LAMA. *Foundations of Tibetan Mysticism.* (n.e.) Rider, London 1969; Wehman, Hackensack, N.J. 1970.

MARQUES-RIVIERE, J. *Tantric Yoga.* Weiser, New York 1970.

TRUNGPA, C. *Born in Tibet.* Allen & Unwin, London 1966; Penguin, Baltimore, Md. 1971.
Meditation in Action. Robinson & Watkins, London and Shambala, Berkeley, Calif. 1969.

WENTZ, W. Y. E-. *Tibetan Book of the Dead.* Oxford University Press, London and New York 1956.
Tibetan Book of the Great Liberation. Oxford University Press, London and New York 1954.
(ed.) *Tibetan Yoga and Secret Doctrines.* Oxford University Press, London and New York 1958.

ZEN BUDDHISM

BLOFELD, J. (trans.) *The Zen Teaching of Huang Po.* Rider, London and Grove, New York 1959.
(trans.) *The Zen Teaching of Hui Hai.* Rider, London and Weiser, New York 1969.

BOWNAS and THWAITE (ed.) *The Penguin Book of Japanese Verse.* Penguin, Harmondsworth, Middx. 1960; Peter Smith, Gloucester, Mass. 1972.

CHEN-CHI, C. *The Practice of Zen.* Rider, London 1960.

CHUNG-YUAN, C. *Original Teachings of Ch'an Buddhism.* Random House, New York 1971.

FROMM, E. *et al.* (ed.) *Zen Buddhism and Psychoanalysis.* Allen & Unwin, London 1960; Harper & Row, New York 1970.

HARDING, D. *On Having No Head.* The Buddhist Society, London and Harper & Row, New York 1971.

HERRIGEL, E. *The Method of Zen.* Routledge & Kegan Paul, London 1960.
Zen in the Art of Archery. Routledge & Kegan Paul, London and Pantheon, New York 1953.

KAPLEAU, P. (ed.) *The Three Pillars of Zen.* Harper & Row, New York 1966.
The Wheel of Death. Harper & Row, New York 1971; Allen & Unwin, London 1972.

LEGGETT, T. *A First Zen Reader.* Tuttle, Tokyo and Rutland, Vt. 1960.
The Tiger's Cave. Rider, London 1964.

MERTON, T. *Mystics and Zen Masters.* Farrar, Straus & Giroux, New York 1967.
Zen and the Birds of Appetite. New Directions, New York 1968.

MIURA, I. and SASAKI, RUTH F. *The Zen Koan.* Harcourt Brace Jovanovitch, New York 1965.

REPS, P. *Zen Flesh, Zen Bones.* Tuttle, Tokyo and Rutland, Vt. 1957.

ROSHI, R. F. *The Way of Zazen.* Cambridge

Buddhist Association, Cambridge, Mass. 1961.

ROSS, NANCY W. (ed.) *The World of Zen.* Random House, New York 1960; Collins, London 1962.

SHIBAYAMA, ABBOT Z. *A Flower Does Not Talk: Zen Essays.* Tuttle, Tokyo and Rutland, Vt. 1970.

SOHL, R. and CARR, AUDREY. *The Gospel According to Zen.* New American Library, New York and New English Library, London 1970.

STRYK, L. and IKEMOTO, T. *Zen: Poems, Prayers, Sermons, Anecdotes, Interviews.* Doubleday, Garden City, N.J. 1965.

SUZUKI, D. T. *Essays in Zen Buddhism.* (First, Second and Third Series) Rider, London 1968, '69 & '70; Paragon, New York 1971. *Living by Zen.* Rider, London 1972. *Manual of Zen Buddhism.* Grove, New York 1960. *Sengai, the Zen Master.* New York Graphic Society, Greenwich, Conn. 1970; Faber, London 1971. *Studies in Zen.* Rider, London and Dell, New York 1955. *Zen and Japanese Culture.* Routledge & Kegan Paul, London and Princeton University Press, Princeton, N.J. 1971. *The Zen Buddhist Monk's Life.* Olympia Press, New York 1972. *The Zen Doctrine of No Mind.* Rider, London 1969; Hillary House, New York 1970.

WATTS, A. *The Spirit of Zen.* Grove, New York 1958; J. Murray, London 1959. *The Way of Zen.* Thames & Hudson, London and Pantheon, New York 1957.

WEI, W. W. *Ask the Awakened.* Routledge & Kegan Paul, London 1963.

TAOISM

BLOFELD, J. (trans.) *The Book of Change.* Allen & Unwin, London and Dutton, New York 1965. *The Secret and Sublime.* Allen & Unwin, London 1973.

COOPER, J. C. *Taoism: the Way of the Mystic.* Aquarian Press, London and Weiser, New York 1972.

GRAHAM, A. C. (trans.) *The Book of Lieh-Tzu.* J. Murray, London 1961; Paragon, New York 1969.

ISHIHARA, A. and LEVY, H. S. *The Tao of Sex.* Harper & Row, New York 1970.

LAU, D. C. (trans.) *Tao Te Ching.* Penguin, London and Baltimore Md. 1968.

LIU, D. *T'ai Chi Ch'uan and I Ching.* Harper & Row, New York 1972.

MERTON, T. *The Way of Chuang Tzu.* New Directions, New York 1969; Allen & Unwin, London 1971.

WATSON, B. (trans.) *The Complete Works of Chuang Tzu.* Columbia University Press, New York 1968.

WILHELM, R. and BAYNES, C. F. (trans.) *The I Ching or Book of Changes.* (2 vols.) Routledge & Kegan Paul, London 1968.

YUTANG, L. *The Wisdom of Confucius.* Michael Joseph, London 1938. *The Wisdom of Lao Tzu.* Michael Joseph, London 1948.

SUFISM

ARBERRY, A. J. (trans.) *Discourses of Rumi.* J. Murray, London 1961; Transatlantic, Levittown, N.Y., 1972. *The Doctrine of the Sufis.* Cambridge University Press, Cambridge and Weiser, New York 1951. *Sufism.* Allen & Unwin. London 1950; Harper & Row, New York 1970.

BAERLEIN, H. (trans.) *The Diwan of Abu'L-Ala.* J. Murray, London 1908; Paragon, New York 1969.

ED-DIN, A. B. S. *The Book of Certainty.* Rider, London 1952; Weiser, New York, 1954.

GIBRAN, K. *The Prophet.* Heinemann, London and Knopf, New York 1970.

HAPPOLD, F. C. *Mysticism.* (r.e.) Penguin, Baltimore, Md. 1963; Harmondsworth, Middx. 1965.

HUSAINI, M. S. A. Q. *Ibn Al 'Arabi.* Theosophical Publishing House, Madras 1931.

KHAN, I. *The Way of Illumination.* The Sufi Movement, London (undated).

KRITZECK, J. (ed.) *Anthology of Islamic Literature.* Penguin, Harmondsworth, Middx. 1964; New American Library 1965.

MUNSHI, K. M. and DIWAKAR, R. R. *Sufis, Mystics and Yogis of India.* Bharatiya Vidya Bhavan, Bombay 1971.

NICHOLSON, R. A. *Mystics of Islam.* Routledge & Kegan Paul, London 1966. (ed.) *Rumi, Poet and Mystic.* Allen & Unwin, London and Hillary House, New York 1968. *Studies in Islamic Mysticism.* Cambridge University Press, Cambridge and New York 1967.

RICE, CYPRIAN. *Persian Sufis.* Allen & Unwin, London and Humanities Press, New York 1964.

SHAH, I. *The Sufis.* W. H. Allen, London 1964; Doubleday, Garden City, N.J. 1971. *The Way of the Sufi.* Cape, London 1968; Dutton, New York 1970.

SINGH, SIR J. (trans.) *The Invocations of Sheikh Abdullah Ansari.* J. Murray, London 1959.

SMITH, MARGARET. *Rabi'a the Mystic.* Cambridge University Press, Cambridge. *Readings from the Mystics of Islam.* Luzac, London 1950. *The Sufi Path of Love.* Luzac, London 1954.

WATT, W. M. (trans.) *Confessions of Al Ghazzali.* Orientalia, New York 1971.

ZAEHNER, R. C. *Hindu and Muslim Mysticism.* Schocken, New York 1970.

INDEX